DAWN OF D-DAY

GREENHILL MILITARY PAPERBACKS: WORLD WAR II

DAWN OF D-DAY
These Men Were There, 6th June 1944

David Howarth

Greenhill Books, London

Stackpole Books, Pennsylvania

This edition of *Dawn of D-Day*
published 2001 by Greenhill Books, Lionel Leventhal Limited,
Park House, 1 Russell Gardens, London NW11 9NN
www.greenhillbooks.com
and
Stackpole Books, 5067 Ritter Road, Mechanicsburg, PA 17055, USA

British Library Cataloguing in Publication Data

Howarth, David, 1912–1991
Dawn of D-Day: these men were there, 6 June 1944. – (Greenhill military paperback)
1. World War, 1939–1945 – Campaigns – France – Normandy
2. World War, 1939–1945 – Personal narratives
I. Title
940.5'42142

ISBN 1-85367-439-7

Library of Congress Cataloging-in-Publication Data

Howarth, David Armine, 1912–1991
Dawn of D-day/David Howarth
p.cm.
Originally published: London: Collins, 1959
ISBN 1-85367-439-7 (pbk.)
1. World War, 1939–1945 – Campaigns – France – Normandy. I. Title

D756.5.N6 H694 2001
940.54'2142-dc21

00-066103

Publishing History

Dawn of D-Day was first published in 1959 by Collins (London) and reprinted in
paperback by Fontana Books in 1961. This *Greenhill Military Paperback* now
appears exactly as the original edition.

Printed and bound in Great Britain by CPD (Wales), Ebbw Vale

CONTENTS

ILLUSTRATIONS

Appearing between pages 96 and 97

MAPS

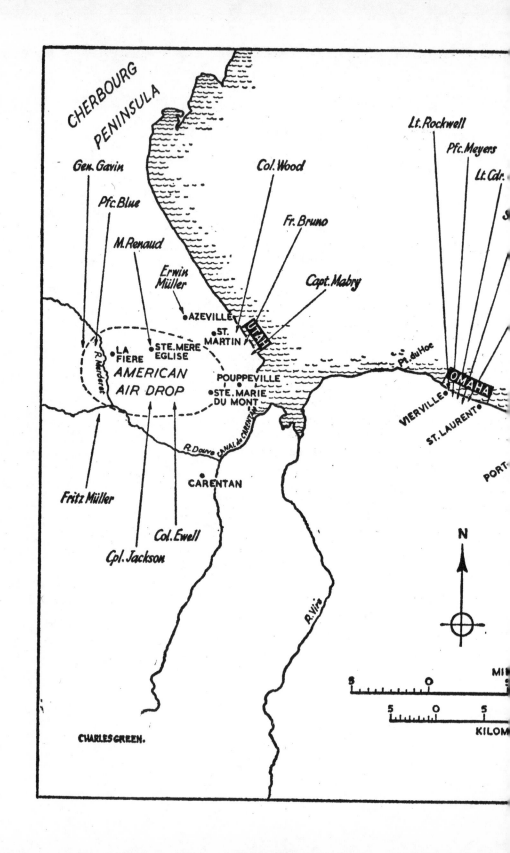

CHERBOURG PENINSULA

Gen. Gavin

Pfc. Blue

M. Renaud

Erwin Müller

Col. Wood

Fr. Bruno

Capt. Mabry

Lt. Rockwell

Pfc. Meyers

Lt. Cdr.

• AZEVILLE

• ST. MARTIN

LA FIERE

• STE. MERE EGLISE

R. Merderet

UTAH

AMERICAN AIR DROP

POUPPEVILLE

• STE. MARIE DU MONT

Pt. du Hoc

OMAHA

VIERVILLE •

• ST. LAURENT

R. Douve CANAL de CARENTAN

Fritz Müller

• CARENTAN

Col. Ewell

Cpl. Jackson

R. Vire

PORT

N

CHARLES GREEN.

MI

5   O   5
KILOM

5   O   5

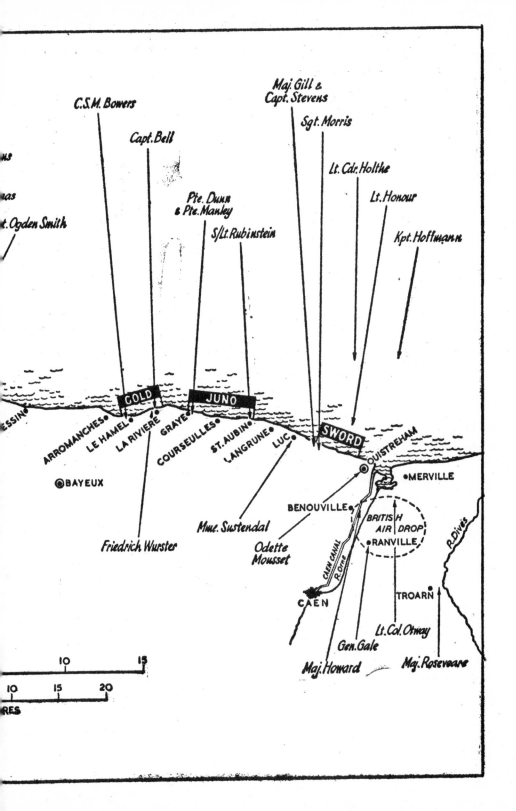

C.S.M. Bowers

Maj. Gill & Capt. Stevens

Capt. Bell

Sgt. Morris

Lt. Cdr. Holthe

Pte. Dunn & Pte. Manley

Lt. Honour

S/Lt. Rubinstein

Kpt. Hoffmann

t. Ogden Smith

GOLD   JUNO   SWORD

ESSIN   ARROMANCHES•   LE HAMEL•   LA RIVIERE•   GRAYE•   COURSEULLES•   ST. AUBIN•   LANGRUNE   LUC•   OUISTREHAM•

●BAYEUX

MERVILLE

BENOUVILLE•

BRITISH AIR DROP

Friedrich Wurster

•RANVILLE

R. Dives

Mme. Sustendal

Odette Mousset

CAEN CANAL

R. Orne

TROARN

CAEN

Lt. Col. Otway

Gen. Gale

10   15

Maj. Howard

Maj. Roseveare

10   15   20

RES

FOREWORD

THIS IS not a military text-book. Military histories of battles deal with military units, and the way their generals manœuvred them; they do not usually tell their readers what individual soldiers saw or did, or what they thought or feared. But this is the aspect of battles which interests me: not only the actions and opinions of the generals who planned them, but also those of the soldiers and junior officers who had to fight them.

There are several technical works already about the invasion of Normandy, and several generals' memoirs; and there is Chester Wilmot's brilliant analysis in *The Struggle for Europe*. What I have tried to do is simply to give an impression of the experience of the men who landed in the night and dawn of D Day: an impression of what it was like to be dropped from the sky that morning, or pitched ashore from a landing craft under fire.

This is a simple intention, but it can only be carried out with limitations. Churchill himself said the invasion of Normandy was the most complicated and difficult operation that has ever taken place. Tens of thousands of men took part in even its earliest stages. One can only give an impression of such a vast sum of activity by choosing the experiences of a few men as examples of the rest. However many one chose, they could only be a small proportion of the whole; and I think that to choose too many would make the story dull and repetitious. Therefore I have only chosen just over thirty; but I have chosen them carefully, to make the impression as balanced as I can.

One result of this method is that if readers who were there look in this book for the names of their units, or descriptions of the exact parts of the action which they saw, the chances are they will not find them. But I hope they will understand why, and will be equally interested to learn what other people were doing there; for although I have left out many details for the sake of clarity, I have certainly been able to tell far more of what happened that morning than any single man knew when he landed.

I have depended on the help of a great many people. The main characters in the book have taken endless trouble to tell me all they remember. For facts about the town of Ste. Mère Eglise, I am indebted not only to the conversation of M. Renaud, the mayor, but also to his charming book *Sainte Mère Eglise: Première Tête de Pont Americaine en France*. In America, Britain and Germany, I have met with equal kindness from officers of Defence Departments and veterans' organisations in my search for representative men. In America, Mr. David Legerman helped me enormously to find my way around. I have failed in good manners if any of these people do not already know how grateful I am to them.

In talking to all the people in the book, and many others, about the events of the morning of D Day, I have noticed how widely their impressions of what happened vary. Some of them disagree with official reports. Naturally, a battle looks quite different to an old soldier and to a man who has never been shot at before. I have even met one American officer whose impression was that Omaha Beach was quiet. It is often impossible to give a purely objective account of events which were only observed by people in the stress of intense emotions.

My general outline of this battle is objective, and I believe it is accurate: the details are accurate too, but they are deliberately subjective. So, if any reader says of his own beach or his own dropping zone that it was not like this at all, I shall truthfully answer that this was how it looked to the men I have chosen to describe it.

I

ENGLAND

ALL OVER the south of England, on the night of the fifth of June, people awoke, or else, if they were going late to bed, stopped what they were doing and went outside to listen. Those who had lived there for the past four years were used to noisy nights. The noise at nights had changed through the years, from the distinctive beat of German bombers and the din of air-raids, to the sound of British bombers outward bound at dusk and homeward bound at dawn. But people who heard the noise on the fifth of June remember it as different from anything that had ever been heard before. Life in war had made them adept at guessing what was happening from what they could hear, and as they listened that night, with increasing excitement and pride, they knew that by far the greatest fleet of aircraft they had ever heard—and therefore the greatest fleet that anyone had ever heard—was passing overhead from north to south.

Nobody had much doubt of what the noise implied; even those who had nothing to do with military secrets had known it would happen soon. They simply said to themselves or to each other " This is it " ; and probably most of them heard the sound with such deep emotion that they did not try to put their feelings into words. It was the invasion, as everybody either knew or guessed ; and the invasion, if it succeeded, was to be the redemption of the defeat of Dunkirk, and the justification of the British refusal to admit defeat when everyone else in the world believed they were finished. It would be a reward for the four years' grinding labour by which they had dragged themselves up from the depths of 1940 to a state of national strength which made them an equal partner of the United States. And personally, to the British, it had a significance like a first gleam of sunshine after rain ; it would be a sign, if it succeeded, of hope that the worst was over, the first glimpse of the beginning of the end of the sorrow, boredom, pain and frustration in which they had lived for so long.

That was to be its significance if it succeeded : what if it failed ? People could not bring themselves to imagine what would happen if it failed ; but they knew that failure would be a military disaster which at best would take years to retrieve, and in the back of their minds they doubted their own ability, exhausted by war as they were, to survive such a disappointment and start again, as they had at Dunkirk, and build everything up anew.

They went to sleep that night, if they slept any more, with a sense of great events impending, and of comradeship in a vast adventure, knowing the day would bring news of a battle which would influence all their lives for ever more. On the whole, they were certainly thankful the time had come to put everything to the test ; but of course they thought anxiously of the thousands of their own people who even then, in the night, were on their way to battle, and of the Americans, whom many of them had met for the first time in the past few months. And many of these people, perhaps most, thought with special anxiety of one man who they imagined, rightly or wrongly, was on his way to France by air or sea.

In the morning, the main news in the papers and on the radio was still of the fall of Rome, which had been announced on the day before, and nothing was said of events which were nearer home. But just after nine o'clock the bare announcement came : " Under the command of General Eisenhower, Allied naval forces supported by strong air forces began landing Allied armies this morning on the coast of France." Within a few minutes, this news, which the people of southern England had anticipated, was repeated all round the world.

The purpose of this book is to give an impression of what happened in the English Channel and on the coast of France that morning, roughly between the time when the aircraft were heard over England, and the time when the news was given. But to make the impression clear, one must start with a summary of eighteen months of concentrated thought and work which preceded the invasion, and of the reasoning which decided when and where it should be made, and the plans of what the high commanders intended to happen that morning.

The idea of an invasion of the continent from England could be said to have started at Dunkirk in 1940, when the more far-sighted British soldiers, struggling across the shore to escape from the German army, already knew that a British army would have to cross the shore of Europe in the opposite direction before the war was won. At that time, it seemed a very distant project: distant, but never impossible. In that same year, while most of Britain was preoccupied with improvising its own defence, the organisation called Combined Operations had already been founded, and was studying the technique of landing on hostile coasts. Eighteen months later, when Captain Lord Louis Mountbatten took over command of Combined Operations, Churchill told him " to plan for the offensive." When Russia and America joined Britain in the war, the prospect had become less distant; and in January 1943, Churchill and Roosevelt, meeting at Casablanca, agreed to appoint a joint staff to make a definite plan for the invasion. The head of this staff was Lieutenant General F. E. Morgan, who was appointed Chief of Staff to the Supreme Allied Commander—COSSAC for short—although the Supreme Commander himself had not yet been chosen.

For six months in 1943, COSSAC studied the coasts of Europe, and the Allied and German forces which might be joined in the battle, and the complicated technical details of the

project. It was in that period—a year before the invasion—
that the question of where to land in Europe was decided : a
decision which had to remain an elaborately guarded secret till
the very moment when the invasion fleet was sighted from the
shore.

Many considerations were weighed and balanced in this
decision : beaches suitable for landing, and country suitable for
deploying an army behind the beaches ; weather and tides ;
the distances from bases for short-range fighter aircraft, and
from foreign ports which could be captured to help to support
the army ; and of course, the German defence. Of the whole
of the coast of Europe from Norway to the Bay of Biscay, strict
military logic narrowed the choice to two places : the district of
Calais, or the coast of Normandy between Cherbourg and Le
Havre. In the choice between these, there was room for opinion.
Of course, Normandy is much further than Calais from English
ports, but that made very little difference. The fleet which was
planned was so large that all the ports from the Thames to the
Bristol Channel would be needed to load it, and so most of the
ships would have a long crossing wherever the landing was made.
The Americans favoured Calais, although it was the most
strongly defended part of the whole of the coast, because it
offered a more direct route to Germany. The British rather more
emphatically favoured Normandy, because its defences were
weaker and because it could be cut off from the rest of Europe
by bombing the bridges over the Seine and Loire. In the end,
the COSSAC staff agreed to recommend Normandy, and their
plan was approved by Churchill, Roosevelt and the Combined
Chiefs of Staff at the conference in Quebec in August 1943.
In Quebec it was also agreed that the Supreme Commander
should be American, and that his deputy and his three commanders-in-chief should be British, and May 1944 was fixed
as the target date.

It was not till December, after some weeks of hesitation,
that Roosevelt appointed General Eisenhower, who was then
Supreme Commander in the Mediterranean, to take command

of the invasion of France ; and in January the names of his British subordinates were announced : Air Chief Marshal Tedder as Deputy Supreme Commander, and Admiral Ramsay, General Montgomery and Air Chief Marshal Leigh-Mallory to command the navies, armies and air forces. Already, at the Teheran conference at the end of November, Stalin had shown himself very impatient for the opening of what was called a second front, where the Americans and British could take a fairer share of the burden of fighting from the Russians. Roosevelt and Churchill had promised him the invasion would start in May ; and so, when the commanders took up their appointments in January, there were only four months to go.

When Eisenhower and Montgomery saw the details of the COSSAC plan for the first time, they both declared the area of the landing was too narrow and the troops for the first assault too few. General Morgan had thought so himself, but as a chief of staff without a commander, he had had to plan with the forces which the two governments had told him could be used ; and the size of the whole operation had been limited by the number of landing craft which existed or could be built in time. At Eisenhower's demand, landing craft were gathered in from all over the world ; but still there were not enough for the extra forces he wanted. As a last resort, the landing was postponed till early June, so that another month's production of new craft would be available, although Churchill was worried by the thought of what Stalin would say when May was ended and the promise had not been fulfilled.

The exact date which was chosen in June was decided by the tides, the plan of attack, and the German defences. Reconniassance photographs of the coast of France were taken by aircraft every day that spring ; and they showed Germans and French civilians hard at work building new gun emplacements and installing several kinds of obstacles on the beaches. The obstacles were wooden stakes and ramps, and steel barricades and spikes. Some of them were mined.

As the Germans intended, these obstacles offered a choice

of evils. If a landing were made at high tide, when the obstacles
were submerged and invisible, a large proportion of the landing
craft might be lost by hitting them. If it were made at low tide,
the troops would have to cross an open beach under German
fire ; and in Normandy the beaches slope gently and the range
of tide is large, so that at low tide some beaches are three or four
hundred yards wide.

Eisenhower and Montgomery chose to take the latter risk,
and to minimise it by landing tanks ahead of the infantry, and
by bombarding the defences very heavily just before the landing.
They decided to land just after low tide, and planned to demolish
the obstacles at once, so that landing could continue as the tide
rose.

The navy wanted to approach the coast under cover of night,
but both navy and air force needed an hour of daylight for the
bombardment of the defences. These considerations fixed the
time of the landing at an hour after dawn ; and by combining
this time with the state of the tide, the date of the landing was
fixed. Low tide in Normandy was an hour after dawn on June
6th. On June 5th and 7th, it was near enough to be acceptable.
After that, of course, the tides were not right again for a fortnight, until about June 20th ; but by then the moon would have
waned, and the airborne forces preferred moonlight for the
parachute and glider landings which were planned. Besides,
by June 20th, fulfilment of the promise to Stalin would be another
fortnight overdue. So June 5th was chosen as D-Day, with
the next two days as alternatives if the weather was bad. H Hour,
the moment of landing, was 6.30 a.m. at the western end of the
area of the landing, which the tide reached soonest, and 7.30
at the eastern end.*

* D-Day and H-Hour are standard military expressions. In most operations,
preparations have to be made at specific intervals of time before the operation
begins, and they usually have to be planned and discussed before the date of the
operation is decided. It is convenient then to refer to the.date of the operation as
D-Day, so that the preparations can be dated D-1, D-2 and so on. D-Day has come
to mean the date of the invasion of France because that was the most important
operation in which the expression was ever used, and because the general public
thought of it as D-Day for so long beforehand.

Of course, the Germans knew an invasion was coming. At that moment, the only front where America and Britain were fighting Germany on land was in Italy, and there was nothing like enough scope in Italy for the Allies to deploy their whole strength. To try an invasion of north west Europe was the only way they could get to grips with Germany. Just before Montgomery was appointed to command the invading army, his old adversary of the desert war in Africa, Field Marshal Rommel, was appointed to the defence of the coast of Europe. For two years, German propagandists had talked of the Atlantic Wall, which was supposed to be a chain of impregnable defences all along the coast. But Rommel found the Atlantic Wall was very little more than propaganda. Its strength had been exaggerated to discourage British or American raids, and to encourage the Germans. But in fact, the building of it had been given a low priority, its materials had often been diverted to other works which had seemed more urgent, and on many parts of the coast its construction had been neglected by local commanders who regarded an appointment to France as a rest cure from the Russian front. But Rommel was a man, as the British had reason to know, of tremendous energy, and during the last few months, while preparations for the invasion were being completed in Britain, he was working at top speed to build fortifications to defeat it : it was his work which reconnaissance showed in progress. But the work was still made difficult by shortages of material, and even more difficult by differences of opinion among the high command. Rommel himself believed an invasion could only be halted at sea and on the shore. His immediate senior, Field Marshal von Rundstedt, thought that was impossible, and put his trust in reserves which he proposed to keep intact till the exact intentions of the invading forces could be seen. The whole of the German high command, using the same logic which had guided COSSAC, had decided on Normandy or Calais as the most likely points of invasion, but they could not agree in the choice between the two places. Von Rundstedt was convinced the main landing would be in Calais, and so was the higher command of the army in Germany. Rommel favoured Normandy, and so, it is said, did Hitler.

These disagreements were the result, at least in part, of deliberate deception by the Allies. Having decided on Normandy, they did everything they could to persuade the Germans they had decided on Calais. While the armies and fleets were assembling in the south-west of England, dummy army camps and dummy fleets were assembled in the south-east. All the radio activity of an army was simulated in Kent. General Patton, whom the Germans knew well, was brought back from the Mediterranean to England with ample publicity to command this non-existent army. More reconnaissance flights and more preliminary bombing attacks were made in Calais than in Normandy. At the last moment, while the fleets were sailing to Normandy, dummy fleets of ships and aircraft sailed to Calais, using devices which made them appear on radar much larger than they were.

The British secret service was also at work to implant this false belief in the minds of the German commanders. Its task was probably simplified by disagreement between the German secret service and the Nazi leaders. Admiral Canaris, the head of the secret service, had recently been dismissed, and most of his organisation disbanded. A new all-Nazi service had been started under Himmler; but its agents are said to have been clumsy and amateurish, and easy game for the practised cunning of the British. After the war, in German files, about 250 reports from Himmler's men were found to predict the place and time of the invasion. All of them were wrong except one. The wrong ones simply repeated the rumours and false information which were circulated by British agents; and nobody in Berlin had taken any action on the single report which was right.

The deception was so successful that von Rundstedt, for one, went on believing for several weeks after the invasion that the landing in Normandy was a feint and that the main attack was still to come in Calais, and he still kept his reserves in the Calais area. In fact, it was much more successful than anyone expected at the time, and looking back at it now, it seems likely that some kind of deception more convincing than dummies or rumours was in use, and that the British had a direct method of giving false information to the German high command, and giving it with such authority that the Germans could not bring themselves to disbelieve it. Students of spy stories may imagine what the method might have been; but whatever it was, it is still kept secret and probably always will be.

During May, the troops who were to lead the attack had finished a long and arduous and often dangerous training. The seaborne forces had landed in exercises against live ammunition on beaches in Britain which resembled the beaches in Normandy, especially on Slapton Sands in Devon and at Burghead in the Moray Firth; and each unit had practised assaults on replicas of the particular German defences it was expected to attack. But none of them yet had been told where they would be going, or when. Most of the training had been as thorough as it possibly could have been; but the troops could not appreciate its thoroughness till they were told precisely what it was for, and in May, packed into great camps in the south of England with very little to do, men began to feel first bored and then apprehensive. The weather was perfect that month. There seemed to be no reason why they should not start and get it over. Waiting was enough to make anyone nervous.

Most of this feeling disappeared at the end of the month when briefing began. The briefing gave every man the feeling that he was being told exactly what he had to do, and that whoever was planning the thing was making a good job of it and not leaving anything to chance. Every man was shown maps and models of his own objective, and photographs of the shore which were taken from aircraft flying low above the sea, and were so good and clear that in some of them the individual German soldiers manning the defences could be seen. Everyone was allowed to study these for as long as he liked, and officers explained in the greatest detail exactly what each unit was to do and what other units would be doing in the neighbourhood. The only fault that could be found with this briefing, in retrospect, was that it was so good that it made some units over-confident.

Once the briefing had started, the whole vast process of the invasion was irreversible : it had to go on, or else for ever be abandoned. Its success depended entirely on surprise and secrecy. Even during the briefing, the maps had no real names on them, only code names, and nobody except individually selected officers had yet been told what part of the coast they represented. Most men were not told this final secret till after they had actually embarked. But of course everybody could make his own guess ; and in fact anybody who knew France well, or had an ordinary map for comparison, could easily have discovered that Poland meant Caen and that Sword Beach, for example, was at Ouistreham. And as for the time, anybody, not only the soldiers in the camps but anybody who lived near the coast, could tell that it was coming very soon.

The camps in which men were briefed were therefore cut off from the rest of the world. Men and materials were allowed in, but nobody was allowed out again except on the strictest compassionate grounds : the only way out was on a ship to France. The people of England, who had put up with so much already, had to submit to new sets of restrictions. Mail was stopped, and travel was restricted. A zone along the coast was sealed off. As a second line of defence against leakage, the few remaining ways out of the country were closed, and diplomats of neutral countries found they could not communicate with their governments, which was an unprecedented breach of inter-national custom. Ireland was specially under suspicion, because the Germans still had a flourishing embassy in Dublin. But this state of readiness could not be kept up for long, and the longer it lasted the more chance there was that the secret, now shared in whole or in part by hundreds of thousands of people, would leak out of the country and somehow reach Germany.

The people responsible for security had a series of minor scares. Early on, an American major general was sent home to

America as a colonel for what was thought to be careless talk in Claridges; and on a hot morning in May, when a window was open in the War Office in London, all twelve copies of a top-secret signal which gave the whole show away blew out and fluttered down into the crowded street below. Distraught staff officers pounded down the stairs and found eleven copies, and spent the next two hours in an agonised search for the twelfth. It had been picked up by a passer-by, who gave it to the sentry on the Horse Guards Parade on the opposite side of Whitehall. Who was this person ? Would he be likely to gossip ? Nobody ever knew, and the only comfort was that the sentry said he had very thick glasses and seemed to find it difficult to read.

A railwayman who retired in 1957 announced then that in 1944, just before the invasion, he had found the plans of it in a briefcase in a train, and had given them to the station master at Exeter, who had kept them in his safe, watched by the Home Guard, till an officer came to claim them the next morning.

The oddest of all the scares was the *Daily Telegraph* crossword puzzle of May 22nd. When this puzzle was solved, it included the name Omaha, which was the code-name for one of the beaches where the Americans were to land, and the word dives, which might have been the River Dives, on which the left flank of the whole invasion was to rest. Another vaguely suspicious name in it was Dover. It caused some concern to staff officers who still retained the English middle-class habit of doing the *Telegraph* crossword after breakfast, and in after years it provided a story with unlimited scope for growth. Everybody enjoyed stories against the security forces, and stories of narrow escapes from disaster, and sooner or later most of the dozens of code-words in the invasion plans were said to have been revealed in this puzzle.

After Eisenhower had extended the original COSSAC plan, the area of the landing covered sixty miles of the coast of France, from the River Dives near Caen to the east side of the Cherbourg peninsula. At each end of the area, large forces of airborne troops, Americans at the west end and British at the east, were to land by parachute and glider during the night to protect the flanks of the seaborne forces. In the first light of dawn, great fleets of naval ships and aircraft were to bombard the coast, and as the bombardment stopped, the seaborne forces were to land on five separate stretches of beach, each three or four miles long. Again, the Americans were on the west and the British on the east. The Americans had two stretches of beach, one on each side of the estuary of the River Vire ; it was these which had the code names Utah and Omaha. The three other beaches were known as Gold, Juno and Sword. Gold and Sword were British objectives ; Juno was mainly Canadian. The British and Canadian troops for the first assault were about equal in number to the Americans. The air forces were also equal. About three quarters of the naval forces were British.

Everything about the plan was superlative. The fleet of 5,333 ships and landing craft was the largest ever assembled anywhere ; so was the fleet of 9,210 aircraft.* No landing either from the sea or air had ever been attempted on anything like such a scale. The bombardment before the landing was the heaviest and most concentrated ever planned. The logistics and staff work were by far the most complicated that any armies had ever undertaken. Dozens of new devices, from artificial harbours to swimming tanks, had been invented to solve new problems. The naval operation orders, three inches thick on foolscap paper, were the fattest and probably the most indigestible ever printed.

But individual soldiers and sailors were only vaguely aware of these superlatives. Nobody could see five thousand ships or ten thousand aircraft at a glance, and nobody, not even the highest commanders, had any first-hand impression of the whole

* Figures like these always need explanation. The number of ships includes landing craft carried on larger ships, and some vessels which did not cross on D Day. On D Day itself, 2727 vessels crossed the Channel on their own bottoms. The number of aircraft, on the other hand, does not include the heavy bombers and other aircraft indirectly supporting the invasion. Including these, 25,275 sorties were flown between 9 p.m. on June 5th and 9 p.m. on June 6th : on the average an aircraft took off from England every three and a half seconds all through that night and day.

of the tremendous undertaking at the time. Each man who dropped from the sky or plunged into the surf that morning was aware only of what was happening within the short distance he could see, and of the hope and fear and resolution within himself; and it is from that point of view, rather than in terms of enormous figures, that the only true impression of the morning can be given.

Several of the senior officers who commanded the forces of invasion—Eisenhower among them—have commented that the first assault was a soldier's battle, and not a general's battle. The plans were completed in the utmost detail, and explained with meticulous care to the men who had to carry them out ; but once that was done, and the order was given for the operation to begin, and the aircraft had taken off and the ships sailed out from the English harbours, there was absolutely nothing more, for the time being, that the high command could do. Not one of the famous leaders went ashore on D-Day. Events had passed out of their hands. The beaches were attacked, the Atlantic Wall destroyed, and the Allied armies led ashore on the continent, not by generals but mainly by officers and men from the rank of colonel downwards. While they were doing it, they had neither the apparatus nor the time to send any full reports of what they were doing to England, and the few reports which did come back, mostly from ships off-shore, were delayed because the system of signals was overloaded. So it happened that Eisenhower himself, in his headquarters in Southwick House near Portsmouth, knew practically nothing of what was happening until well after the first phase of the battle had been completed. At the moment when the seaborne forces began to storm ashore, the Supreme Commander, according to his aide, was in bed reading a cowboy story, and in the circumstances, that was much the wisest thing for him to do.

The names of the high commanders therefore have very little place in the narrative of the landing. But when everything was ready, one final act remained for them to do. That, of course, was to give the order to go ; and this order was fraught with unexpected anxiety and drama.

Absolutely everything was organised except the weather. For a landing on Monday, the 5th of June, some naval units had to sail on Friday the 2nd ; these included the heavy ships for the bombardment, which were starting from Scotland and Northern Ireland. The movement of men and materials out of the camps and into the landing craft and transports also had to start on that day. It would still be possible on the 3rd to postpone everything for twenty-four hours ; but by dawn on the 4th, the leading ships would have gone too far to be recalled. Weather which was reasonably calm and clear had been regarded all through the planning as absolutely essential for the landing ; and thus, accurate weather forecasts forty-eight hours in advance were needed to ensure success—or twenty-four hours in advance to avoid disaster.

A committee of meteorologists had been assembled for what was certainly the most important weather forecast ever made. All through May, forecasting had been successful, and the weather had given no reason for worry at all. But on June 1st, it turned dull and grey ; and on June 2nd, the meteorologists reported a complex system of three depressions approaching from the Atlantic. On June 3rd, they forecast high winds, low cloud and bad visibility for the 5th, 6th and 7th—the only three days when low tide was at the right time in the morning.

This forecast, and the grim problem which it caused, were presented at 9.30 p.m. on June 3rd in Southwick House, at a conference of Eisenhower, his deputy, his three commanders-in-chief and their chiefs of staff. The first ships had sailed ; tens of thousands of men were cooped up in discomfort in landing craft and transports ; the camps they had left were being filled by follow-up troops ; the whole immense machine was in motion. The problem at that moment was whether to let it go on, or to stop it for twenty-four hours ; and either way, the possibilities of disaster were very clear.

Many accounts have been given of this all-important meeting, and of three which followed it in the next thirty-six hours. In their details the accounts are all different; and that is not surprising, because only nine men were present at the meetings, and even the most junior of them carried a fearful responsibility. Nobody was there as an observer. However high a rank a man achieves, his capacity for thought and feeling is only human, and one may imagine that the capacity of each of these men was taxed to the limit by the decision they had to make, so that none of them had the leisure or inclination to detach his mind from the problem and observe exactly what happened and remember it for the sake of historians. The men were General Eisenhower, Air Chief Marshal Tedder, Admiral Ramsay, General Montgomery and Air Chief Marshal Leigh-Mallory; and the four chiefs of staff, Lieutenant General Bedell Smith, Rear Admiral Creasy, Major General de Guingand and Air Marshal Robb. It seems strange in retrospect that only two of them were American, and seven British; but for the moment, the British could only advise; the ultimate responsibility was Eisenhower's, and he carried it all alone.

In looking back at that moment of decision, one may also glance back further at the life of the man who had to make it. The story of Eisenhower's rise to fame is a typically American romance. He came of German stock, and people often commented on the irony that the Supreme Commander bore a German name; but his family had been in America for over two hundred years, and nobody could have been more purely American in character. An irony which was less widely known at the time was that his family had always been strictly pacifist; his mother, who was still alive in 1944, was a member of the sect called Jehovah's Witnesses, and was a conscientious objector.

Eisenhower was born in Texas in 1890, and brought up in poverty in Kansas, in the American middle west. His father was night watchman at a creamery, and his biographers describe a boyhood which might have been the story of any of the least privileged of the hundreds of thousands of Americans who were to come under his command: a story of working a way through high school, of interest more in athletics than in class, of boyish fights and disgraces, and of only the vaguest of plans or ambitions for the future. Yet the marriage of David and Ida Eisenhower, his father and mother, was one of those strange and rare unions which produce children far more brilliant than their ancestry would lead one to expect. All of their seven sons, except one who died young, hauled themselves up out of poverty and achieved distinction, each in a different profession. The influence which made their third son choose the army came from outside the family and shocked his mother; but she had made it a principle never to stand in the way of her sons. He put himself in for the entrance examination for West Point, and passed top of his class. After that, his career in the military academy was not very distinguished, and when he graduated at the age of twenty-four, he was sixty-first in a class of one hundred and sixty-eight. That was in 1915. During the first world war, he was never sent overseas, and never saw battle, and between the wars, his promotion was very slow. He remained a major for no less than sixteen years, and only just over three years before the invasion of Normandy, he was still a lieutenant-colonel. At that time, his highest hope was to end up as a colonel.

His quick rise through the ranks in those three years was largely due to General Marshall, the American Chief of Staff. Of course, Marshall did not push him up without reason. During all his years as a junior officer, Eisenhower had collected an enormous fund of miscellaneous military knowledge, and he had the clear and analytical brain which high command requires. But probably another reason for his appointment to the European command was simply that everybody liked him. An American general in command of British armies—and especially of British generals — not only had to have military judgment which everyone would respect; he also needed exceptional tact and charm and sense of humour. Eisenhower certainly had those qualities. He could be strict and tough, as generals have to be; but in spite of his position he still seemed a modest and even humble man. He never considered himself to be a genius. He had no pretensions, and none of the flamboyance which generals find so irritating in other generals. The British liked him as much as the Americans. At the time, they said he really might almost have been British; and afterwards, General Morgan wrote that his grin was worth an army corps.

This was the man who, after fifty years of obscurity, had to preside over the meeting of his British commanders-in-chief at Southwick House, and balance their opinions, and make the decision on which the course of history and the lives of countless men could clearly be seen to depend.

At the meeting on Saturday evening, June 3rd, the report of the meteorologists and the advice of the commanders-in-chief made him almost certain that the operation would have to be postponed. It was a most unwelcome prospect. Plans had been made by which everything could be brought to a standstill for twenty-four hours, but Eisenhower was sure that postponement would be hard on the morale and the physical condition of the troops already at sea; and any delay would add to the risk of the secret leaking out. The decision was none the easier because at that moment, outside the windows of Southwick House, the skies were clear and there was hardly any wind at all.

He decided to hold another meeting at 4.30 the next morning, Sunday, June 4th, in the hope of some improvement in the forecast. In the meantime, some of the convoys of American landing craft sailed from their ports in south Devon and Corn-wall, and began their voyage along the English coast.

The next morning, the forecast was just as bad, though the weather outside was just as good. At this meeting, Montgomery was willing to go ahead in spite of the forecast, but Ramsay doubted whether his smaller craft could cross the Channel in the seas which were predicted, and Leigh-Mallory was certain the air forces would not be able to play their full part in the plan. By then, the main forces were due to sail in two hours' time. But Eisenhower gave the order to postpone the sailing for twenty-four hours and recall the ships at sea. The fleet of big ships steaming south down the Irish sea turned about, to steam north for twelve hours. A flotilla of minesweepers was only thirty-five miles from the Normandy coast when it got the order to return, and a convoy of landing craft on its way to Utah Beach did not receive the signal and ploughed on southwards. Destroyers were sent to turn it back, but they could not find it. At 9 o'clock, it was spotted by a naval seaplane a third of the way across the Channel. The landing craft from Devon, which were then off the Isle of Wight, put back towards harbours which were already full. At Portland, there was the most tremendous traffic jam in maritime history. During the morning, in rising wind, it seemed that the landing craft would have to go back to Devon to sort themselves out and start again, and if they had, they would not have been ready for at least two days. But order was restored, in a struggle which lasted all day, and not very much damage was done except that one tank landing craft drifted into the tide race off Portland Bill and foundered.

But the postponement had not solved Eisenhower's problem. On Sunday evening, he faced the same terrible choice in a different and even more difficult form. Instead of good weather outside and a bad forecast, the weather outside was then visibly impossible, but the forecasters offered a chance, and only a chance, of a slight temporary improvement on Tuesday morning. Ramsay reported that the convoys which had been recalled could only make one more attempt without refuelling. The choice was therefore between launching the invasion on Tuesday the 6th, in weather which was nothing better than a gamble, or postponing it for a fortnight till the tides were right again. Again, Eisenhower put off the final decision till early the following morning.

During that night, he carried as heavy a burden as has fallen to the lot of any man. Everyone who had been at the evening meeting remembered one phrase he had used: " The question is, how long can you hang this operation out on a limb and let it hang there ? " The troops could not stay in their ships for a fortnight. But they had been briefed, and had now even been told the real names of the places they were to go to ; and if all the tens of thousands of them were brought ashore again— even supposing it were possible to accommodate them—it was impossible to hope that the secret would not leak. So far, the German air force only seemed to have spotted a small proportion of the fleet, and had never attacked it. That luck was too astonishing to last. The Germans were known to have " secret weapons " (soon to be given the familiar name of doodle-bugs) which were nearly ready and might be used, with effects which nobody could foresee, in attacks on the crowded harbours. In postponement for a fortnight, there were such risks of confusion, of loss of security and of counter-attack that the whole plan might have to be abandoned. These were possibilities which Eisenhower himself has said were almost too bitter to contemplate.

But the alternative of launching the invasion in uncertain weather was almost equally risky. If the forecast was exactly right, all might be well ; but if it was only slightly over-optimistic, landing craft would be swamped, naval and air bombardment would be inaccurate, German bombers might be able to take off while Allied fighters were grounded, and the invasion might end in a slaughter of troops and the greatest military disaster which either America or Britain had ever suffered.

And finally, if it failed, whether it had been postponed or not, it would be impossible to try again that summer, perhaps impossible ever to try again. All the hopes and power of America and Britain had been put into this one attempt to bring the Germans to battle in western Europe. If it failed, hope might also fail, not only in America and Britain but in the countries which the Germans had occupied ; the Russians might decide their allies were useless and make a separate peace. The ordinary troops, and the ordinary people, had never wasted time on the thought that the war might be lost, but Eisenhower, with expert and dispassionate knowledge, knew that if the invasion failed it might be impossible ever to win the war.

He himself, being a soldier, has never described his own feelings on that night of decision, but perhaps some indication

of them is given by the announcement which he drafted, without
telling anyone, some time on June 5th.

" Our landings in the Cherbourg-Havre area have failed
to gain a satisfactory foothold and I have withdrawn the
troops. My decision to attack at this time and place was
based upon the best information available. The troops, the
air, and the navy did all that bravery and devotion to duty
could do. If any blame or fault attaches to the attempt it is
mine alone."

When he had written this, he put it in his pocket in case it
was needed. Six weeks later, he found it again, still in his
pocket.

By the time he wrote this announcement, he had already
decided to commit his forces to the hazard of landing, whatever
the weather might bring. All through the meetings, Montgomery
had been willing to start. Ramsay had agreed, but reluctantly.
Leigh-Mallory, speaking for the air forces, had wanted to wait ;
but at the last meeting, just after four a.m. on Monday, he also
had agreed that the chance must be taken, and Eisenhower had
launched the invasion with the words " O.K. We'll go."

That evening, when the ships had sailed and there was
nothing more that he could do except wait for the result of his
decision, he drove to an airfield fifty miles inland near Newbury,
where American parachutists were waiting to take off. He had
a particular interest in these men, and a particular concern for
them. Some thirteen thousand of them were to drop that night
in the Cherbourg peninsula, while British parachutists dropped
near Caen. Ever since the outline of this plan had first been
made, four months before, Leigh-Mallory had opposed the
American drop because it had to be made in wooded and well-
defended country ; he had predicted that 80 per cent. of the troop-
carrying aircraft would be lost. Only a week before, he had
come to Eisenhower again to protest against what he called the
futile slaughter of two fine American divisions.

Eisenhower had never agreed with his pessimistic view, but

it was no light matter to disregard the advice of his air commander-in-chief. At Leigh-Mallory's insistence, he had retired alone to his quarters and analysed the airborne plan again with the greatest care, and then—again carrying the burden alone—he had decided to over-rule him. But the doubt still remained in his mind that his air adviser might be right, and his own judgment might be wrong, and of all his personal worries that day, the worst, he said afterwards, was the thought that his own conscience might find him guilty of the blind sacrifice of these thousands of young Americans.

At the airfield, concealing this thought, he strolled round among them talking cheerfully to anyone who caught his eye. They were full of confidence, and knew nothing of his fears. One of them, who had a ranch in Texas, offered him a job when the war was over. As darkness fell, they embarked in their aircraft, and Eisenhower waited and watched the aircraft take off into the gathering night; a Supreme Commander is always a lonely man. At the same time, others were taking off from airfields all over England, and soon the sky overhead was full of the sound of them.

Probably Eisenhower had hardly noticed the countryside around the airfield, but the parachutists knew it well. When they left their depot at Fort Bragg in Carolina, England had been described to them as a combat zone. Many of them, after crossing the Atlantic, had arrived at their camps in Wiltshire in the dark, and had had a surprise at what they saw the next morning : gentle green hills, ancient stone pubs and churches, thatched villages with incredible names—Chilton Foliat, Straight Soley and Crooked Soley, Ogbourne St. George, and the place which was written Mildenhall and spoken of as Minal. There was no sign of combat, but every symbol of ancient peace and calm. One of the parachutists said he felt as if he had passed out and woken up on a Hollywood movie set.

It was true that almost nothing could change the peaceful ways of those English villages. Most of their young men and

D.O.D.   B women had gone away. All through the years from Dunkirk, the people who remained had plodded on, working rather harder than they ever had before, urged on by government officials, and by their own consciences, to grow more than the land had ever been made to produce, and spending what leisure time was left in the Home Guard, the civil defence, the first aid, or the fire watchers. When the Americans came, the people of the villages watched the most extraordinary activities with interest, but without very much surprise. Mass parachute drops on the neighbouring parks and farms became such a common sight that they hardly bothered to go outside to watch.

But when the Americans suddenly disappeared, the villages seemed very strange without them. On the evening of the fifth, when Eisenhower was at the airfield, the bar of the Stag's Head in Chilton Foliat a couple of miles away was a desolate place. Nobody was in, except the local regulars sitting over their mild and bitter. The bottled ale and the strictly rationed whisky, which had usually all gone by nine o'clock, were left on the shelves that night. The landlord and the regulars, in desultory conversation, wondered where the Americans had gone, and agreed that they really rather missed the noise and hustle, and reflected how dead the place would have been all winter if they had never been there.

At closing time, with these thoughts still in his mind, the landlord locked the bar, and washed up the few glasses, and then went out to shut up his chickens ; and it was while he was out there in the meadow behind the pub that the airfield came to life. The aircraft came up over the elms in the park where the American camp stood empty now and silent : in twos, in dozens, in scores, they circled overhead and took up formation, and others came over from further north in hundreds. Standing there in awe, he called to his wife to come and listen. " This is it," he said.

Even in London, veterans of the air-raids were woken by the sound. There in the capital, there were many staff officers who knew the secret and had known it for months, but Londoners in general had known less of what was going on than country people. Out in the countryside, there was hardly a village without its own local airfield or camp or dump of equipment, in which the people had taken a personal interest and pride; but in London none of the preparations could be seen, except down the river where some of the colossal concrete sections of the two artificial harbours had been built: the harbours which were to be towed across the Channel and put together on the coast of France within a few days of the landing. In villages, there were still some things which people could gossip about, because there were things which everyone in the village had seen; but in London security was such an ingrained habit by then that even people who had seen some clue to the invasion told nobody else about it. Invasion was in everybody's mind, but was seldom discussed at all.

It was not till nearly dawn that the aircraft began to cross London. Then they flew over the city without a single pause for two and a half hours. Nothing like this had happened before; the fleets of aircraft which had been bombing Germany had normally kept clear of London so that its defences were not confused. Some people woken by the noise thought at first, half asleep, that they must have missed hearing the siren; but then they woke more, and remembered that the days were past when Germany could send such fleets of aircraft over, and realised that London was hearing for the very first time a bomber fleet without an air raid warning. People got up and looked out of their windows across the blacked-out city, but the sky was cloudy and there was nothing to be seen.

Down on the coast, everybody knew, even before the planes came over and flew in formation out across the sea. In the coast-guard hut on the top of St. Alban's Head, the watch had just been changed, and a man called Wallace had come off duty; and during the day he had been witness of a spectacle vaster and braver than had ever been seen on that historic shore, or

on any sea in any age of history. St. Alban's Head is high, and
from the top of it the view extends across the Channel to the
south ; to the east across Weymouth Bay to Portland ; to the
west across the approaches of Southampton Water to the Isle of
Wight ; to the north, through the gentle folds of the Purbeck
Hills to the grey stone village of Worth Matravers.

The village and the coastguard cottages and the hut on the
top of the cliff had been home for Mr. Wallace for many years.
He was a veteran of the Dover Patrol of the First World War.
Originally, he had come from Bristol, but his wife had been
born in Worth Matravers, and it was on her account that he had
come home there in his middle age, and settled down to a perfectly
contented life as a coastguard, a churchwarden, a chairman
of the parish council, and an organiser in general of most of the
activities of the village.

That was before the war, before Worth Matravers had become
in a sense a front-line village, and before the coastguard hut had
become an outpost looking over no-man's land. In those days,
the village had been peaceful and even sleepy, but the part of
the Channel off St. Alban's head had always been busy with
ships. In 1940, both village and sea had changed. Tired men
without weapons, straight back from Dunkirk, had been put
into camps among the hills. Farmers had sharpened pitchforks,
the Local Defence Volunteers had paraded with pikes, the coast-
guards had armed themselves with knobbed sticks to repel the
invasion ; and the sea, for the first time in centuries, had been
absolutely empty. For week after week, that year, not a single
ship had been sighted from the hut, and the only entries in the
coastguard log were of German aircraft patrolling the English
Channel unmolested.

Ever since those days, four years before, Mr. Wallace and
the three men who alternated the watch with him had seen
increasing drama as the Channel, from being a German preserve,
became a battlefield. They saw the first coastal convoys, attacks
by E-boats, sinking ships, crashing aircraft, deaths and rescues.
And all through those years, they had the sense of standing on

the very edge of the world; for the known, orderly, civilised world ended then within gunshot of the cliffs of England. It was plain to see that anyone who ventured beyond the edge took his life in his hands; while over the south horizon was implacable and impersonal hostility, as hard to visualise as the terrors which the ancients imagined beyond the Western Ocean.

This feeling, which was widespread in England, of an uncrossable frontier which hemmed the country in, made the sight which Wallace saw on the fifth of June more wonderful. For several weeks, the harbour at Portland, seventeen miles to the westward, had been filling with ships. In the past week, when he looked at it through glasses, the whole of its area had seemed black. Then it had begun to overflow, and all the seventeen-mile sweep of Weymouth Bay had begun to fill. A screen of destroyers had been thrown across the bay. The destroyers turned close in below his hut, and steamed in a straight line, back and forth, all night and day, across the mouth of the bay to Portland Bill; and inside the screen, ever more and more ships had anchored. Then, on the day before, between the squalls of rain, he had seen still hundreds more come in: these were the landing craft and escorts which had come up from Cornwall and Devon and then, on Eisenhower's order, turned back to shelter.

And that morning, the fleet had sailed. He could not possibly count the ships, or even guess the numbers; in fact, much more than a thousand ships were before his eyes. Close under the cliffs of the headland, he looked down on landing craft, and could see the troops on board. Beyond them, line after line of tank landing craft passed by, escorted by motor launches. There were armed trawlers, and ocean tugs, and far out and ahead, there were echelons of minesweepers. Hundreds of ships were flying barrage balloons. Destroyers and frigates took up their stations out to sea; French, British and American cruisers; tank landing ships, and infantry transports carrying small landing craft in davits; and on the horizon, coming up from the west beyond Portland, battleships and monitors and heavy cruisers.

Fighter planes wove patterns overhead. Then in the east, more landing craft and escorts emerged from Poole, and in the far distance another separate fleet steamed out of the Solent and turned south in silhouette against the white cliffs of the Isle of Wight. Wallace stood on the head of the cliff, entranced and exalted by a pageant of splendour which nobody had ever seen before, and nobody, it is certain, will ever see again. Before evening, the last of the ships had gone, hull down on the southern horizon, and once more the sea was empty.

He was on his way home when dusk had fallen and the sound in the sky began. At home, his wife was listening. " This is it," he said to her ; and later that night, when they were ready to go to bed, he said : " A lot of men are going to die to-night. We should pray for them." They knelt by the side of the bed.

II

THE BRITISH AIR DROP

In the dark cloudy sky above the lush pastureland of Normandy, at twenty minutes past midnight, the first of the parachutists jumped and the first of the glider pilots cast off from their tugs, and the vanguard drifted down in silence on the wind.

At the eastern end of the invasion shore, there are three waterways : first the Caen Canal, which runs from the sea to the city eight miles inland ; then the River Orne, which is close to the canal ; and then, five miles farther east, the River Dives. The main German armoured reserves were in the area east of Caen, and the rôle of the British 6th Airborne Division was to drop in the five-mile strip between the two rivers and protect the seaborne forces against armoured counter-attack while they were landing.

This task called for speed and good timing, and for novel and daring techniques. The division was not allowed to take off from England before dark, in case its aircraft were detected ; and before dawn it not only had to win a territory of twenty-five square miles and demolish its main defences, but also be ready to fight off German tanks. Its anti-tank guns and other defensive equipment were too massive for parachutes, and could only be carried in gliders ; but nobody before had ever attempted an accurate landing in enemy country of large numbers of gliders in the dark. Nevertheless, under Major-General Richard Gale,

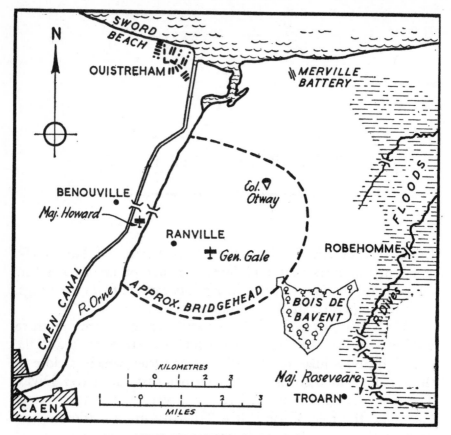

THE BRITISH AIR DROP

the division evolved a plan which it was confident could lead to success. The keys to it were seven small bridges, five over the River Dives, one over the Orne and one over the canal.

The Dives is a small river, which winds gently among flat water-meadows and willow trees; but the Germans had flooded its valley as part of their scheme of defence and made an impenetrable marsh from half a mile to two miles wide. No doubt they assumed that control of the five bridges which crossed it would be in their hands; but Gale decided to destroy them by surprise attacks, and so turn the barrier of the marshes to his own account. With these bridges down, a German armoured counter-attack from the east would be impossible, and he could concentrate his anti-tank defences to the south.

The Orne and the Caen Canal, on the other hand, lay between his own landing zones and the British beaches from which he would ultimately be reinforced; and therefore, while the Dives bridges had to be destroyed, the Orne and canal bridges had to be captured intact. Only one road crosses the Orne and the canal between the city and the sea.

When the division's plan was completed, the main events of the night appeared as follows :—

12.20.   A force in gliders to land on the Orne and canal bridges.

12.20.   Pathfinders to drop by parachute, to mark out dropping zones for the main parachute forces.

12.50.   Main parachute drop to begin. Objectives : to demolish the Dives bridges, reinforce the defence of the Orne and canal bridges, capture a coast defence battery, seize the territory between the rivers, and clear landing zones for the main glider force.

3.30.   Main force of 72 gliders to land with anti-tank armament, transport and heavy equipment.

Each of these separate actions depended on the quick success of those before it. The division's defence depended on the gliders. The gliders depended on the parachutists to clear their landing zones within one hour and forty minutes. The parachutists depended on the pathfinders. The final relief and reinforcement of the whole division depended on the capture of the Orne and canal bridges. And dawn began at 5.30. Much had to be accomplished in the seven hours' darkness of the summer night.

Since that night, there has been plenty of argument, mostly light-hearted, between units which claim to have been the first to land. It is an argument which can never be decided. The pathfinders and the first gliders of the British army came down in groups, here and there between the rivers, with no more than a minute or two between them; and at almost the same moment American landings started 50 miles away. But whoever was the first to land, the first troops in action were probably three platoons of the Oxford and Buckinghamshire Light Infantry, and certainly they were the first to achieve their objective; for this was the force assigned to capture the bridge on the Caen Canal. At midnight these platoons were already close to the coast of France, each platoon cooped in the pitch-dark inside of a Horsa glider towed by a Halifax bomber. In the leading glider everyone was singing. " Abie, my boy " was the most successful song. Almost all that first platoon were Cockneys, and wisecracks flew around. Somewhere over the Channel, somebody dropped a machine-gun magazine with a loud metallic clang on the steel floor. " Old so-and-so's dropped 'is false teeth," a voice said cheerfully. It seemed tremendously funny at the time, but heaven knows what doubts and fears were hidden behind the laughter; for apart from the apprehension of the coming battle, these men all knew that their glider was going to crash.

Most passengers in aircraft think of a crash as the end of everything: to begin the day with a deliberate crash appears a bizarre conception. But logic, and the situation of the Caen canal bridge, demanded this desperate measure. The bridge is a large steel structure which can be raised to let ships go through. At its western end there are a cross-roads and the first houses of the village of Benouville. A quarter of a mile down the road in the other direction is the bridge across the Orne.

British Intelligence had learned from the local amateur French spies that both these bridges were wired for demolition and defended by permanent guards. Air reconnaissance had shown trenches and barbed wire on the approaches to the bridges, and during March concrete pill-boxes had also appeared on the photographs. Nobody knew precisely what orders had been given to the German guards, but as they had wired the bridges it was only common sense to assume that they intended to blow them up, rather than allow them to be captured. To capture them intact was therefore a matter of split-second surprise. It had to be done before the guards knew what was happening or had time to make up their minds to press the button to explode them.

That was the reason why the attack on these bridges was the first action in the airborne plan ; and it was also the reason for the decision to use gliders for the attack, rather than parachutes. Parachutists are always more or less scattered when they drop, and take at least a few minutes to assemble. A glider provides a possibility of landing up to thirty men together on a given spot, ready for action within a matter of seconds of their landing.

But it remained no more than a possibility. First, the glider pilots had to find the bridges in the dark. Secondly, the bridges were surrounded by fields too small for a normal landing ; and that was why a crash was inevitable. But the Glider Pilot Regiment, upon whom this duty was to fall, took pride in achieving feats with gliders which seemed impossible, and they confidently promised to try to do what General Gale demanded : to crash six gliders within three minutes of 12.20 a.m., three at each bridge and all within a few paces of the abutments— and to do it, if all went well, without killing their passengers.

The passengers in this deadly experiment were led by Major John Howard, one of the company commanders of the " Ox and Bucks " ; and on the flight across the Channel, while his men were so cheerfully singing, Howard sat in the seat next to the door in the leading glider, keyed to the utmost pitch of tense anticipation ; for much of the plan of attack was his own creation, and he had looked forward to and yet dreaded this moment throughout the past three months.

Howard was a regular officer of 30, and he had volunteered for airborne duties, like many other men in the division, as a matter of self-respect. For the first year of the war, he had commanded a training company, but in 1942 he had heard that the Ox and Bucks were going airborne, and he had made up his mind to join them. Nobody he had asked knew very much about airborne warfare, but it sounded the sort of thing he needed to counterbalance that year which he felt had been ignominious. He lived in Oxford, so it was only a matter of getting transferred to his county regiment.

But not very long before he made that decision, John Howard had married a very pretty girl called Joy ; and on the day when he told her he had decided to become a parachutist, she told him she was going to have a baby. That was an unpromising beginning for an airborne career ; but Joy understood his professional pride, and did her best to hide her anxiety from him. A month before D-Day, their second child was born ; and all through the months of training, Howard's wife and children had never been far from his mind.

The flight across the Channel was scheduled to take one hour and twenty-four minutes. It was a curious pause, between the end of the preparations and the beginning of battle, in which a man's thoughts—unless he could stifle them with songs and laughter—were all too prone to dwell uselessly on the possibility that something essential had been forgotten. Howard's thoughts were a mixture of the personal and the military. He thought about Joy. He thought with surprise that it was a wonder he was not being sick ; for he had always been sick on training flights, even when nobody else was, so that it had become a standing joke in his company. And he thought with pride of his 160 men. Many of them were hardly more than boys, and most of them had never seen action. Before they had embarked, he had thanked them for their patience in the long and tough and often boring training ; and his voice had not sounded like his own to him, because he felt the emotion of the moment very keenly. They had always done everything he told them, and so he felt responsible for their fate. Next to him in the glider, for example, was Lt. Den Brotheridge, the platoon commander. Brotheridge had been a cadet in Howard's own training company, and Howard himself had persuaded him to join the airborne forces. Howard reflected now that without his persuasion, Brotheridge would not have been there at all ; and he knew that Brotheridge, like himself, had a young wife and that she was expecting a baby any day. But in fact Brotheridge had no regrets, and would never have thought of Howard as responsible for his fate. He had bet him 50 francs he would be out of the door before him when the glider crashed, and so lay claim to be the first Allied soldier to land in the invasion.

On the other side of Howard, at the controls of the glider, was his pilot, Staff Sergeant Wallwork of the Glider Pilot Regiment. It was Wallwork who had done most to calm Howard's worries in the last few weeks. For Howard, the whole three months of planning and training had been a worrying time, and his worry had reached a climax on May 30th. On that day, he had been shown new aerial photographs of his bridges, and in all the fields round them, white spots could be seen which had not been there before. These, he was told, were holes for posts which were intended to make it impossible for gliders to land. The interpreters of photographs could not tell him whether posts had been put in the holes yet or not. Gloomily, he had shown the photographs to his pilots. They seemed delighted. "That's just what we needed," Wallwork had said. "We'll land between the posts. The posts will break the wings off and slow us down, and we shan't hit the bridge so hard."

It was impossible not to trust a pilot who could say a thing like that. Yet Howard, on his way across the Channel, was still wondering whether he had asked Wallwork and the others for something impossible. He had told them he wanted the first glider to stop with its nose inside the wire defences of the bridge, and the others to stop ten yards behind and five yards to the right. He had no idea how such precision could be achieved, but they had made light of it, and his troops had caught their mood of confidence.

Sitting there in the dark, half listening to the singing and the roar of the rush of air, Howard thought over these special worries of his own, and also the worry which beset almost every man who was crossing the Channel that night: did the Germans know they were coming? Would the surprise come off, or were they running their heads into an ambush? In a pause between songs, he heard a friendly anonymous shout from the back of the fuselage : " 'Asn't the major bin sick yet ? "

12.16 : Wallwork half turned in the pilot's seat and shouted back to him : " Casting off." Howard called for silence, and the singing and talking died as the order was passed down the two lines of men who sat facing each other on each side of the body of the glider. The glider checked : the tow rope was gone : as the speed fell off, the roar of the wind on the flimsy structure also died, to a hiss which seemed like silence ; and in the silence fears rose up which the cheerful noise had held in check till then. The nose dropped, and the glider swooped, bumping through the torn clouds. Brotheridge undid his safety belt and stood up, with Howard and the platoon sergeant holding him, and swung open the forward door. Cold air streamed in. The glider levelled out from the dive and banked steeply to the right, and peering down through the open door into the darkness of space beneath, Howard glimpsed for a second a dimly gleaming ribbon : the Caen Canal. But the sight of it only elated him for a moment, because he was not really thinking of what lay below him and ahead. He was thinking of Joy and the children asleep in bed at home in Oxford, and he was thankful they did not know what he was doing.

" Hold tight," Wallwork said ; and all the platoon linked arms and lifted their feet off the floor and sat there locked together, waiting.

The concussion was shattering. The glider tore into the earth at ninety miles an hour, and careered across the tiny field with a noise like thunder as timber cracked and split and it smashed itself to pieces. The stunning noise and shocks went on and on for a count of seconds ; and then suddenly for a split second everything was perfectly still and silent. But even in the stunned silence, training worked. Howard found he had undone his belt and was on his feet. The doorway had crumpled into wreckage. But in front of him was a jagged hole in the glider's side and he went through it headfirst and fell on the earth of France, picked himself up and felt his limbs for broken bones and looked up : and there against the night sky, exactly and precisely where it should have been, twenty paces away, was the steel lattice tower of the bridge. Brotheridge came running round the tail : he had got out of a hole on the other side. " All right ? " he said. " Yes," Howard said. " Carry on." Brotheridge shouted his platoon letter, " Able, Able," to rally the men who were tumbling out of the wreckage, and the action began which they had rehearsed on bridges all over England. A phosphorus smoke bomb was thrown at the pillbox by the bridge. A machine gun opened fire from it, but one man ran forward under cover of the smoke and dropped a Mills bomb through the gun port, and the platoon scrambled across the wire which the glider had demolished, up an embankment on to the road, and with yells of " Able, Able," they dashed across the bridge against the fire of a second machine gun on the far side. Howard made for the spot he had named as his command post, followed by his radio operator, Corporal Tappenden, and as he ran he heard a crash behind him, and then another : the other two gliders coming in. Soon above the noise of small arms fire he heard his second and third platoons come running through the darkness, shouting " Baker " and " Charlie," not only to identify themselves, but also because men shout by instinct when they charge into a battle.

The sentry on the bridge was a young German called Helmut Römer, and when he saw the first glider crash he naturally thought it was a bomber, because there were heavy air-raids going on in Caen and along the coast, and he had been watching the anti-aircraft fire. Nobody had told him anything more than an air raid was expected. So when men with black faces charged across the bridge at him, he was totally taken by surprise. He dived for the trenches : it was the only thing he could do. There was no time for the guard to turn out, much less for the whole platoon to be called from their billets. But the N.C.O. of the guard fired the machine gun and shot down the first of the men who were coming across the bridge. Then the wave of them broke into the trenches, and the garrison scattered and ran.

Within three minutes of the crash, the attack had succeeded. Engineers searched for the demolition wiring and disconnected it. The charge itself had not been put in place : they found it afterwards in a store by the bridgehead. With the bridge in their hands, the infantry went on to clear out the houses beyond it. One man from the leading platoon came back across the bridge to tell Howard they were through. " But Mr. Brotheridge is hurt, sir," he said. By Howard's side, Corporal Tappenden was trying to call the other half of the company which by then should have landed at the Orne Bridge down the road, but he could not get an answer. A man was struggling up the steep bank to the road, and Howard bent down to help him and saw a face which was a red mask of blood. It was Wallwork, the pilot, injured but still bringing up ammunition from the glider. Men came back over the bridge carrying Brotheridge on a stretcher. Howard looked at his friend. He was still alive, but unconscious, and Howard knew by instinct that the man he had persuaded to go airborne, the man who had bet him he would be first to land, was going to be the first to die in action.

Howard called for the doctor, and he was found wandering dazed across the bridge : for the second glider, in which he had travelled, had broken in half in the middle, and many of the men in it were injured. One had been thrown out of it into a little pond and drowned. Tappenden looked up from his radio and shouted : " I've raised them, sir. They got the other bridge."

The attack on the Orne bridge had been a walk-over. The landing had not been so precise as the landing at the canal. One glider was close to the bridge, but the next was a quarter of a mile away. The third was cast off from its tug in the wrong place, and landed beyond the marshes of the Dives. Even the first of the three was a minute or two behind the first at the canal, and the leading platoon, commanded by Lt. Fox, got to the bridge just in time to see the German defenders running for their lives. One of Fox's N.C.O.s jumped into an empty machine-gun post and turned the German gun against the retreating Germans ; and his were the only shots which were fired. It was just like an exercise. The commander of the second platoon, running breathlessly on to the bridge some minutes late, found Fox in the middle of it, staring down at the dark water of the Orne. " How's it gone ? " he asked anxiously. " It's gone all right," Fox said. " But where the hell are the umpires ? "

The code words which Howard had been allotted to signal the success of his attack had none of the air of modest triumph which might have suited the very first success of the invasion. The capture of the canal bridge intact was to be reported by radio to brigade headquarters by the word ham. For the Orne bridge the word was jam. Corporal Tappenden could not get an acknowledgment from brigade, and for half an hour, squatting by the roadside, he broadcast those pregnant words : " Ham and jam. Ham and jam. Ham and jam." Meanwhile, the six platoons, weakened now by the losses of the crash and the fighting, attended their dead and wounded and prepared to defend what they had won ; for a counter-attack was expected as soon as the Germans had recovered from their surprise, and until Howard's men could be reinforced by the main body of the parachutists, they were in a perilous position.

Nobody at Brigade Headquarters heard Howard's signal because the brigade signals equipment had all disappeared in the drop—the first symptom of a difficulty which was to bring the whole airborne attack to the edge of disaster.

The pathfinders of the division were a company of parachutists carried in six aircraft. Their job was to land at the same moment as Howard in his gliders, but farther east, and to set up lights and radio beacons on which the main parachute forces would be dropped. Their navigators and pilots, of course, were picked men, but even they had trouble, in the wind and cloud, in dropping their troops exactly. The parachutes themselves were carried by the wind. The errors accumulated, and when the pathfinders landed they found they were scattered and much farther eastward than they should have been. But they only had

half an hour to prepare the dropping zones. There was no time
to march back to the zones which had been planned, and so they
had to set out their beacons where they were, although one of the
zones which they improvised was dangerously close to the woods
called the Bois de Bavent, and another was near the floodlands
of the Dives.

Close behind the aircraft of the pathfinder company were
those of the 3rd Parachute Brigade, whose missions were to
destroy the five bridges across the River Dives and a powerful
coast-defence battery at Merville, near the mouth of the Orne.

The capture of the Merville battery was important, because
it commanded the beaches on which the left flank of the British
3rd Division was to land, and the anchorage where by dawn the
fleet would be assembled. If it were still in action at the break
of day, it would certainly cause havoc, and might even prevent
the landing of the 3rd Division. The job of silencing it was
given to the 9th Parachute Battalion, whose commander was
Lt.-Col. T. B. H. Otway; and when the Brigadier had first
given Otway his orders, he had described the job, quite rightly,
as a stinker.

Reconnaissance had shown that the guns of the battery,
in their bomb-proof emplacements, were surrounded first by
machine-gun positions and a belt of barbed wire. Outside this
was a minefield thirty yards wide, and outside that a second
barbed-wire entanglement. Beyond this again were a further
100 yards of mines surrounded by a wire fence. Intelligence
estimated that it was held by 200 men with ten machine guns
and two dual-purpose cannons. Otway's battalion had to drop
at ten minutes to one, assemble, march a mile and a half to this
stronghold, and capture it by 5.15; for at that moment, if
they had not fired a signal of success, the navy were to begin
to shell it. The only support which Otway was offered was a
bombing attack, in the early hours of the morning, by 100
Lancasters of the R.A.F. But neither shelling nor bombing
was expected to destroy the battery, which of course had been

built to withstand that kind of attack. The only way to destroy
it was to get inside it.

Terence Otway was 29, and looked younger ; and at that age
he commanded 750 of the toughest of British troops. He was
slim and lightly built. His face was lean and gave an impression
of keen intellect and an ascetic and sensitive character. One might
almost have been forgiven for putting him down, at first sight,
as an artist rather than a colonel of paratroops. But such appointments are more than a matter of chance. Otway's father had
been killed in the First World War, and his mother had had a
long struggle to bring up her son on a war widow's pension.
When he left school he was nearly articled to a solicitor in
Brighton ; but he had hated the idea of settling down in an
office before he had seen the world at all, and so, when he was
19 he had entered the Royal Military College, Sandhurst, and
been commissioned into the army, only intending to stay for
five years. The army took him to the north-west frontier of
India and to China. The five years expired a few months before
war began. By then, he had come to despise a good many things
about army life, especially life in an officers' mess in India, and
he had tried to get out. But he had not been allowed to go ; and
so, by D-Day, he had served for ten years and had revealed—
perhaps to his own surprise—an extremely acute and incisive
military brain.

When he had been told, four months before the invasion,
of what his battalion was expected to do, he had set to work
to prepare his plan and train his men with fantastic thoroughness.
He went out with the secret maps and photographs of Merville
to find a stretch of the English countryside which resembled
the surroundings of the battery, and he found one near Newbury
in Berkshire. Within two days, he had had it requisitioned, and
persuaded the government to pay for £15,000 worth of crops
which he had to destroy, and he fenced the place in with barbed
wire and began to build an exact replica of the battery and its
defences. When the surrounding fields and woods did not
exactly fit the maps and photographs, they were bulldozed till

they did. On this artificial stage, in the strictest secrecy, the battalion rehearsed its attack again and again, using live ammunition, first by day and then by night.

Otway had heartily agreed with his Brigadier from the very beginning that the job was a stinker; and studying its details and watching his rehearsals, he began to doubt whether it was possible for his men, with their light armament, to break open the defences within the short time they were allowed. At best, there was a risk of failure; and logical analysis made him decide that there was only one way to make reasonably certain of success: to put sixty of the men in three gliders and crash-land them inside the defences, right against the walls of the gun emplacements, at the moment the attack began. This, he thought, would tip the balance; but it was obvious that the sixty men would have even less prospect than the rest of living through it. He chose his " A " company, and told them what he had planned, and called for volunteers. As usual, this procedure was no more than a formality, because the whole company took a smart pace forward; and it was left to him and the company commander to select the sixty men.

By the time this glider attack had also been rehearsed, and the battalion had moved into its closed embarkation camp, Otway's military mind was satisfied that his plan was as good as it could be. But he was young, and perhaps too intelligent and introspective to find life easy as a military commander; and as D-Day came nearer, he began to torture himself with doubt. The lives of his 750 depended on his clear reasoning; and he had also been told that a large and essential part of the invasion itself, and therefore the lives of innumerable other men, would hang on his success. It was a fearsome responsibility for a man still in his twenties. On the night of June 3rd, the night before he expected to embark, he had not been able to sleep at all, and had walked round the camp all night in a state of nervous tension which he had had to hide from his officers and men, turning over and over in his mind the utmost details of the operation, trying for the hundredth time to weigh imponderable chances, glancing from time to time at the familiar unworried faces of the men who were on duty, and wondering how many of them would live to another dawn.

For him the postponement had been a godsend. By the night of the 4th, he had worried himself into exhaustion, and that night he had gone to bed and slept soundly. On the 5th, he was himself again, calm and confident; and when his men had assembled that evening to embark, he had walked round and exchanged a few words with every one of them. In the aircraft, by midnight, he was sleeping.

For the twenty-four hours before the attack, Otway had put a ban on drink, in case anyone, under the strain of waiting, drank too much and went into battle with a hangover. But he had broken his own rule to the extent of taking a bottle of whisky with him, and somewhere over the Channel he woke up and passed it round the twenty men in his aircraft. They did not drink much, or perhaps they had quietly thought of providing themselves with something. The bottle came back to him before it was empty.

Soon after this interlude, the anti-aircraft fire began as they crossed the coast of France; and not many seconds later, Otway had his first warning that the drop was going to go wrong. The pilot began to throw the aircraft about in violent evasive action. The effect on the drill of the parachutists was chaotic. When they tried to move down to the door to jump in the quick compact succession for which they were trained, the sudden lurches threw them off their balance. Some fell on the floor, encumbered by their heavy equipment. Others tripped over them in struggling cursing heaps. Out of the mêlée, Otway shouted to the pilot: "Hold your course, you bloody fool."

"We've been hit in the tail," one of the aircrew shouted back.

"You can still fly straight, can't you?" Otway asked angrily. But before he was given an answer, the signal came to jump. Otway's turn was early. He clambered along to the door, and found he was still clutching the half-empty bottle of whisky. He thrust it at the R.A.F. dispatcher. "You're going to need this," he said ; and with that parting shot, he jumped.

In those few seconds of heavenly quiet which reward a parachutist between the shock of the jump and the shock of the landing, Otway looked down at the familiar land below him. He could see it quite clearly in the diffused moonlight and the gleam of searchlights reflected from the clouds. There was the dark square of the wood which was his rendezvous. Beyond it, the sodden marshlands of the Dives, which the Germans had flooded, gleamed where the bog was wettest. Below him were fields with thick black hedges, and across the fields, down wind, a farmhouse which he knew particularly well. It was the last place he wanted to land ; for it was ringed with blue on his map and marked as a German battalion headquarters.

Otway was still angry at the way his men's training had been nullified by the pilot's tactics. He was made angrier by finding now that the aircraft had been off course, and angrier still by seeing that somebody was shooting at him. Tracers were passing him ; looking up, he saw them tearing through his parachute. It struck him as damned impertinence, but there was not much time to worry about it because the wind was drifting him straight to the German headquarters. He tried to manipulate his parachute to keep clear of the place, but there was nothing much he could do. Inexorably, as he fell, the wind took him, at 15 miles an hour, across the last field and then across the farmyard. He hit the wall of the house itself, some feet above the ground, and dropped out of his harness into what seemed to be a garden. Two of his men were there already. A German threw open an upstairs window and leaned out. One of the men with Otway picked up a brick and threw it. It was a good shot. There was a crash of glass and the German put his head in, and Otway and his companions—he never knew who they were—ran by instinct to the back of the house and got out of the garden while the German headquarters staff poured out of the front door.

Otway learned later that only seven of the twenty men in his plane had managed to disentangle themselves in time to jump while it was over the dropping zone. It had to make three more runs to get them all out. Among the seven who jumped with him was his batman, whose name was Wilson. Wilson, before the war, had been a professional boxer and a professional valet, and nobody could have had better qualifications as an airborne colonel's batman; but his drop was even unluckier than his colonel's. In fact, no parachutist could have dreamed of a more grimly humorous landing; for the German headquarters building had a greenhouse attached to it, and Wilson went plumb through the roof of it and landed in a shower of broken glass among the pot plants. At that moment, the Germans were rushing out of the building, and he rushed out behind them, and found himself being shot at by some Canadians. None the worse, he set off for the rendezvous alone.

As Otway hurried on towards the rendezvous, he picked up a few men heading for the wood in twos and threes. Before they got there, they had an experience which was harrowing even to the toughest of them. Strangled cries came from the darkness of a shallow valley, and following them they found in the valley bottom one of the tentacles of the flooded bogland of the Dives. There in the mud, not far from the bank, was a parachutist, struggling, sunk to his shoulders in the ghastly slime. They reached his parachute, and hauled in the lines till they were taut. Half a dozen men were on the lines before the end came: but fighting for a foothold themselves, they could not overcome the suction of the bog. Still shouting for help, the man sank lower. They never saw who he was. He gave a last cry of anguish before the mud silenced him.

When Otway got to the wood, the first man he recognised was his second-in-command, who said, " Thank God you've come, sir."

" Why ? " Otway asked him.

" The drop's a bloody chaos. There's hardly anyone here."

This was no exaggeration. It was nearly two o'clock. Otway himself was late, but only a few men had reached the wood before him. Glancing round at the group of them, he became aware of Wilson, ever the perfect servant, standing at his side, proffering a small flask as if it were a decanter on a silver salver.

" Shall we take our brandy now, sir ? " Wilson said.

As time crept on, in the darkness below the trees, more men arrived, but only a few at a time ; and Otway began to force himself to face a disaster worse than anything he had imagined. His plans had been flexible ; no parachute commander expects a drop to be perfectly successful. But nobody could have planned for a drop in which only a handful of men survived and only a few odds and ends of equipment could be found. There was very little encouragement in the reports which were brought to him. By half past two, one hundred and fifty men had come in : six hundred were missing. They had one machine gun. Their mortars and anti-tank guns and mine detectors and all their heavy equipment had disappeared, and so had their radios and all their signal equipment except, ironically, the Very lights which were to be fired to signal the success of the attack. There were no engineers and no doctors ; but six medical orderlies, who were conscientious objectors, had arrived with first-aid kit. There was no sign so far of a reconnaissance party which had been dropped a little earlier than the main body to penetrate the first belt of wire and the minefield.

Otway was in a terrible dilemma. He had to decide whether he ought to throw his remaining men into an attack which seemed to be suicidal and doomed to failure, or whether he ought to preserve their lives for the other secondary objectives which they were supposed to tackle later in the day, and leave the Merville battery to the air force and the navy. And if he decided to attack, he had to decide exactly when to move. There was still a mile and a half to go, and the Germans were thoroughly alerted. If he moved too soon, he would lose the help of any men who might still turn up at the rendezvous. If he left it too late, he would not be ready when the gliders came in, and their troops would probably be captured. It was a problem he could not discuss with anyone, for the only thing which might still save the day was the self-confidence of his men, and a hint that he was in doubt would have destroyed it. So for an hour, in the solitude of command, Otway prowled round the groups of men who were waiting in the wood, and wrestled with his conscience all alone. The only man to whom, for a moment, he showed his fears was Wilson. At a quarter to three, the time of final decision had arrived.

" What the hell am I going to do, Wilson ? " Otway said.

" Only one thing to do, sir," Wilson answered. " No need to ask me."

Otway laughed. " Yes, I know," he said. " Get the officers and n.c.o.s. We'll move in five minutes."

Wilson's confidence had settled the problem for him. The officers and N.C.O.s gathered round him, and he told them they were going to attack with exactly one fifth of the battalion. None of them gave the slightest sign that they thought he might order the attack to be abandoned. At ten minutes to three, they moved out of the wood in single file.

Otway had ordered secrecy and silence on the march, but some of the men were tempted by an anti-aircraft battery. They skirted round it, still in single file, a hundred yards away. It was firing at gliders of their own division, which were passing overhead to land further in from the coast. Every time a gun fired, its crew were revealed, caught in mid-movement like a flashlight photograph, an easy target for a quick shot from a Sten gun. Otway's officers went back down the line of men, grabbing guns which were levelled at the Germans and shoving men back into file.

Soon after this Otway, at the head of the file, saw a figure and challenged and got the right reply. It was the commander of the reconnaissance party, coming back to report to him. Some of his news was good, and some was bad. He had cut the outer wire fence and crossed the large minefield, and had lain by the inner belt of wire for half an hour listening to the conversation of the Germans inside the battery. There was no sign of any tougher defences than Intelligence had expected. The wire was not so bad as it might have been. The engineers who had

landed with him to clear a path through the mines had lost their
mine detectors and the tape with which the path was supposed
to be marked; but they had got through, searching for the
mines with their fingers and "delousing" them one by one,
and they had marked the path as well as they could by scratching
two lines in the earth. But the attack by the hundred Lancaster
bombers had been a wash-out. Their pathfinders had put down
their markers not on the battery, but half a mile away on the
dropping zone of the reconnaissance party. Consequently, the
reconnaissance party's drop had been very alarming. Some of
them, drifting down on their parachutes, had heard bombs
whistling past them and seen them explode below their feet.
One man said he had been swung above the level of his own
parachute by the blast of a bomb below him, but he had got
down alive. So far as they knew, not a single bomb had hit the
battery.

The 150 men reached the outer wire without any other
incident, except that a herd of terrified cows alarmed them by
stampeding through their file; and there, when he could actually
see the casemates of the guns against the sky, the final blow
awaited Otway's plans. It was 4.30. His gliders were due.
Until that last moment, he had clung to a hope that somebody
would turn up with the mortar flares with which, in accordance
with his plan, he should have signalled the gliders in to land.
But nobody came. Precisely on time, he saw two of the three
gliders and their tugs approaching. The tugs flashed their
headlights—a private signal to him that they were casting off
their tows. The gliders circled down. But he had no way whatever of telling them he was there and was ready to attack.
Without such a signal, he knew they would conclude that his
force had got into trouble and would land anywhere they could,
except on the battery. He saw one glider skim over the battery,
a hundred feet up: but he could only watch it as it turned away
to come down in the countryside behind him. With this last
hope gone, he gave the signal to attack.

The battle was short and terrible and bloody. Otway had

no romantic idea of leading his men in the charge. The logical place for the command post was at the rear, where anyone could find it, and logic was always his guide. His first post was beside the gap in the outer wire, and there he waited, in a bomb crater with Wilson and his adjutant and signal officer, while the first men crept forward to blow gaps in the inner wire. He saw the explosions : and at once, a fury of fire burst out from the battery defences. Silhouetted against the streams of tracers, his men were moving across the minefield, running and dropping down to shoot, or else to lie where death had found them. In the flashes of mortar bombs he saw the first of them fight through the gaps and into the trenches beyond.

That was his own moment to advance. Like many men with imagination, Otway had no great fear of being killed, but a horror of being mutilated. That horror attacked him when he had to get out of the crater and run forward into the flood of fire. Irrelevantly, the thought flashed through his head of what Wilson would think of him if he hesitated. He shouted, " Come on " and ran for it. Running, he forgot about the minefield which had become a minor danger. In the gap, the officer beside him, his adjutant, fell, shot through by a machine gun. He flung himself down inside the wire. The remnants of a company he had kept in reserve came through behind him, and dropped down, waiting for his orders.

He had planned that the leading companies were to go straight in for the guns, without wasting time on any troops outside the casemates. This they did. In a few minutes, he could see them right up against the casemates, pouring their fire through the openings. He ordered the reserve company up to clear the trenches. Soon shouts in German were heard—" Paratroops ! " —and Germans began to surrender. In twenty minutes from his first order, it was over. His men were in the casemates and had done their best to blow up the guns by stuffing German bombs into the breeches, since they had no more explosives of their own. The Very light to signal success was fired. A spotting aircraft, circling over the battery, saw it and passed on the signal to the navy, fifteen minutes before the shelling was due to begin. Otway's signals officer extracted a battered pigeon from the blouse of his battledress and set it free. Back across the Channel, below the host of aircraft, this solitary bird flew through to its loft in England with the news that the Merville battery had fallen.

Otway's gallant remnant of a force had won by nothing but the unhesitating fury of their hand-to-hand fighting. But victory gave them no feeling of elation. On the contrary, when the men assembled they were pale and silent; for of the hundred and fifty who had charged twenty minutes before, seventy-five, exactly half, were now lying dead or wounded, and of the two hundred Germans in defence, only 22 could still rise to their feet to surrender.

There was no time for rest, because immediately the battery had fallen, another German battery to the west began to shell it. Otway set everyone to work to carry the wounded away from the shell-fire to a barn beyond the minefield. Among the German survivors was an elderly doctor; and in the barn, this man started with impartial care to attend to the worst of the wounded, both British and German. Before long, both British and German medical supplies in the barn were finished. The German doctor knew where extra supplies had been stored in the battery, and he set off alone through the fire to fetch them. On the way, he was killed by a German shell.

The battalion had other assignments to carry out that morning, and before dawn Otway marched off, with one out of ten of all the men who had embarked with him when the night began. This skeleton of a battalion was extremely angry with the Air Force for the chaos of their drop, and later, when they began to hear what had happened to their comrades who had vanished, the news did nothing to calm their feelings. Some had been landed twenty or thirty miles away. Navigators had mistaken the River Dives for the River Orne, and without identifying the countryside below them had cast out their troops on the wrong side of the marshes. Some of these scattered men got back to their unit in the end. One of them swam along the shore for two miles, with all his equipment and his Sten gun, to get past the mouth of the Dives. One sergeant turned up four days later, bringing with him the whole of his plane-load of men who had dropped thirty miles inland, and bringing also, like scalps, the pay-books of a number of German officers. But a great many of the scattered troops were killed or captured; and of Otway's 750, no less than 192 men were never heard of again alive or dead. Perhaps they were dropped in the sea; but more likely the ghastly quagmires of the Dives closed over their heads and their bodies lie buried there to-day.

Of course the parachutists were inclined to blame the pilots and navigators, but that was not fair. They had done their best. It might have been fairer to blame the R.A.F. commanders who had sent them out with training which was clearly inadequate; but of course the size of the efforts of the Allied air forces that night had strained their resources to the utmost. The army's analysis of the drop suggested that one of the two R.A.F. groups which took part in it had been much more successful than the other. Conditions were the same for both groups, and the difference certainly looked like a difference of training. Probably all the navigators could have found their targets if the night had been calm and clear, but on the evidence they had not been taught enough to cope with wind and cloud. As for the pilots, some had been sent on bombing missions to give them experience of anti-aircraft fire; but others had never been shot at before, and had to make their own assessments of how dangerous the fire might be. Many of them, in their anxiety to get their passengers through, flew too high and too fast, or disorganised the jumping drill by "weaving." Yet the fire was not really intense: of the 373 aircraft which dropped the 6th Airborne Division that night, only nine were reported missing from all causes, and seven damaged. On the other hand, to be fair, it must be said that the night was difficult for aerial navigation; for even some of the best trained men of Bomber Command, the pathfinders, missed their targets—like the Merville battery; and the Americans fared no better than the British.

The dispatch of the Air Commander-in-chief which described this air-lift afterwards ended with a very curious statement. Leigh-Mallory wrote: "The accuracy with which these forces were delivered to the allotted zones contributed greatly to the rapid success of their *coups-de-main*." Otway and his 75 survivors would have had a word for that; but it was not published till three years later, and by that time their tempers had cooled. Meanwhile when these men, soon after dawn, were marching wearily along a road on the way to their next objective, they were bombed by the American Air Force. That only confirmed their opinion of all airmen.

Fortunately, Major-General Gale, the divisional commander, took a less gloomy view of the scattering of his forces, and was not in the least depressed. His equanimity probably had two causes: one was that he saw the division's landings as a whole, and knew that no other battalion had suffered quite so much as Otway's; the other was that he was an old soldier, used to the setbacks of war.

Age of course, is a matter of comparison. Richard Gale was forty-eight; much older in years than his subordinate commanders, but no older in mental and physical agility. Thirty years in the army had moulded his appearance and his character; he had fought in the bloodier battles of the First World War, and had won his Military Cross in 1918. He was six feet three in height, stood as straight as a ramrod, and wore a fiercely bristly moustache; and he would have been delighted to think that his juniors feared his displeasure—as they did—much more than they feared the Germans. But his martial appearance and manner seldom quite hid his robust sense of humour, and it never hid the quickness and originality of his brain. Among the qualities which helped to make him a great airborne commander were a passionate hatred of red tape, and, more subtly, an understanding of human frailty; for he had made a study of fear, and knew it is impossible to predict how a man will behave in a battle before he has been tried.

The General himself landed with the main glider force at 3.30. With him in his glider were his A.D.C., his jeep and driver, a dispatch rider with a motor cycle, and two or three headquarters staff. Before the action, Gale was confident, and elated at the greatness of the occasion. Privately, he was also delighted, in an almost boyish fashion, at being the first British general to land in France, and so stealing a march on his contemporaries. When his glider was airborne, he told his A.D.C. to call him when they crossed the coast of France, and then he went to sleep. His landing was rough. The glider ran across a sunken lane, and the bump rammed the undercarriage up through the fuselage. But nobody was seriously hurt, and the general stepped out to a scene which in less experienced eyes appeared disastrous.

The parachutists had cleared the glider landing zone in time, removing the posts which the Germans had planted, and most of the natural obstacles, with two airborne bulldozers which had been brought by isolated gliders earlier in the night. The mass-landing was amazingly accurate. Seventy-two gliders were dispatched. Forty-nine of them landed on time, and right on the meadow which was cleared. For two or three minutes before and after 3.30, they converged from all directions in the dark. Almost all of them crashed. Wheels, undercarriages, wings were torn off. Some buried their noses in the soft ground, some collided. One went right through a small cottage and emerged bearing with it an old-fashioned double bed : rumour said that a French couple were still in the bed when everything came to rest. Troops who climbed out of the earlier gliders seemed in danger of being mown down by others swooping in ; the headquarters staff had to duck as a latecomer swished over their heads. By 3.35 the meadow was covered with wrecks grotesquely silhouetted against the sky. At a glance, one would have expected a terrible death-roll. Yet most of the passengers survived. Upwards of a thousand men scrambled out, and dragged with them their jeeps and ten out of eighteen of the all-important anti-tank guns.

The General's jeep was stuck in the wreck of his glider, and rather than wait he set off for his headquarters in Ranville on foot.* As soon as he was established, reports began to come in of tremendous casualties among the parachutists. They seemed alarming, but Gale remained unmoved. He knew that the immediate aftermath of a big night drop would seem chaotic, and he was convinced, through his own long experience, that casualty reports on the battlefield were always twice as high as they should be. And besides, he knew his own troops, and firmly believed they would carry out their missions whatever their losses had been.

The night passed without any news of the demolition of the five bridges on the River Dives, by which the division's flank was to be protected. Blowing bridges is work for engineers, and detachments of Royal Engineers had dropped to do it. By the time the General landed, several small isolated parties were out to the eastward ; and they were justifying his faith by tackling jobs which he had allotted to much larger, more powerful units. One troop of the engineers, assigned to destroy a road bridge in the village of Robehomme, had fallen mostly in the marshes, and one of their aircraft had taken such vigorous evasive action that the men in it were thrown flat on the floor and jumped in a " stick " which was over two miles long. The survivors of this troop struggled through to their bridge after seven hours in the marshes ; but they found it had already been blown by a solitary sergeant who had happened to drop very near it and had borrowed explosives from some Canadians who had also come down there by mistake.

The most important of the bridges, and the farthest away, was the one where the main road from Caen to Rouen and Le Havre crosses the river, just beyond the small town of

---

* In the height of the battle which followed, supply headquarters in England are said to have received an urgent request by radio for a horse.

Troarn. This bridge was four miles outside the area which the division intended to hold. It was planned that a troop of engineers under Major J. C. A. Roseveare, protected by infantry, should dash for this bridge while the Germans were still confused. They were to carry their explosives in jeeps with trailers, which were to land in gliders. But this plan also went astray.

The troops dropped on time, at 1.50; but when Roseveare came to earth he could not see any landmarks which he knew. It seemed to him, as he stood in the dark in a field which he could not recognise, that aircraft were coming in from every direction and dropping parachutists from every unit in the division. Some gliders were landing nearby, but not the gliders which were carrying his jeeps. A mile away to the south-west there were sounds of fighting, and he guessed rightly that the last men out of each of his aircraft were already involved with the Germans.

However, he rallied what men he could, and they collected all the equipment they could find. At length, he had six officers and about forty other ranks; but of the protecting infantry there were only twenty men and no officers at all. Between them, they gathered up plenty of explosive, but there was nothing to carry it in except trolleys which had to be hauled by hand.

This rather forlorn and yet determined party set off about half past two, under mortar and machine-gun fire, to haul the trolleys up a steep hill in one of the winding Norman lanes. Many of them were already limping from injuries of the drop. Before long, they came to a crossroads with a signpost which confirmed what some had already come to suspect: they had dropped two miles too far north, and the Troarn bridge was seven miles away.

There was very little hope of hauling the trolleys so far before dawn, and no hope at all, of course, of hauling them through the town in daylight.

In this unpromising situation, a motor was heard approaching, and a jeep with a trailer appeared from the darkness. It was not an R.E. jeep, it belonged to the R.A.M.C., and it was full of medical stores ; but if the R.A.M.C. men had wanted to argue, they would probably not have had much chance. They surrendered their jeep, and the engineers turned out the medical stores in a timber yard, and loaded it with explosives. By then, it was four o'clock : just over an hour to dawn, and five miles still to Troarn. There was no time to think about anyone on foot. Roseveare dispatched the greater part of his force across country to another nearer bridge. He himself took the wheel of the jeep, and piled on the jeep and trailer one officer and seven other men. Including them, the load was a ton and a quarter. They drove off alone down the lane, into country where no British troops had landed.

Their first encounter was at a level crossing. The gates were open, but there was a barbed-wire barrier across the road, and Roseveare drove into it before he saw it. A German sentry fired a single shot and ran away. The jeep was so tangled in wire that it took twenty minutes' work to cut it free : a tense twenty minutes, for it had to be assumed that the sentry had gone to call a guard. Clear of that obstacle, they reached the main road on the edge of the town, and Roseveare sent two scouts ahead. As the scouts reached the crossroad, a German soldier rode past it on a bicycle. They pulled the unlucky man off his bicycle, and because he began to shout they killed him ; but they foolishly did it with a Sten gun and so gave the alert to the town.

Stealth was useless after that ; Roseveare trod on the gas and they went into town at full speed ; but the overloaded jeep and trailer would only do about thirty-five miles an hour, and it seemed to be crawling. Soon they were under fire from the houses. One man by then had dropped off somewhere and been left behind : the remaining seven passengers all fired back with Sten guns and a Bren. At a bend in the road they saw the long, wide, straight main street of the town stretched out for a mile before them, downhill towards the bridge. There the firing was intense : every doorway seemed to be hiding a German with some sort of gun : a cone of tracer came up the street towards them. Roseveare drove on, with his foot hard down on the floorboards.

The overloaded jeep ground slowly forward. The passengers blazed away in all directions. It was the hill which saved the situation. On the downward grade, the jeep picked up speed, went faster and faster, swerved from side to side of the road as the trailer swayed behind, and tore out of the town and down to the river valley pursued by shots of a heavy machine gun. They came to the bridge, and found it had not been guarded. One man, who had acted as rear gunner with the Bren, had disappeared ; none of them knew if he had been shot, or had lost his balance and fallen off the trailer. They unloaded their charges, and five minutes later the job was done and the centre span of the bridge had dropped in the river. They drove the jeep up a side track as far as it would go and then ditched it, just as the sun was rising ; and by wading through bogs and swimming over creeks, they reached the airborne perimeter again that afternoon.

By dawn, in spite of the scattered drop, the division had achieved every one of its immediate objectives. All the five bridges on the Dives were blown up. The canal and Orne River bridges, intact, were in Howard's hands, and parachutists were approaching to relieve him. The Merville battery would never fire again. The territory which the plan demanded was all under control, although there were plenty of Germans still at large inside it ; and in the south, facing Caen, a tenuous line of anti-tank defences was in position. It was a fine feat of arms.

Not all this news had yet reached Gale's headquarters. Even if it had, it was still too soon for him to congratulate himself or his commanders. The ground which was won still had to be defended until the seaborne forces were ashore. For the moment, the Germans were showing no signs of anything but confusion, but a counter-attack was certainly still to come.

The achievement had not been cheap in terms of suffering ; nobody had expected that it would be. Men were still creeping lost through the hedgerows and forests, or lying alone in pain. Many who had started the night in hope and vigour had already watched their own death approaching and surrendered to it. But at dawn the living heard a sound which encouraged them : beyond the sound of aircraft and bombs and small guns close at hand, an even deeper thunder from the north which shook the earth. On the canal bridge, one of Howard's corporals paused and listened. " Hear that, sir ? " he said. " That's the navy."

Before long, the enormous naval shells were passing overhead, ranging on targets ten miles inland. One could hear them rumbling across the sky from north to south. The corporal, hearing this extraordinary and distinctive noise for the first time, looked up as if he hoped to see the shells. " Cor," he said, " what next ? They're firing jeeps."

III

THE AMERICAN AIR DROP

FIFTY MILES to the west of the scene of these events, in the peninsula of Cherbourg, the German 709th Infantry Division had been waiting for a year, scattered in farms and villages along thirty miles of the channel coast and in the countryside behind it. It was a force without much pride or much cohesion. It had been formed eighteen months before, with a core of German veterans from the Russian front and a large proportion of more or less unwilling conscripts. Most of its men were too young or too old or too unhealthy to fight on more active fronts. Its average age was 36. Some of its private soldiers were Germans who had been living abroad when the war began, in France, Holland, Belgium, Denmark and other countries which since had been overrun. They had been dragged into the German army when the authorities caught up with them. There were also Poles and Russians who had fought for Russia and been captured and agreed to fight for Germany. Most of these were merely ignorant men dazed by events, who hardly knew one authority from another and would have fought dumbly for anyone in power over them. Others, captured at the height of the German successes in Russia, had declared themselves anti-communist, but as the Germans retreated, their anti-communist zeal had quickly cooled, and now they were rated officially as unreliable. In short, the 709th Division was a third-rate fighting

unit. Of course, it was far from typical of the German army :
but the German army, defending Hitler's vast perimeter, and
weakened by its losses in Russian and Africa, was stretched too
far and was forced to use motley divisions like this to man the
static defences of the Atlantic Wall.

The division had been where it was for much too long. It
grumbled at boredom and bullying and apparently useless chores,
as all soldiers of all armies grumble from time to time ; but it
grumbled with a venom seldom known in American or British
armies, because it was not allowed to grumble : grumbling, in
itself, could be called disloyalty. It was divided from top to
bottom by an uncrossable rift : on one side, the men who still
believed in the Nazi ideals and in Hitler as a leader, and on the
other those who had never believed, or had lost their Nazi
faith ; on one side, keen soldiers still ready to die for Germany,
and on the other the men who thought the war was lost already
or should never have been started, and were only interested to
come out of it alive. Neither side trusted the other. The
believers spied on the doubters, and the doubters were afraid.
Newcomers to the division were treated with care and suspicion
till they made their opinions known.

The whole division knew that invasion was coming, and
knew there was a chance it might come on their stretch of the
coast. Probably very few of them thought they could stop it if
it came, with the weapons and organisation they possessed.
They were given pep-talks by their brigade commanders, aimed
not at increasing their faith in themselves, but at persuading
them that they could count on good support. They were told
that the coastal artillery batteries were powerful enough to control the whole shore, and that secret weapons existed which
would not be used unless an invasion came, but then would
destroy it before it reached the land. Some of them—but only
some—believed this.

These unhappy men, divided against each other, far from
their homes in an alien land among resentful people, were
scattered as usual in their posts and billets on the night of the

5th of June, with no suspicion that their doom was already approaching ; for nobody had warned them.

About midnight an air-raid alert was sounded in their district. That was nothing unusual. There had been one already, earlier in the evening, which had only lasted for half an hour ; and indeed there had not been many nights in the past few weeks without a warning. It was merely a nuisance. But in one section of an infantry platoon, stationed on a farm south-east of the town of Montebourg, the alert was almost welcome, because it put an end to an argument which was becoming dangerous. The argument may not have been typical, but it was symptomatic.

One of the antagonists was a private soldier called Friedrich Busch, who had been a schoolmaster in Dresden. He was in a mood of desperate depression that night, and rashly said that he was fed up with soldiering for a cause he had never believed in, and wanted nothing in the world except to go home to his wife and baby. He was overheard by an N.C.O., who told him that the only thing he was fit for, and the only thing he could do for Germany, was to get himself killed as soon as any fighting started. The argument grew angry, and Busch's friends were afraid he was heading for arrest and a charge of sedition. One of the men who listened anxiously was a German called Erwin Müller. His wife was Danish, and he had lived in Denmark for twenty years and thought of himself as a Dane ; but he had never thought of applying for Danish citizenship until it was too late. So after Germany invaded Denmark, he was called up for the German army ; and he went quietly, for fear of getting his wife and children and his parents in Germany into trouble.

Müller wholeheartedly agreed with Friedrich Busch, but he thought it was foolish to say so. When he left home, he had promised his wife he would come back to her alive, and fulfilling that promise was the only thing he really cared about. Long before, he had made up his mind what to do : to keep out of trouble and to hide his own thoughts, except from the friends he could trust. If it ever came to fighting, he intended to fight, if that was the only way to save his own life, but to let himself be captured if that seemed a better chance. He expected to fight, because he expected to find himself up against paratroops, and the division had been told that American and British paratroops never took prisoners. But he did not care in the least about fighting for Germany. There was Jewish blood in his family, and under the Nazis his father, still living in Germany, had led a difficult and precarious life.

When the second alert sounded, Müller felt relieved for the sake of Busch. As the section turned out for its air-raid posts, he heard Busch fling a parting shot at the N.C.O. " I hope I'll see you in a battle," he said. " I wonder which of us will be the first to get himself killed."

Sheltering in their trenches and bunkers, the platoon began to wonder whether something more than an ordinary air raid might be brewing, because there seemed to be so many aircraft overhead, and because some of them were showing lights. Soon after midnight, an order was passed round to fall in on the road and march to a village called Azeville. Few of them had ever been to Azeville, although it was their battalion headquarters. The order surprised them, but it also reassured them. On exercises in the past, they had always carried blank ammunition in their rifles and the pouches of their equipment; their live ammunition was stowed in their haversacks. They had always supposed they would know the real thing when it came because they would get the order to load live rounds. But nobody gave them the order that night, so they set out on their march with blanks still in their rifles, believing the whole thing was another boring and ill-timed exercise. The first shock and disillusionment came on the outskirts of Azeville. They were shot at from the churchyard in the middle of the village, and the ammunition was unquestionably live.

The whole platoon dropped into ditches beside the road, and without waiting for orders they delved in their haversacks and reloaded their pouches and guns; and then, led on by their N.C.O.s, they crept forward by devious routes to surround the churchyard. An eerie battle of hide and seek began against the

unknown enemy hidden among the gravestones. Men with
their nerves on edge fired at any shadow which seemed to move
or to have a human shape : and sometimes, the shadows returned
their fire. Very slowly, from grave to grave, the Germans
crawled in towards the church. As they closed their ranks,
dark figures dashed out between them and escaped, and
the firing died away ; but by the church porch a man was
lying dead ; and Müller, looking down at him, recognised the
equipment of an American parachutist and knew the day had
come.

Events moved swiftly in Azeville after that, towards a dawn
which Müller was to remember with horror all his life. The
platoon was posted round the village to defend it, under the
disadvantage that the men had never seen the place in daylight
and did not know their way about it. They wondered, but never
discovered, what had happened to the headquarters platoon
which should have been billeted there. Müller and another
man were placed at a garden gate in a hedge and told to keep
watch ; and peering nervously over that gate, entirely ignorant
of what they might expect, they witnessed a spectacle which
they had never imagined at all : for all of a sudden the whole
night sky to the south and west was filled with uncountable
parachutes.

Müller and his companion stood there and watched them,
with awe and with a certain admiration for an army and air
force which could launch an attack of such a majestic size. They
believed from the moment they saw it that they were beaten ;
for the force and efficiency which they knew must lie behind it
were far beyond anything they had ever experienced in their own
inferior division. Some of the parachutists drifting down
were within an easy rifle shot, but the two Germans, inexperi-
enced as they were in total war, were held spellbound by an
instinctive feeling that it was unfair to shoot a man on a parachute.
So they simply watched them come to earth. Only one of the
parachutes came down in the village itself. That one was carrying not a man but a large container with a red light on it. Some

of the Germans gathered it in and opened it, and found it was full of delicious things to eat.

It was not very long before the first Americans entered the village. Probably this was not a planned attack, but merely a group of men on their way to their rendezvous. They got into a farmyard opposite Müller's garden gate, and his section was sent to clear them out again. The N.C.O. went first, through an archway into the yard, and nothing happened; and Friedrich Busch went second, and a single shot was fired and killed him instantly.

Müller was shocked by the first death he had ever seen in battle; the more so when he remembered what Busch had said about his wife and baby. It was the first of a series of terrible events of that night in Azeville which haunted his mind for years afterwards as nightmare memories. They were memories of skirmishes in the dark; of a white-faced man who dashed through the village shouting that all his section had been killed, of the writhing body of a friend of his, not yet quite dead, being pushed down the road on a hand-cart by somebody looking in vain for a casualty clearing station; of a man, American or German, who screamed and screamed in an orchard not far away; of a rumour that Americans were shooting from the church, and of searching the church, and of a priest who watched him in silence as he committed this sacrilege; and of confusion and moments of paralysing fear and the belief that nobody in command knew what was happening. The fighting in this insignificant village went on till dawn; and Müller fought as best he could all through the night, because there seemed to be no alternative.

By dawn his platoon was cut off and the village seemed to be surrounded. They had no radio, and the telephone had gone dead. The platoon commander told the sergeant to take a patrol to try to get through to brigade headquarters and ask for orders; and the sergeant picked Müller and a couple of younger men. There was an angry argument, because the platoon commander told them to go on bicycles and the sergeant told him that that was lunacy—as it certainly was—in daylight. But soon after dawn the four men stole out of the village on foot across the fields. As they crept along beside a hedge out in the no-man's-land of the open countryside, they had a most strange encounter. They heard voices, and saw two American soldiers in a meadow. Leaving the two young men to cover them, Müller and the sergeant crawled down a ditch until only the thickness of the hedge divided them from the Americans, who seemed preoccupied. Looking through the branches, Müller was astonished to see that one of the parachutists had a large painting of a pin-up girl on the back of his tunic, and the other had the words " SEE YOU IN PARIS " on the back of his. Müller, who had learned to speak English in Denmark, poked his rifle through the hedge and said " Hallo." At this surprising greeting, the Americans wheeled round. " Hands up," Müller said ; and he and the sergeant broke through the hedge, and then saw a third American, lying badly wounded.

" I'm sorry, but we must search you," Müller said.

" O.K., if you say so," the younger of the two Americans answered ; and as Müller began to go through his pockets he added : " But don't take the picture of my girl."

" I take nothing but your weapons," Müller said.

The collection of stuff which he found in their pockets surprised him again. Among it were chocolate, silk stockings and elegant lingerie. " What's this for ? " he demanded, rather shocked at this flippant equipment.

" That's for the little girls in Paris," the prisoner said. " And the candy's for me. Have some ? Say, how far is it to Paris, fella ? "

" I don't know, I've never been there," Müller said, and accepted the chocolate.

" Don't eat it, it might be poisoned," one of the young Germans shouted.

" What does he say ? " the American asked, and Müller told him.

The American laughed. " It's not poisoned," he said ; and

their eyes met, and Müller felt a bond with this casual self-confident young man, who seemed to take war so lightly, as if they shared decency and sanity and could laugh together at mad suspicions and enmities. He ate the chocolate.

When the second of the prisoners was disarmed, Müller turned his attention to the man who was lying wounded. He was very badly hurt, and it was only a minute or two before he died.

" I'm sorry," Müller said ; and he said it sincerely, for the body of this enemy lying there seemed as pathetic to him as the body of Friedrich Busch.

The young American knelt down and closed the dead man's eyes and crossed his arms on his chest ; and then he began to say the Lord's prayer. Müller and the other American joined in ; and then the sergeant and the two young German soldiers, recognising the rhythm of the words, took up the prayer in German, and the six men in their two languages prayed together, grouped round the man who had died.

Müller and his sergeant got their prisoners back to the village in the end, and handed them over to their platoon commander. Probably they escaped very soon. Müller himself was taken prisoner after a week of wandering, and so, years later, he returned to his wife alive.

Suspended from one of the multitude of parachutes, which Müller had watched with such awe through the garden gate, was a farmer's boy from North Carolina, and his name was James R. Blue. Blue looked down, as they had taught him, while he dropped, and tried to make the countryside fit his recollection of the map of the dropping zone ; but nothing fitted. Below him he could see tracers from machine guns, not aimed upwards at him but criss-crossed along the ground. To one side was a darker patch of land without any visible signs of battle, and he was glad to find he was drifting towards it. He manipulated his parachute as well as he could to hit this quiet area, and as the ground came up to him he got ready for the bump.

It was not a bump, it was a splash : a psychological more than a physical shock. Expecting the solid earth, he fell into three feet of water. It closed over his head and in panic—not knowing what had happened, thinking the water was deep—he struggled and lashed out with his arms and legs, felt the muddy bottom and came floundering to the surface. Before he found his balance, his parachute dragged him over backwards and he went under again, weighed down by his seventy pounds of equipment, fumbling at the buckles of his harness.

Blue was a man of exceptional strength ; and the bottom of the marsh where he fell was hard enough to stand on. Without those two advantages, he would have drowned as so many Americans and British drowned that morning. Even with them, he was half dead when he got clear of his harness and stood up, waist deep in the stinking soupy water. He was sick from the water he had swallowed, and trembling from the shock. He peered round at the empty menacing countryside and felt quite lost and desperately lonely. And then he heard a familiar angry voice which filled the night with good rich American curses, the voice of a buddy of his who had jumped just before him.

" Hi there," Blue shouted when the other man paused for breath.

" Is that you, Blue ? " the voice said in the night. " I've lost my goddam helmet."

The journey from the Carolina farm to the marsh in Normandy had started when Blue was twenty-one, and had taken two years. It was quite a straightforward journey which he had made of his own free choice ; and he had never regretted his choice, except perhaps in those seconds when he thought he was drowning. He had volunteered as a parachutist because General William C. Lee, the outstanding pioneer of American airborne forces, was a native of North Carolina like himself, and had been quite a near neighbour of his family in the small town of Dunn. The General had been the hero of his boyhood ; and in a slightly more grown-up way, he still was.

Army life suited Blue very well, and he enjoyed it. It came

easily to him, because he had been brought up to hard work; and because he was an amiable, kind-hearted, friendly young man who nevertheless enjoyed a good fight from time to time; and because he was six feet three and invariably won a fight once it had started. He had a reputation of making a good friend or a dangerous enemy, which is a useful reputation to have in any army.

Blue had a good measure of that unexpected humility and capacity for wonder and admiration which the British—perhaps because it flatters them—find so endearing in Americans whenever it comes to the surface. He always knew and sometimes said that in spite of being a private first class, he was still just a farm boy inside. Let loose on a pay day in Nottingham or Leicester, he was amazed at the luck which had brought him on a free trip to Europe—a thing he had never dreamed of as a boy—and had put money in his pocket and extended his horizon so far beyond the streets of Dunn and the fields of Carolina. He was ready to appreciate everything he saw, from quaint pubs to quaint policemen. It was inevitable that he should fall in love with an English girl, and perhaps equally inevitable that the love should not outlast the war. His three months in England had been a riot of new experience and excitement. He had won in fights, and won at cards, and won in love, and he went to Normandy in just the same spirit, expecting still to carry all before him.

This supreme self-confidence, for one reason or another, was typical of the American airborne forces. Perhaps it had its roots in a national characteristic, but it was also cultivated in the men by their senior officers. Of course, it is the policy of all successful armies to assure their men that they are the finest soldiers in the world. The German soldiers had always been told it, and so had the British in a less flamboyant way. So now, and with no less reason, were the Americans. In them, the belief in their own prowess sometimes took novel forms and induced the light-hearted attitude to war which had shocked Erwin Müller. The more callow youngsters among them wore slogans on

their backs, or war-paint on their faces, or shaved their heads
except for a scalp-lock, like Red Indians, or relished dare-devil
names for their units, believing for example that the Germans
often referred to American parachutists with awe as the Devils
in Baggy Pants. This exuberance shocked plenty of people in
Europe besides Erwin Müller, but it certainly did some good.
For one thing, it provided the French with a welcome contrast
to the grim formality of the German army. The American forces
looked like liberators.

Blue himself, with a majority of the parachutists, was rather
embarrassed by these eccentric signs of courage, because they
offended his pride in his regiment, and because he suspected that
the braver a man is, the less he needs to say so. All the same,
as he flew the Channel, he was perfectly certain his outfit was on
its way to lick hell out of the Germans. Perhaps, through no
fault of his own, he was almost too certain; for in one respect,
American confidence had been carried a little too far. Some
senior officers, unnecessarily trying to encourage men who
had plenty of native courage of their own, had made them
believe the invasion would be easy. Some men, new to battle,
suffered for this when they found themselves face to face with
horrors they had never been led to expect. But with that exception, self-confidence carried Americans into France with a
momentum all their own.

As soon as Blue heard his friend's voice, his moment of
panic and loneliness ended, and he was himself again. The two
men waded toward each other, sloshing through the mud. The
level surface of water covered with weeds stretched as far as they
could see in all directions, and there was nothing to show the
way to the nearest dry land. But tracer bullets were still flying
about to the westward. Neither of the two, with a rifle full of
water, was in any condition to fight; so they waded away from
the shooting, hoping to find somewhere to dry their equipment,
if not themselves, before they joined the battle. Blue regretted
this afterwards, because he heard that the first fight going on
just behind them had been led by Brigadier-General James

E. Gavin, the assistant commander of the 82nd Division, a man whom Blue admired next only to General Lee.

General Gavin, who at that moment was only leading a few dozen riflemen, was the very type of the young intelligent officer to whom the American army often successfully entrusts its high command. He was thirty-six. He had started his army career as a private soldier ; soon after the invasion, at the age of thirty-seven, he was promoted major-general. This extraordinary rise in rank was a measure of his energy and brains, and of the passionate interest and belief in airborne warfare which he had held since its earliest days under Lee.

Gavin had jumped with the 82nd Division in Sicily, and since then he had worked with COSSAC as an airborne advisor on the plans for the Normandy invasion. This must have been a frustrating task, because the plans for the use of American airborne forces in Normandy had often been changed. At one period of the planning, there was talk of a landing near Paris. At another, the parachutists were to land all along the invasion beaches, and attack the shore defences from behind. Then they were assigned to capture Bayeux, and occupy a river valley at the back of Omaha beach. In March, in a plan which seemed at last to be final, two airborne divisions were employed, the 101st to land behind Utah beach, on the east coast of the Cherbourg peninsula, and the 82nd to land near the west coast, so that between them they could cut the peninsula and isolate Cherbourg. But even this plan, after the intervening months of detailed work, was abandoned just over a week before the invasion started.

These changes, hard though they were for the airborne commanders, were nobody's fault. The eastern end of the invasion area, all through the planning, had been fixed at Caen and the River Orne ; but the western end was limited by the forces which were available. When Eisenhower was appointed in January and supported Montgomery's demand for more forces, the extra forces were used to extend the invasion area to the west, into the Cherbourg peninsula. Thus the objectives

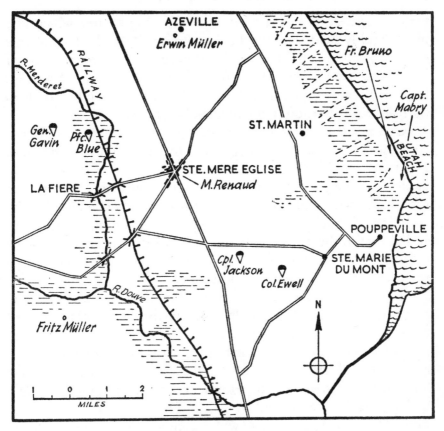

THE AMERICAN AIR DROP

for the British airborne troops were fixed from an early stage, but those for the Americans were moved as the plans expanded.

However, the final change of plans was caused by the Germans. For a long time, two divisions of Germans had garrisoned the countryside of the Cherbourg peninsula. One was Erwin Müller's, and the other was also a static division of something less than first-class quality. But during May, French railwaymen reported through their underground that a new and better division was moving into the district of St. Sauveure-le-Vicomte; and this was the very area where the 82nd was to drop. The German move was not due to any leakage of Allied plans, it was simply a matter of strengthening an area which was more weakly held than most ; but the 82nd, in the face of this new opposition, might easily have been cut off and tied down in self-defence. So on May 27th, at a meeting of the American high command in Bristol, a new plan was devised : to drop both airborne divisions close to Utah beach.

One result of these changes was that the American airborne commanders never had enough time to study and rehearse their attacks on specific targets. There was no chance of the elaborate tactical training which the British had leisure to apply to the Merville battery and the Caen Canal bridge. By comparison, the American airborne attacks were improvised, through necessity ; and although the airborne divisions fulfilled their general rôle of protecting the landing on Utah, their successes, with one exception, were not so quick or so spectacular.

The ultimate last-minute plan, like the British plan, was based upon rivers and floods, and the bridges which crossed them. The floods which the Germans had made in the Cherbourg peninsula were even more extensive than those in the British zone. Behind the sand dunes on the coast, they had flooded a long strip of low-lying meadows and saltings roughly a mile wide. These were crossed by half a dozen causeways ; and the capture of these causeways was essential, to get the seaborne forces off the beach. To the south, and about seven miles inland, they were also known to have flooded the valley of the River Douve. The seven-mile gap between the two belts of floods was the rich, lush pasture land which is typical of Normandy, a maze of tiny fields, thick hedges and winding lanes ; and here the majority of the parachutists were to drop. The 101st Division was to capture the inland ends of the causeways which led from the beach ; to capture or destroy the bridges and a lock on the River Douve, and so protect the southward flank of the area ; and to form a defensive line towards the north. The 82nd Division was to drop on both sides of the River Merderet, a small tributary of the Douve. It was to capture the town of Sainte-Mère-Eglise, and so cut the main road and railway from Carentan

to Cherbourg; and to capture intact two bridges across the
Merderet and a wide area beyond it, which could be used by the
seaborne forces in a westward drive to cut the peninsula itself.
It was this latter force of paratroops which General Gavin
commanded during the night of the landing until his divisional
commander, Major-General Ridgway, had built up a headquarters staff.

In the space of two minutes before he jumped, Gavin had to
adjust his mind to yet another sudden drastic change in the
prospects and plans of the assault. Crossing the Channel,
absorbed in the kind of problems which concern a high commander about to give battle, he had glanced back in the clear
moonlight and had seen the twenty aircraft which were flying
in close formation with his own, and beyond them, as far as the
eye could reach, the stream of other formations which carried
his seven thousand men. All was well. The host of aircraft
passed through the Channel Islands, where ineffective fire came
up from Guernsey and Jersey; and it reached the mainland
coast, on the west side of the peninsula, and turned east to fly
across it. The anti-aircraft fire was heavier there, but that had
been expected. Gavin watched it with detached interest from the
open door of his aircraft, and guessed that one dense array of
flashes was the town of Barneville, where a concentration of
guns had been reported.

But suddenly the view was blotted out. One minute beyond
the coast, the aircraft flew into cloud, so thick that Gavin could
not see the wing tips. He thought of the chances of dropping
blind. In seven minutes and thirty seconds, they ought to be
over the drop zone. In eleven minutes, they would be over the
sea again, on the other side of the peninsula. But before he had
come to terms with that idea, the aircraft was in the clear again.
He looked down and ahead, and saw with surprise a wide gleaming sheet of water. By its size, he thought it could only be the
flooded valley of the Douve, but it seemed to run from north to
south, instead of from east to west, and he could not recognise
it or find his bearings. And then he looked astern, and saw

something worse. The tight formation of planes had disappeared. In the few seconds while he watched, two stragglers came out of the cloud bank, wide on either side ; and that was all. At that crucial moment, he did not know where he was, or what had become of his troops. The green light flashed ; for three more seconds, he searched the ground for a landmark ; and seeing none, he jumped.

He landed unhurt in an orchard full of cows, and looked up through the branches of apple trees at the empty sky which should have been full of parachutes. There was nobody to be seen on the ground, neither German nor American nor French. He started to walk to the eastward, to round up at least the twenty men who had dropped from his plane. That took longer than usual, because of the hedges, but he found most of them in the end ; and the search brought him to the edge of the water he had seen before he jumped.

The water still puzzled him ; and it was a couple of hours before he discovered where he was. He saw a flashing light on the far side of the water, and sent an officer to try to get across to find out who was there ; and the officer came back to report that he had waded for an hour, sometimes up to his neck, and had found a railway embankment. That identified the place. There was only one railway embankment in the district, and that was in the Merderet Valley just north of Sainte-Mère-Eglise. The water must be the Merderet ; and yet the Merderet had appeared on all the aerial photographs as a narrow winding brook.

Gavin was very surprised that the ample floods which he saw before him had never been spotted by air reconnaissance ; and this is still one of the many minor mysteries of the invasion. The explanation seemed to be that grass and weeds had grown up through the water and lay in a mat on the surface, so that most of the valley looked solid. From the air, it looked solid to Blue, but it looked liquid to Gavin, who perhaps had chanced to see the direct reflection of the moonlight. But whatever the explanation, the important facts, as Gavin soon discovered, were that the bank of cloud and the anti-aircraft fire had broken up the close formations of planes, and that most of the regiment which should have dropped with him had overshot its dropping zone by a few seconds, and had fallen with its equipment in the water. Many of the men were able to save themselves, like Blue ; but it was much more difficult to salvage the equipment.

During the night, one hundred and fifty men from different units attached themselves to Gavin. Many were soaking wet, some injured, and a few wounded in skirmishes with a German patrol which was approaching. Not one of them had a weapon heavier than a carbine or a rifle. Gavin assembled all comers in a meadow beside the water, placed some along the hedges for defence, and set the others to search the flood waters for equipment—especially for any weapon which could be used against a tank. The German patrol closed in, and began to attack. For the moment, the General was acting as a company commander.

Blue and his friend staggered on through the marsh till they also saw the railway embankment ahead, and they dragged themselves up it while water poured out of their pockets and the legs of their uniforms. On top, by the railway track, were a dozen sodden men from different regiments, in charge of a lieutenant. Blue had never seen any of them before, but he was glad of their company ; and at dawn he followed them southwards, stumbling across railway sleepers, still very wet but still as full of confidence as ever, sadly regarding with his farmer's eyes the waste of good land beneath the floods on both sides of the railway. A mile or two down the track, they came to dry land, and then to a bridge where the railway was crossed by a lane. This was the road from Sainte-Mère-Eglise to the river bridge at the hamlet of La Fière, the capture of which was one of the principal aims of the division.

A good many other men had collected near the road. The lieutenant handed over his dozen to a captain ; and then, about forty strong, in open order in both the hedges of the lane, a party began to advance towards the bridge, and Blue went with them. The party had one bazooka and one machine gun, which brought up the rear. At last, Blue thought, things were getting interesting. This was what he had come for.

Then he saw his first German. A motor cycle and sidecar came up from the bridge, and the rider did not seem to see the parachutists before it was too late to stop. He came on, and succeeded in passing all forty riflemen at point blank range, because none of them could fire without a risk of hitting their friends on the opposite side of the road. He nearly got through with his life, but not quite. The machine gunner shot him in the back as he rode away towards Sainte-Mère-Eglise, and the motor bike crashed into the hedge. It was terribly easy.

A hundred yards farther on, the party was shot at from a group of farm buildings just before the bridge, and a short sharp fight developed ; the first for Blue, and for most of the men who were with him. The officers told them not to use the bazooka, because they only had a few rounds for it ; but they fired at the windows with their rifles and machine gun, and soon a white flag appeared. A paratroop lieutenant walked up to the door of the farmhouse and pushed it open ; and a single shot was fired from inside it. He ran back holding his ear, for the bullet had gone through the lobe of it, and he angrily called for the bazooka, after all. Two rounds were fired through the downstairs windows. They exploded inside and set the house on fire. In a minute or two, a German officer and fifteen men came out of it with their hands up.

Blue was elated with this quick and easy victory ; so much so that he believed the bridge was won and the war as good as over. But then his high spirits were dashed. Two elderly Frenchmen slowly hobbled out from the back of the burning house, and one of them was pushing a wheelbarrow ; and in the wheelbarrow was a very very old woman.

That glimpse of another aspect of war went straight to Blue's heart, and hurt him deeply. She looked just like an old country woman from Carolina. He suddenly pictured this happening in a farmhouse at home, and for a moment, it made him ashamed of the brave intentions and the military pride he had brought with him to France. What sort of liberators must they think we are ? he wondered. Surely somebody should tell the old people they were sorry they had set their house on fire ? But instead, the order came to cross the bridge.

Quite a force of parachutists walked unmolested over the bridge and a causeway four hundred yards long which crossed the marsh beyond it. Most of them spread out and vanished on the other side, and Blue was left to look after the bridge with three or four officers and half a dozen men. The position did not worry him ; like any good private soldier, he expected somebody else to do the worrying. He sat in what little sun there was, to get dry.

A German armoured counter-attack caught them with over-whelming strength. Blue saw the tanks come down the lane, but then his awareness of what was happening shrank to a confused impression of hellish noise and violence and a feeling of utter frustration as he pressed himself into the sweet-smelling grass by the side of the lane, because he had no weapon to hit back with. The man with the bazooka did some damage but not enough and Blue heard an officer shout, " Every man on his own." He ran crouching towards the tall reeds in the marsh beside the causeway and plunged in and began for the second time to wade through the flood, keeping his head down among the reeds while tanks came roaring along the causeway close behind him. He reached the abutment of the bridge. The river was deeper there. He wondered whether to swim, but decided to try the bridge. He lay on the steep slope of the abutment while some of the weight of water drained out of his clothes. Somebody shouted " Run soldier ! " and he got up and ran like a snipe across the bridge, the bullets whipping past him, and fell down gasping on the other side, back where he had started just over an hour before. The farm was still burning. The three old French people had gone, and Blue never saw them again ; but he never forgot them, any more than he forgot his first victory, or his first defeat.

Blue as a private never knew what had gone wrong; but just about the time when the bridge was lost, General Gavin arrived there with his one hundred and fifty men, and began to sort out the dangerous situation.

Gavin had already fought a long defensive action while half of his men searched the floods for the lost equipment. By dawn, not a single anti-tank weapon had been found. Gavin was impatient to reach the bridge. He had the choice of fighting his way, ill-armed, down the western bank of the river, or crossing the flood and marching down the railway, where he had heard that his other regiments were in reasonably good shape. He decided to cross; and in the early morning light, leaving their injured and wounded, his body of miscellaneous men began to wade under fire from German snipers. Most of them made the crossing; but delayed by the unsuccessful search, they were too late to save the bridge.

Like General Gale fifty miles away on the British zone, General Gavin was not perturbed by the apparent chaos of the drop; he knew his men would get on with the job wherever they happened to be. But the loss of the bridge was more serious, because it spilt his division in two and left parts of two regiments to fight without hope of reinforcements on the other side of the river valley. It had been lost through a misunderstanding. The main body of troops who had crossed it were men who had dropped on the wrong side of the river and crossed over simply to get to the other side where they ought to have been. They thought others behind them were following to defend it, but nobody came, except the dozen with Blue. Gavin, however, was not concerned to find out what had happened; he set himself to try to force a second crossing, not only at La Fière but also at another bridge a little farther south, and at an ancient ford. But without the support of any heavy weapons, the parachutists could not shift the Germans, and nobody crossed the river again till seaborne tanks arrived there four days later.

But although they could not take the bridge, they did achieve something almost as important; they stopped the Germans crossing it, and so held the German tanks not only away from the beach, but also away from the town of Sainte-Mère-Eglise, a mile behind the bridge, where another of Gavin's regiments, in the very early morning, had won an unqualified victory.

Sainte-Mère-Eglise is a little market town of grey stone houses which stand on each side of the main road from Cherbourg to the south. It has relics of the time when Roman legions marched up that road, and of William the Conqueror's armies; but for six or seven centuries it traded humbly in farm implements and horses and cattle and cheese, and had no military interest. Even on the night when it suddenly formed the stage of high drama, its importance was only fortuitous. It was the beach, the roads and the rivers which were important. Sainte-Mère-Eglise just had the luck, good or bad, to be there, at a crossroads on the map, in the middle of the area of the airborne forces' drop, and so to win the double-edged honour of being the first town in France which the Allied forces planned to liberate.

For precisely four years, an enormous swastika flag had flown from the flagstaff outside the town hall, and Sainte-Mère-Eglise, patient and cynical, had watched the progress of the German occupation. It remembered the early days in 1940 when the pick of the German army, proud and confident, had marched up the road singing " *Wir fahren gegen England,*" and promising that Britain in three weeks would be *kaput*. These German soldiers compelled some grudging admiration from the people who watched them pass; but even then, the town's small boys had perfected a technique of making sea-sick and drowning noises which ruined displays of military pomp; and the town had witnessed the first tarnishing of German pride when the invasion of England had had to be postponed. Since then, the occupation of Sainte-Mère-Eglise had mirrored the creeping defeat of the Germany army. Little by little, the finer troops had disappeared to face their doom in Russia or North Africa or Italy; old men and boys replaced them, men who were sick or

partly disabled by wounds, and finally the dregs of the foreign
conscripts.

In the meantime, the town submitted to the gloom of occupation : the nagging fear, the rising prices, scarcity, black markets,
the occasional rumours of sudden tragedy. It never suffered
acutely. Perhaps the worst of its hurts was humiliation ; the
thought that after all the centuries of good Norman husbandry,
the present generation had surrendered to an upstart foreign
power.

Through the B.B.C., Sainte-Mère-Eglise followed the news
of the war and waited from season to season for its liberation.
At first, it clutched at every hint that the invasion was coming,
and so it often suffered disappointment. As early as the spring
of 1943, the B.B.C. told people to move from the coasts. A great
spring offensive was expected. Churchill broadcast, and people
understood him to mean that France would be invaded before
the leaves fell in autumn. But the leaves fell, and no invasion
came, and Sainte-Mère-Eglise found it hard to maintain its faith
through another winter.

In March and April of 1944, there were signs of new German
activity. Troops passed through the town at night, going
north, using requisitioned horses and farm carts to carry their
equipment. An anti-aircraft battery moved into the town and a
new battalion was stationed in the villages round about. Exercises were held continuously. These were the local results of the
arrival of the new division which upset the airborne plan, and
of Rommel's energy. In May, the Germans demanded the
help of able-bodied Frenchmen in putting up their anti-glider
posts. Their demand was naïve. The quicker the job was done,
they explained, the better it would be, because once it was
finished the " Tommies "* could never land near Sainte-Mère-
Eglise, and the town and countryside would be spared from
destruction. The Frenchmen were astonished to learn that the
Germans really thought the district might be invaded ; for they

* This word for a British soldier, almost forgotten in Britain since World
War I, is still in use in France.

themselves, by then, hardly believed that the British would ever invade, and were certain that if they did, they would go to the district of Calais, or else to Holland. Not even the increasing air bombardment of the coast in the first days of June made them change their opinion. The swastika flag had flown so long outside their town hall that people hardly dared to hope to see it hauled down again. But on June 5th, at an airfield in England, the commander of a parachute regiment showed his men an American flag, and told them it was the flag which the regiment had hoisted in Naples when it fell; and he promised them they would fly it in Sainte-Mère-Eglise before the morning.

The delicate task of representing the town in its relations with the Germans had fallen upon the mayor, Alexandre Renaud. M. Renaud was proprietor of the chemist's shop in the square in the centre of the town. Chemists usually know their townsmen well, and so do mayors; being both, M. Renaud knew almost everything there was to know about Sainte-Mère-Eglise. In his shop, behind his counter, intent on his prescriptions, with his glasses on his nose, he appeared such a gentle and scholarly person that no stranger would have suspected how shrewd or how tough he could be. But all through those four black years, he defended the rights of the townspeople, such as they were, and yet avoided provoking the Germans to violence; and that was no small achievement.

M. Renaud was a veteran of the great days of the French army. He was proud to have fought at Verdun. As an old soldier, he could still appreciate military standards of behaviour, and found he could size up most of the German officers who followed each other as garrison commanders of his town. Most of them were only intent on carrying out their orders, and were strictly correct in the demands they made on him, and never showed their feelings. A few were bullies, and a few were openly unhappy in the rôle of conqueror. The commanders of the two units, the infantry battalion and the anti-aircraft battery, which were in the district in May, were of opposite types. The infantry commander was a swashbuckler who made the mistake of thinking the mayor was as meek as he sometimes looked. He tried to humiliate and frighten him; and when that only made him angry, he threatened him with instant execution if the " Tommies " landed. Perhaps the threat was empty, but Renaud was not at all sorry when the battalion moved away. Then only the anti-aircraft unit was left in the town. Its commander was an elderly Austrian. It was said that before the war he had been the music critic of a newspaper in Vienna. If he was, it is easy to imagine why he seemed miserable, as he did, in his post at Sainte-Mère-Eglise. Gossip said that his only remaining interest was in wine. This man was in charge of the town on the night of the landing.

The night began with a house on fire on the opposite side of the square to the chemist's shop. M. Renaud had just gone to bed, uneasy in his mind, for he had spent the evening at an up-stairs window, watching the flashes and flares of a tremendous air raid somewhere in the direction of the coast. He was roused by somebody banging on his front door; the fire brigade wanted all the men they could muster to help them by carrying water. He dressed quickly, and put on his coat and hat, and leaving his wife to look after the children he crossed the familiar square, beneath the chestnut and lime trees in front of the church. The house was blazing. Nobody knew how it had started. It might have been just an accident, but the sky was full of aircraft and it seemed more likely that something—not a bomb, but a flare perhaps—had fallen on the roof, which was well alight. The firemen in their bright brass helmets were trying to save the thatch of a barn nearby which was threatened by sparks, and volunteers were carrying water in canvas buckets from the pump in the cattle market. M. Renaud joined them. The flames lit up the bell-tower of the church, where German machine-gunners, posted on the roof, were shooting aimlessly at the aircraft overhead, filling the sky with arches of tracer bullets. Other men of the anti-aircraft unit, waiting the order to fire, watched the firemen from their positions in the square. The earth below the trees vibrated with the explosion of distant bombs.

Then above the sounds of war, the church bell rang. It continued to ring, urgently and quickly : the tocsin, the ancient signal of alarm. M. Renaud stopped on his way to the pump, with a new clutch at the heart as he asked himself what more disaster the clamour of the bell foretold. He instinctively looked up towards the tower, and so he saw what was coming : low over the rooftops and the trees, almost in silence, a host of aircraft sweeping across the town, their lights burning, their wings and bodies black against the moon ; and then as the first of the waves of them receded, the giant confetti which drifted in their wake.

M. Renaud and the firemen stood amazed, neglecting the fire, unable to believe that the thing which they had thought about so long was really happening, and was happening in Sainte-Mère-Eglise itself. High up, the parachutes were seen in silhouette against the sky ; as they fell, the men on them were also seen, in the light of the fire. The machine gunners on the church tower and in the square saw them too and fired lower. The watchers, horrified, saw the convulsion of a man who was shot as he was falling. They saw a parachute which draped an old tree : the parachutist began to climb down, the machine-gunners saw him and left him swinging limply in his harness. They also saw a man fall into the fire and crash through the burning roof. Sparks spurted out, and the flames blazed up afresh. More squadrons of planes were passing over : the bell still ringing ; shots cracking through the square. The German soldiers ordered the Frenchmen indoors, and M. Renaud, anxious for his wife and children, hurried home. A German beneath the trees, pointing at the body of a parachutist, shouted to him with satisfaction : " Tommies—all *kaput*."

This fatuous optimism may have been shared, for the moment, by other Germans in the square of Sainte-Mère-Eglise, for the few parachutists who had the bad luck to drop within the firelight presented easy targets. It was not the intention, of course, to drop on the roofs of the town itself. The men who did so were only stragglers from a whole regiment which landed between the town and the river, and this regiment had the most accurate drop of any parachute unit that night. A thousand of its 2,200 men fell in the dropping zone and assembled at once. Most of the rest were not very far away, and came in before daylight. Within an hour of dropping, the regiment had begun its first task of clearing Sainte-Mère-Eglise and blocking the road to the north and south of it.

The old soldier in M. Renaud made him sally forth before long to see what was going on, and he happened to pass a pond, which had once been the public laundry, in the nick of time to seize the lines of a parachute and haul out a man who had had a ducking there. But after that adventure, he spent the rest of the night indoors with his wife and children, listening and trying to interpret the sounds from the streets of the town ; for the moon had set, and it was too dark to see anything from the windows. The firing had died away, except for the machine guns on the church. He heard cars and motor cycles in the square, but saw no lights, and he guessed that the anti-aircraft battery was retreating. For almost an hour from two o'clock to three, there was a strange and ominous silence. About three, he saw matches lit below the chestnut trees, and the glow of cigarettes, and the light of a flashlamp, and he and his family debated who was there : the Germans, or the " Tommies." And at last, day began to break, and as the light penetrated below the trees, he was astonished to see that his square was occupied not by Germans, or by " Tommies," but by men in the round helmets he had seen on American troops in German newspaper pictures. The people of Sainte-Mère-Eglise, through all their years of listening to the B.B.C., had never dreamed that their liberators, in the end, would be American.

Very soon after dawn, a parachute captain knocked on the door, and introduced himself, and offered the mayor a piece of chewing gum. The new régime had started. The captain asked the way to the headquarters of the German commander of the town. M. Renaud escorted him there himself; but during the night, the Viennese music critic and all his men had gone. The swastika flag had gone too; the American flag from Naples flew instead.

So Sainte-Mère-Eglise received the honour of being the first town in France which was liberated; an honour which it proudly remembers still, especially at its annual fête on the sixth of June. But the honour was costly, and the price had still to be paid; for during the next two days, till tanks and reinforcements came through from Utah Beach, the Germans turned their batteries on the town and shelled it heavily; and many of M. Renaud's townspeople who had lived through the four dark years were killed in the first two days of the freedom for which they had hoped so long.

The capture of the town was the only specific objective which the American airborne troops achieved before dawn; they got off to a much slower start than the British. There were reasons for this. Through the changes of plan, their training had been shorter. Their drop, on the whole, was even more chaotically scattered; and their stretch of the Norman countryside was even more labyrinthine than the British. But quick tactical victories were not the only way to success. What did happen during the night, far out from such centres as Sainte-Mère-Eglise and the bridge at La Fière, away in the damp dark silent woods and meadows, was equally important: it was a gigantic and lethal game of hide-and-seek. Over ten thousand Americans were taking part in it, and probably at least five thousand Germans. It covered an area over ten miles square, and grim isolated games were being fought twenty and twenty-five miles away from the centre. In this unique contest, the Americans knew what was happening, but few of them knew where they were; the Germans knew where they were, but none of them knew what was happening.

At first, almost every parachutist was alone, lost in the dark in strange country where every rustle and shadow seemed hostile, like the forests of children's dreams. General Maxwell Taylor himself, commander of the 101st Division, spent his first half hour on the battlefield all alone, searching for even a single one of his 7,000 men. If he had given an order, he remarked afterwards, nobody would have heard it except the cows. And even he, when at last he did find an equally lost and lonely trooper, was so relieved that the two of them embraced each other warmly. The fact is that most grown men, even soldiers, of any nation, have traces of their childish fear of the dark; and when the dark forest is really full of enemies, the first thing that any man will look for is a friend. The Germans who were out alone that night, or in small groups on patrol, had just the same instinct: they tried to find other Germans, or to get back to headquarters and band together for self-defence, and for moral support. So all through the four hours from the drop to the dawn, hundreds and hundreds of little groups and solitary men, American and German, were prowling about the country, trigger-conscious, but put on the defensive by sheer loneliness. Anything which moved or made a noise, and could not give a split-second answer to a challenge, was liable to be shot at; the cows and horses suffered considerably. No German who ventured out by car or motor cycle succeeded in travelling far; even a general was ambushed and killed that night. Here and there, where two groups met face to face, there were sharp exchanges of shots at close range. But both sides, with a few individual exceptions, felt they had enough trouble on their hands without looking for more, and these small engagements seldom lasted long.

This curious kind of Red Indian warfare had never been planned, and would never have happened if the drop had been more successful and concentrated; yet it was most effective. For about eight hours, it totally paralysed the Germans. Their garrisons were in small units, like Müller's platoon at Azeville. They were not connected by radio, only by telephone and by dispatch riders. The parachutists cut telephone wires whenever they saw them—including the main cable from Cherbourg to the south—and dispatch riders, of course, were sitting ducks.

Briefing: American troops and English countryside

Ships assembled off the Isle of Wight. The fleet filled all the ports from the Thames to the Bristol Channel

Concealing his fears Eisenhower talked cheerfully to American paratroopers before they took off. Corporal Jackson, with his face blackened, is just behind the general.

Equipment: one of Gavin's men on the night of the 5th

Major John Howard

The Caen canal bridge: the wreckage of Howard's glider is behind the trees

"A lethal game of hide and seek." American paratroopers in the Cherbourg peninsula

Utah beach: Mabry's battalion shelter from artillery fire behind the seawall

Colonel Wilson R. Wood

One of Wood's Marauders over Utah,
just before the landing

Infantry landing craft pass the cruiser Augusta in the rough sea off Omaha

Omaha: men under heavy fire tried to shelter behind the German obstacles, and so hindered the work of the demolition teams

Omaha, dawn: the fire-swept beach ahead

Omaha: "The instant transition from the shelter of the boats to the whitest heat of war"

Omaha: afternoon. The tide in high, close to the shingle bank. Beyond it, men follow tracks through the minefields in single file

"Don't help anyone, get ashore": commandos land on Juno beach

"The confusion looked much worse than it really was." The sea beyond this beach is hidden by the row of landing craft

Canadians at Bernières on Juno beach

"Wounded men and vehicles packed together." First-aid on the beach behind a disabled petard tank

Canadians at Bernières: The bombardment was an ordeal, but the people in the villages soon recovered their good humour

The assault is over: the build-up begins

When their telephones went dead and their dispatch riders vanished, the German small unit commanders did not know what to do and were scared to move; while the higher command had no means of knowing what was happening, or which of their scattered units were still in existence. Of course, the German divisions were far more heavily armed than the Americans, but their artillery and even their tanks, in these early hours, were useless; ten thousand Americans spread over a hundred square miles of country, and constantly moving, never offered a target worth a shell.

Among the Germans unwillingly wandering in the woods was a young man called Fritz Müller; no relation of the Müller in Azeville. Fritz Müller was a medical orderly in a mobile artillery regiment. His regiment had moved into the district only a fortnight before, for the specific job of opposing an airborne landing. It was cleverly or luckily placed; his own battery was on top of a hill which commanded most of the area where the Americans landed. It was also well equipped, and its morale was high; and yet it never fired a single artillery shot from the hill, because it never had a target.

Fritz Müller, who was twenty-two, was in France like many other soldiers only because he had already been badly wounded in Russia, and was rated unfit for any more arduous front. He had entered the medical corps in a rather unusual way. He had always wanted to be a doctor; but his father was a monumental mason in a village on the edge of the coalfields of the Ruhr, and he had insisted that his son should follow him in the business. When the war began, Fritz, who was then seventeen, was attending night classes in anatomy, and so the medical corps had been glad to accept him. That was a step towards being a doctor; and nobody knew that his father had only let him learn anatomy to qualify him for carving angels on tombstones.

Müller was not enjoying prowling in the woods, any more than anybody else; but at least he was doing it with a reasonable humanitarian motive, which meant a lot to him; his officer

had sent him out, with a couple of other men, to look for
wounded, either German or American. From the top of the hill,
Müller and his companions had watched the parachutes come
down with a feeling almost of pity for the parachutists. They had
seen their own machine-gunners dispatch a good many before
they landed, and they had seen others fall in the floods of the
Douve ; and they were sure the remainder would soon be
rounded up. All the same, they had no intention of taking
chances with them. They had been told that parachutists never
took prisoners. Some of them had seen the ruthlessness of their
own parachute corps in North Africa. Müller himself had seen
German parachutists shooting their Russian prisoners. To go
down from the safety of the hill and search the dark woods
around it seemed risky enough in itself, and he had been surprised and rather aggrieved when the officer suddenly told him
he would have to go unarmed.

All Müller's experiences as a medical orderly had been in
Russia, where neither side had taken much notice of the Geneva
Convention. He had worn a red cross, but carried a rifle too,
and used it when he had to ; and so he had brought it to France.

" But these are either British or Americans," the officer said,
" and you can't carry arms against them."

Müller said : " That's like sending me into the lion's cage
and telling me they won't bite."

Orders were orders, he decided, but common sense was
something different. He left his rifle, but when nobody was
looking, he put a revolver in his trouser pocket.

Down in the woods, it was eerie and quiet. Many of the trees
were draped with parachutes. From some of them, corpses
dangled, victims perhaps of the battery's shooting while they
dropped. On others, the harnesses were empty, and the parachutists had disappeared. By and by, Müller and his two companions heard German voices, and pressing on, they came to a
glade where an American was lying, dead or unconscious, on the
ground. A German soldier was rifling his pockets and making
lewd comments on the picture of a girl he had found in his

wallet. Müller was rather offended, and he said so. The German told him to mind his own business. He finished the job by taking a ring from the American's finger, and then stood up and walked away. When he had gone a few paces, a rifle shot was fired from somewhere close at hand, and he fell like a log.

The medical orderly's work often needs courage; no doubt it needed it then. Müller walked across the glade to the German. He was quite dead. He went back to the American. He was still alive, although he was unconscious. Müller began his usual routine of first aid. No sooner had he started than a shower of cigarettes fell round him, apparently from the sky. Absorbed in his task, he was only a little surprised. So many amazing things had happened already that morning that his faculty of wonder was overworked. The Americans were dropping cigarettes, presumably from aircraft: that was all. He did not smoke himself, but most of his patients asked for a cigarette as soon as they came to their senses, so he picked up a few and put them in his pocket.

It was quite a long time before he thought of a rather less whimsical explanation: that parachutists had still been up in the trees around him, and had shot the robber, and then done their best to reward him for giving first aid to their friend.

Quite close to Fritz Müller, completely lost, was another young man of exactly his age called Schuyler Jackson. The two men had quite a lot in common beside their age: the same youthful interests and similar senses of humour. Perhaps if they had ever met in normal life they would have enjoyed each other's company. But the only time they nearly met was in the Norman woods, and it was just as well that their devious paths did not quite cross that morning; for while Müller had come there from the Ruhr, Jackson had come from Washington, D.C., and was playing his part with some relish in the one-man battles which were disrupting the German system of defence. Already, with one other man who was also lost, he had come across a German anti-aircraft gun whose crew of six were intent on

targets overhead. It had been easy to creep up to them in the
dark and throw grenades among them and kill them all, and
with that success behind him, Jackson was ready to try his hand
again.

All the same, that kind of chance encounter was not what he
had come for, and he was worried and upset because time was
slipping by and yet he could not find out where he was or get
on with his proper job. He was a corporal, in the 101st Division,
and it was only a few hours since he had been face to face with
General Eisenhower, just before the division took off. He had
been so surprised to find himself so close to so much brass that
he had hardly remembered anything Ike had said, but he had a
vague recollection of being asked: "You know your objective?" That had been an easy one to answer. He knew his
objective as well as he had ever known anything. The division
was to capture the inland ends of the causeways which led
through the floods behind Utah Beach. His own battalion was to
attack a heavy battery which commanded the beach from a
village called St. Martin-de-Varreville. According to the plan,
he should have dropped within half a mile of St. Martin and it
should have been easy to find. But now he had dropped and
St. Martin was not there.

What specially puzzled him, as he hunted for landmarks in
the dark, was not only that he was lost, but that he kept on
meeting men from his own battalion, all going in different
directions, and all as lost as he was. Evidently, the battalion
had made a good concentrated drop; yet none of them could make
head or tail of the maps and the countryside. Jackson simply
could not believe the only feasible explanation: that the whole
of the battalion, or nearly the whole of it, had been neatly dropped
together in the wrong place. But that was what had happened.
The leading aircraft, off course through cloud and anti-aircraft
fire, had spotted the pathfinder's lights on another dropping
zone, three miles south of where it should have been, and dropped
its passengers there; and twenty-seven other aircraft had blindly
followed its example. The battalion was not only lost, it was

leaderless. Its commander, Lt.-Col. Steve A. Chappuis, was in one of the very few aircraft which found the right dropping zone.

This mistake might have been serious for the fleet which was assembling off the beach, for the battery at St. Martin had been powerful. Colonel Chappuis was in an even worse dilemma than Colonel Otway at the similar battery at Merville : while Otway had found one hundred and fifty men of his British battalion, Chappuis could only find a dozen. With that forlorn force, he hurried to the battery to see what he could do : and found it ruined and deserted. Air attacks in the last few nights had been successful ; the Germans had taken their guns away and abandoned the site.

Corporal Jackson, knowing nothing of any of this, went on searching for the battery till dawn, and then gave it up. About dawn, he came on a glider which had crashed. Dead men were lying in it and round about it. Only one man there was still alive : an officer who was sitting on the ground, apparently uninjured. Jackson asked him if he was all right. The officer said he had a few aches, but nothing serious. Jackson was getting tired, and he sat down beside him to rest ; and the officer started to talk and ask questions, not about the war or the glider or the immediate future, but about life at home in America. Jackson told him about Washington, and told him he had joined the airborne forces just to show he was as good a fighting man as his father, who was a naval officer. The irrelevant conversation among the silent corpses was macabre. Slowly Jackson began to understand that the officer had some very serious invisible injury and was in pain and had detached his mind from all the grim surroundings and was living in some time before the present. Jackson offered him morphine. " I've taken some already," the officer said. A few minutes later, he died.

Jackson left that sombre scene and went on with his aimless journey. He joined up with a friend, and soon they saw another man lying in the middle of a field, and went to see if he was still alive. It was the colonel of their own regiment, and he was alive and conscious ; but he had broken his leg very badly in the drop, and had lain where he was for five hours. He told Jackson and his friend to drag him to the side of the field, where a little dip with a stream in the bottom gave some cover. They had hardly started when they were shot at, and Jackson had a glimpse of a German running behind a hedge. The two men dropped the colonel where he was, and gave chase. The German seemed to run down a farm track between thick hedges. Jackson followed him, spraying the hedges with his sub-machine gun. To his astonishment, screams and groans broke out, and a white handkerchief was poked through the upper branches. " *Kamerad! Kamerad!* " Jackson shouted. He hoped that would do as an order to surrender. It did. A dozen men came out from behind the hedge, some with their hands up, some staggering ; and Jackson was shocked to see the result of his casual finger on the trigger. There was a man supported by others clasping his stomach in agony. There were men drenched with blood. There was a boy, who looked fifteen, shot by some evil chance through both his wrists ; when he tried to put his hands up to surrender, they both hung limply down. Something in the faces of these men, together with their readiness to surrender, made Jackson think they were not Germans at all. Whoever they were, seeing them at his own mercy and in such distress, he found he could not hate them, as he had expected to hate the enemy. They merely looked human, and pitiable. Other para-chutists who had heard his fusillade were coming along the track, and Jackson, half ashamed of the hot gun in his hand, and half ashamed of his unsoldierly feelings, let the others take charge of the prisoners and quickly went away. He did not want to look at them any more.

He went back to the colonel, and dragged him to the stream ; but the colonel had a compound fracture and needed treatment. Jackson went to look for something to carry him on, and hit on the same solution which Blue's two Frenchmen had used for their similar problem : a wheelbarrow. He found one in a farm-yard, and he also found someone at last who could tell him where they were : four miles south of the battery of St. Martin. This placed them only a mile or so from a monastery building which had been designated as divisional headquarters : and the colonel, confronted with the wheelbarrow, told Jackson to take him there. Jackson hoisted the colonel into the unusual equipage and trundled him off down the lanes. " It must have hurt him like hell," he said with admiration when he thought of it afterwards. " But I'll say he could still bark out his orders."

The sight at headquarters of a sweating corporal pushing a colonel in a wheelbarrow was incongruous and had possibly never been seen before in war ; but nobody laughed. Everyone there was a parachutist, and had an inkling of the feelings of a professional officer who had broken his leg on jumping into his first—and possibly his last—historic battle. Still full of fight, the colonel reported to General Taylor, who ordered him, in spite of his protests, to the aid post.

Corporal Jackson seemed to be getting among the brass again. He retreated, to take it easy. One way and another, it had been a busy morning, and he felt he had learned a lot.

It was about 2.30 in the morning when General Taylor embraced the first man of his division whom he found. Now, about 2.30 in the afternoon, his divisional headquarters were still far from complete, and he was still out of touch with most of his command. Almost everything was still confused, and he did not yet know the important and comforting fact that the Germans were far more confused than anybody else. But during the morning, in his own travels, he had witnessed the outcome of the most important of his tasks : the attack on the first of the causeways which led to the beach.

The General had landed quite close to his correct dropping zone, which was west of the village of Sainte-Marie-du-Mont, and four miles south east of Sainte-Mère-Eglise ; but not even he had been able to find where he was in the maze of hedges. The fact was that to drop and assemble in the dark in that particular part of Normandy was a wholly impossible task. If

a parachutist had been lucky enough to recognise a landmark—
of which there were few—in the seconds while he was falling, all
would have been well. But hardly any of them did so; and once
they were down, they could seldom see more than a hundred
yards, and all the woods and hedges looked the same.

The General worked his way laboriously eastward towards
the coast, and picked up as he went a motley assortment of
troops, including, by coincidence, far too high a proportion of
officers. When dawn began to break, and the bombing and
shelling of the coast to shake the earth, about eighty men were
with him in the meadows. Among them were one other general
—General McAuliffe, his artillery commander—and at least four
colonels. As the light in the eastern sky increased, they saw
silhouetted against it the only landmark which could have told
them at a glance where they were : the tall, beautiful, and distinctive tower of the church of Sainte-Marie-du-Mont. They
were not more than two miles from the end of the southernmost
causeway. Not one of the officers or men belonged to either
of the two battalions which should have been there and should
have attacked the causeway; but one of the colonels, Lt.-Col.
Julian J. Ewell, was commander of a reserve battalion, and about
half the men were his. The rest were staff officers, artillerymen
without artillery, clerks, military police, the two generals, and a
war correspondent from Reuters. General Taylor put Ewell in
charge of this curious outfit, and told him to do what he could
at the southern causeway. Generals and colonels were nothing
much more than observers. Majors and captains had sections
to command. Lieutenants had nothing at all. As the troop began
to move, General Taylor remarked to Ewell that never before
were so few led by so many.

Julian Ewell was a professional officer, a graduate of West
Point, and young at twenty-eight to be a colonel. This was
his first combat, an important occasion in his career, and he
would much have preferred to go into it with his own well-
trained battalion, instead of a lot of men who had never worked
together and did not even know each other's names. Probably he

would have preferred to try his hand a little less closely under the General's eye. But parachutists learn to be resourceful.

The two-mile march in the growing light brought minor excitements: the first shots, at a German guard post, the first sight of German dead; the first prisoner, who turned out to be a Pole; and the first American death in action—a medical orderly who ran out into the open to help an officer wounded by rifle fire. As the party skirted Sainte-Marie-du-Mont, it grew like a snowball, collecting wandering men in twos and threes. Some of them had landed in the village itself, and said they had already been captured and escaped.

On the road which leads to the causeway, just before the beginning of the salt flats which were flooded, there is a primitive little hamlet called Pouppeville. From the first few of its cottages, rifle fire brought Ewell's column to a halt. He deployed his forces to attack the place.

The fight which followed seemed a stiff one at the time, though later, when Ewell had more experience of fighting, he looked back on it as a very small affair. The Germans had to be fought from house to house with rifles and hand grenades. Ewell himself, intent on organising a coherent attack with his ill-assorted force, was hardly aware of danger until he incautiously put his head round the corner of a wall and was smartly rapped on the top of his helmet by a sniper's bullet. Very slowly, as the Germans retreated, the fight began to converge on the village school; and Ewell, advancing more carefully now down the village street, reached the wall of the playground and looked over it. A German lieutenant ran out of the schoolhouse towards him, shouting. Ewell shot at him with his pistol and missed, and then realised that he was trying to surrender. Twenty or thirty Germans came out of the school behind him; and Ewell's first fight was over.

Beyond the school, the causeway could be seen, a narrow straight road with water on either side, and at the far end of it, the sand dunes of Utah Beach. There seemed to be nobody on it. But soon, in the reeds beside it, a few small orange flags appeared;

and these were the signals of recognition which had been planned for this moment : the first meeting of airborne and seaborne forces.

Ewell sent a few men down the road, and they came back escorting an officer who reported to General Taylor : Captain George Mabry, of the 8th Infantry. The parachutists looked at him rather like a man from another planet ; for he had come by sea. The time was 11.5 a.m.

IV

UTAH BEACH

─────────────────────────────

Mabry had been ashore for four and a half hours, and had covered over two miles from his landing place; and so far, the seaborne infantry's losses had been astonishingly small. That was the real measure of the airborne troops' success. Although the scattered drop and the difficult countryside had made havoc of their plans of battle, they had reacted everywhere with spontaneous guerilla warfare; and the all-important result of it was that the defences on Utah Beach were cut off from the German army command, which was not even told till the afternoon that a landing had started there. No German reinforcements ever got near the beach. This result was achieved with nothing like the casualties which Leigh-Mallory had predicted to Eisenhower. The losses of American troop-carrying aircraft were twenty out of a total of eight hundred and five, instead of the eighty per cent he had feared. The losses of parachutists did appear to be very high at first. At dawn, five out of six of them were missing. By evening, less than half were in organised units. But many of the missing men were still wandering, and turned up in the next few days; and a couple of months later, when there was time to prepare statistics, it was found that about one out of ten of the airborne troops had been killed on D-Day, or were still missing and presumed to have been killed or captured on that day. That was certainly bad enough, but it was

less than the paratroopers themselves expected, and by the
standards of war it was a price that was well worth paying.
By the evening of D-Day, Eisenhower's worst anxiety for the
airborne troops was over, although the 82nd Division was still
cut off from everybody else. On the next day, Leigh-Mallory
wrote him a note to say that it was sometimes difficult to say
that one was wrong, but that he had never had greater pleasure
than to admit he had been wrong about the drop. He congratu-
lated Eisenhower on his wisdom in deciding to go ahead with it,
and apologised for having added to his worries. Captain Harry
Butcher, Eisenhower's naval aide, regarded this as a typically
British sporting gesture, and wrote in his diary : " You simply
can't stay mad at people like this." So this remarkable difference
of opinion ended.

It was only by chance that George Mabry was the first seaborne officer to report to the airborne General. Nobody had
planned it. But his experience of the landing, and all that led to
it, was typical of the experience of most of the six hundred men
who landed in the first wave of troops on Utah Beach that morning. In fact, Mabry was typical in an even wider sense. It would
be absurd of course, to describe him as a typical American,
because there is no such thing ; but his British acquaintances
might have said—and meant it as a compliment—that nobody
could have been more American than he was.

He was twenty-four, and he had lived all his youth in Sumter
County, South Carolina, where his father, who had once been a
celebrated baseball star, was a farmer on a fairly big scale. The
farm grew cotton, the farm workers were descendants of slaves,
and George's pastimes when he was a boy were fishing in the
rivers and hunting in the woods around his home. When an
Englishman heard George speak of his boyhood, it seemed
unexpectedly familiar, and he felt that they must have met before ;
and then he realised that he was thinking of his own boyhood
recollection of Mark Twain.

George's greatest sorrow in his youth was being small. He

overcame that disadvantage in the only way he could in such a he-man's country: by making himself go one better than the other boys, walk farther, swim longer, climb higher trees. He had never heard of complexes, but it became a habit in him to believe he would always have to do this sort of thing to keep his end up. When he left high school, he told his father he did not want to go to college, and his father shrewdly gave him the toughest job he could think of: he put him in charge of a farm which employed thirty men. George ran the farm for a year. By the end of the year, in a boxing ring, he had fought every able-bodied employee to prove, either to them or to himself, that he was the boss; and having done that, he agreed to go to college. As if to complete this picture of an American up-bringing, George played baseball as a professional during his college vacations.

He joined the army impulsively on a reserve commission in the period after Dunkirk and before Pearl Harbour, when people were beginning to believe that America would fight in the end. As a junior officer, his smallness made him adopt literally the age-old principle of never telling anyone to do anything he could not do himself. Even in training, it was sometimes hard for him to live up to that principle; and whenever he thought about combat, he pictured himself out in front, doing all the most dangerous jobs, because he knew he would never be able to tell anyone else to do them first. In the end, the mere fact of being small led him by these devious trains of thought to a belief which is rather unusual in a soldier: he believed he was sure to be killed. The idea did not worry him, once he was used to it. He would not have told anyone about it, but by then he was married, and he had to tell his wife. For one thing, there was the question of children: they both wanted children, but he thought they ought not to have them. When he was sent over-seas, he asked his wife not to expect to see him again, and tried to make her feel as contented about it as he did. At the end of the war, he was surprised to be still alive. Of course, he was pleased at his luck, but he was a little disappointed in himself; he felt that if he had really achieved the standard he had aimed at, he would be dead.

But in the meantime, accepting the idea of being killed had saved him a lot of worry. For example, while he was waiting in England, he had worried much less about crossing the Norman beach than many soldiers whose desperate hope was to put up an honourable show but to come through the war alive.

In England, Mabry's battalion was stationed at Seaton, a small old-fashioned resort on the south coast of Devonshire. The people of seaside resorts are more used to sudden invasions of strangers than the people of inland towns, and to the people of Seaton the American troops did not seem very much more foreign than the city holiday-makers who had come there every summer before the war. Commercially, they were a boon to a little town which had lost its tourist traffic abruptly four years before ; but commerce apart, the people were glad to see them, and eager to do what they could to make them feel at home, because they knew that the invasion was coming, and that the Americans were there to take part in it, and that invasion would bring the first glimpse, after all those years, of an end of the misery and boredom of the war. The Americans on the whole felt the people's goodwill and appreciated it, although it could not cure their homesickness. They did not want to be on foreign service any more than any other citizen army, but if they had to be, there were worse places than Seaton and worse natives than the English, hard though their customs were to understand.

" Say, what kind of a bird is that ? " a soldier once asked, looking in amazement at a swan on the small river which runs through the town.

" That's a swan," an elderly Seaton lady told him.

" Are they good to eat ? "

" So I am told. But swans in England belong to the King, you know."

" Is that so ? Well, whadda ya say we knock one off for dinner ? "

The only memorable complaint from a local person was also concerned with birds. A landowner requested the American commander to put a stop to rifle practice on the shore, because it was disturbing his pheasants in the breeding season. At first, this made the American commander very angry. Then, for quite a long time, he laughed. Finally he began to wonder if the landowner was right, and if it was the army which had lost its sense of proportion, and if breeding and shooting pheasants was not as important in the long run as shooting Germans. Anyhow, he had been told to humour the English, and he moved the rifle range.

George Mabry had been in the same battalion ever since he joined the army, and had been a platoon commander and a company commander. In the waiting time in England, he was staff officer operations; and so, in the last few weeks, after men of his rank had been told the secret, he was engrossed in the detailed plans of what his own battalion had to do. Two of its companies, 300 men, were to land from ten landing craft on the left hand end of Utah Beach, while two companies of another battalion of the same regiment landed on the right. At the same time, or as soon after as possible, thirty-two amphibious tanks were due to land. Five minutes later, the second wave was due : nine hundred men in thirty landing craft, including the rest of his battalion. After them, there were more tanks, and engineers to demolish the obstacles which the Germans had put on the beach, and to blow gaps in the seawall to let the tanks go through. And behind all this was the organisation and power which was to put ashore twenty-one thousand men, and seventeen hundred vehicles, and seventeen hundred tons of stores, on that single beach by nightfall. In military language, the word spearhead is often used, and it was never more appropriate : the battalion in which George Mabry served was the head of a spear with a tremendous weight behind it in the shaft.

The battalion's responsibility kept him up, night after night, poring over the plans and trying to perfect them, although they were as perfect as military plans can ever be. But late one evening, to his surprise, the assistant commander of his division came stumping into his office and sat down and said : " What the hell are you up to, George ? Quit worrying." This was Brigadier-General Theodore Roosevelt, jr. " Whatever you plan," the General went on, " the boys are just going right in there and throw in all they've got. So what do you want with all this paper ? "

General Roosevelt was famous for outrageously unorthodox statements of this kind. They had a way of proving to be right, and this was not an exception. George stopped fussing over his plans ; and as it turned out, the details went for nothing when the battalion landed, and it was the General himself who changed them on the spot ; for in spite of his rank and his age—he was fifty-seven—he had volunteered to land with the first company and co-ordinate the attack.

Roosevelt was not only the most senior in rank, and probably much the oldest, of all the men in the first Seaborne waves of the invasion ; he must also be accounted its most striking personality. He was the eldest son of President Theodore Roosevelt, and a cousin—though not a close one—of President Franklin Roosevelt, and like his father, he had had a career of soldiering, politics and exploring. He had already seen action in North Africa and Italy. Whatever he did always seemed to be done with ten times the gusto and energy of most ordinary men. He was always completely oblivious of his own safety ; he seemed to treat everyone, except laggards, with the same kind of affectionate disrespect ; and he had a lightning wit, and an ability to see life from a private soldier's point of view. He hardly ever looked like a general. All these qualities made him the kind of man—like Churchill—who has innumerable stories told about him, always with a tinge of admiration. In the first four days of the invasion, he was said to have had four personal jeeps shot to pieces. On one of those days, he came into a junior command post and sat down and took off his helmet and wiped his brow. A cook came in, and said " You look as if you needed a cup o' coffee."

" I certainly do," the General said. " What neck of the woods do you come from ? "

" Pittsburgh," the cook said.

" Pittsburgh ? Hell of a place, that. No pretty girls there, and if there were you couldn't see them for the smoke."

The cook clapped him on the shoulder and hotly defended Pittsburgh and its girls. Then he saw the helmet on the table, with the general's stars on it, and rushed out of the room in confusion. " God damn it," he said later, " I thought he was some frazzle-assed old sergeant."

Roosevelt, in fact, was the perfect G.I. General.

George Mabry's journey to France was enlivened by several glimpses of this remarkable man. Indeed every one of the six hundred men of the spearhead on Utah must have been aware of the General's presence on the beach, and have felt better for it : if the old man can take it, they thought, then so can we. One man whom he drove to mock despair was his aide. " The old feller'll get me killed," he lamented to Mabry. " He doesn't give a damn for anything." But it was not so. The General led the men ashore, inspired them through the first of their battles, saw the invasion succeed, risked his own life a hundred times, and fell dead of a heart attack six days later. They buried him at Sainte-Mère-Eglise.

The General was present when the day came at last for the embarkation. The battalion embarked at Torquay. George Mabry stood on the quay of the little harbour, which is normally used by yachts and by boats which take holiday-makers on trips along the coast, and he watched the men carrying their equipment aboard the tender which was to take them out to their troopship anchored in Torbay. At that important moment, he was confident and excited. After four years in the battalion, he knew every man in it by sight. He had helped to weed out and get rid of weaklings ; and now, among those who were left, there was no visible sign of fear, only of a healthy tenseness as they packed themselves on board for the ultimate adventure. The months in England had been rather like a very long time in a dentist's waiting-room ; boring, and full of slight apprehension. Now they were all relieved, he thought, that the waiting was over. A small soldier was staggering up the ramp, carrying the base plate of a mortar, when Mabry heard the General's booming voice : " The army hasn't changed in a hundred years. Always the littlest guy gets the biggest load." The small soldier grinned, and visibly hitched his burden higher.

For the infantry in their large troopships, the channel crossing was much less dramatic than for men in small landing craft. They were quartered below decks, and most of them saw very little of the sea, or of the armada on it—the eight hundred and sixty-five vessels on their way to Utah Beach—or of the forces at sea and in the air which were deployed all round them to protect them. For all they could tell, they might have been sailing north or west, instead of east and then south ; they just had to take it on trust that after a day and a night at sea, in the light of dawn, there would be a coast, and that the coast would be France. When the navy takes charge, soldiers are always reduced to a state of suspended animation. On the crossing, Mabry heard the General shouting to his aide : " Steve, where in hell is my lifebelt ? "

" I've given you four already," the aide replied, with a delicate hint of reproach.

" Well, give me another," the General said. " I've lost the whole damned lot."

" Did you notice his armament ? " the aide asked Mabry. " A pistol and seven rounds, and his cane. He says that's all he'll need."

Drama began at 2.30 a.m., when the engines of the troopship stopped. Mabry went up on deck. It was very dark, and very quiet except for the sounds of the wind. They were stopped in mid-ocean. As his eyes grew used to the darkness, he saw that there was a faint light in the eastern sky, and reflections of it glinted on the waves. The waves looked large. All round, he saw the shadows of other ships, unlit and silent. Far away to the west there were flashes and flares ; he guessed they came from the Cherbourg peninsula, where the airborne fight should already be going on.

The silence was unexpected, and seemed sinister. Nobody knew why the Germans were not attacking : nobody could believe that they simply did not know the fleet was there. There was an uneasy feeling of an enemy lying in wait, of an ambush, of some secret danger which the planners had never foreseen. By instinct, absurd though it was, men were talking in hushed conspiratorial voices, as though Germans might overhear.

The transfer to landing craft had been rehearsed so often that no orders had to be given. The landing craft, launched from their davits, broke the silence by crashing and clanging against the sides of the troopship : it was certainly rough down there. At five minutes past four, the troops of the first wave scrambled into them with hardly a word, so that something the General said was plainly heard. Two soldiers offered him a hand over the gunwale. " Dammit," he said testily, " you know I can take it as well as any of you. Better than most."

Mabry took his turn, and one by one the landing craft cast off to leave room for more, and began to circle round to wait till it was time to set course for the beach.

In this hour before dawn, it was cold and wet and rough ; there was plenty of time for courage to sink, and for seasickness and cramp and discomfort to weaken the strongest will. The square bluff open boats butted the waves and showered the troops with spray. Most men crouched beneath the gunwales, more or less miserable, heads down, trying to preserve a little warmth and present the smallest target for the spray, and not caring to get themselves soaked by trying to watch what was happening.

At 4.55, the landing craft were assembled and started their long run—an hour and a half—towards the beach. They were led by two 173-foot patrol craft, and one smaller boat specially fitted with radar. There should have been two radar boats, but one had suffered the most ignominious of nautical failures : at the critical moment, it had got a rope round its propeller and could not move. Mabry and the infantry knew nothing of this, but it was the first of a series of cumulative mishaps which were to upset every one of their calculations.

As the landing craft turned to the westward and plunged into the head sea, Mabry was so excited and so passionately interested in the military scene that he never thought about getting wet, and stood in the bows of the craft looking over the ramp. He was in a free boat—a boat which was not attached to any particular wave of the assault, but could make its own landing at whatever stage seemed best. It started behind the second wave, but soon passed through it and began to catch up with the first. The shore was still far out of sight, but already Mabry could see part of the concourse of ships: ahead, the battleship *Nevada* and a line of British and American cruisers lying at anchor; astern the command ship *Bayfield*, the transports and tank landing craft. As the dawn light increased, ships more and more distant emerged from the cover of night: destroyers, minesweepers, the ancient British monitor *Erebus*, *Quincy*, and *Tuscaloosa*, incredible uncountable numbers of ships from horizon to horizon. They lay still and silent and unreal, though already the sound of distant guns was rolling in from the north-west, where American destroyers, still out of Mabry's sight, were under fire from the coast, and the British cruiser *Black Prince* was fighting a duel with a German battery which had shelled some minesweepers.

The column of boats—a score of them ahead of Mabry's and a hundred more astern—sailed on towards the line of heavy ships, steering for a gap in the line to the south of *Nevada*; and as they approached the gap, the hands of clocks moved on to the minute for which the ships were waiting: 5.40. Mabry saw the muzzle flashes and the smoke, and then the splitting crash of the first salvoes of the bombardment came across the water like a wall of sound. From then, for forty-seven minutes, there was never a pause in the roar of naval gunfire.

The boats crept in beyond the warships, underneath the shells. Before six o'clock, Mabry could see the shore; or if not

the shore, the smoke and the dust of shell-bursts which spouted
from it. He peered at the coast-line he knew so well from its
maps and photographs, but so far there were no landmarks
to be seen. He saw the bombers come down through the low
grey clouds, squadrons and squadrons of them, and the anti-
aircraft fire go up to challenge them. The firing looked to him
so fierce and thick that he could hardly believe an aircraft could
fly through it. Ahead, he saw a bomber explode in an orange
flame; the sound of the explosion drowned in the sea of noise.
The shore erupted again and again, the bombs being added to
the shells.

His attention was diverted from the shore by events which
were closer at hand. A solitary German fighter broke through
the clouds and dived towards the landing craft. A Spitfire fell
from the sky like a hawk and pounced on it and blew it to
pieces with three bursts of fire. The German's propeller, still
spinning, crashed into the sea nearby. Ahead, a small ship was
floating bottom up. The landing craft passed close to it, and
someone identified it : one of the two patrol craft which were
guiding the boats to the beach. Two men were lying on the
keel. One seemed to be dead—the first dead American Mabry
had seen. The other was waving, and they could see but not
hear him shouting for help, but of course they did not stop.
Soon after they passed, the ship sank. Beyond it, an amphibious
tank was on the point of sinking. Its crew had escaped from it,
and were swimming round it ; but as the landing craft passed
it, Mabry saw an officer, struggling half out of the turret. It
was a man he knew. The tank wallowed and a final wave broke
over it and it sank, dragging the man down with it. Mabry
thought of him sadly, drowning there so near beneath the
surface. (But long after, he met him again : he had been trapped
by his foot, but when the tank hit the bottom he freed himself
and floated up again.)

The shore was now close. Landing craft armed with 4.7-inch
guns were closing in on either side, shooting at close range
against the dunes. Seventeen tank landing craft fitted with rocket

launchers fired salvoes of fifty-pound rockets with a noise which
was fearsome even above the gunfire. Mabry could see the
sandy beach, heaving, drenched with explosives. But smoke
and dust and fine sand were drifting out to sea, and he only
caught glimpses of the outline of the dunes behind the beach.
There should have been a windmill, and a small patch of dunes
called Les Dunes de Varreville which were higher than the rest.
But he could not identify anything. The first wave of landing
craft were just ahead of him, steering for the shore in line abreast,
leaving white wakes in the water. Four hundred yards out, two
of them fired black smoke signals into the sky : the sign to the
navy that the moment of climax had come. Instantly, the barrage
lifted ; the beach lay still. The landing craft drove on to the
narrow line of white where small waves broke quietly on the
shore. To within a minute, the time was H Hour : 6.30 in the
morning.

In the last minutes, Mabry glanced back at the men in the
boat with him. The Colonel's bodyguard, a very small man—
smaller than Mabry—whom everyone in the battalion knew as
Smoky David, was being sick in his helmet. Some others were
grinning, watching him out of the corners of their eyes ; but
several looked green themselves. Looking at all their familiar
faces, each with a hint of serious anticipation or else of exaggerated calm, Mabry had the sense of solid companionship ; and
beside that feeling of *esprit de corps*, he was aware also of himself,
an individual, the real George Mabry beneath the grotesque
helmet and the uniform and equipment and badges of rank ;
aware of home, the farm, the cottonfields in the sun, the hunting
and fishing, his father and mother and wife, all the people and
things which had made him the person he was. He wondered
at seeing George Mabry as a witness of such great events, and
like the bowmen of Agincourt he knew he would remember
this day and this hour for the rest of his life, whether life was
short or long. There was no time then for these thoughts to be
put into words, but he knew they were there, in the back of his
mind. Something like them was in the minds of most men who

landed that morning in Normandy. If Mabry had spoken at all, in those few seconds before the boat's engine slowed down and the bottom grated gently on the sand, he might only have said that this would be something to tell the folks back home in Carolina.

The beach was about three hundred yards across, and on the other side of it, lurking in their dugouts in the dunes, were some hundreds of men of the German army. Looking back on it now, no soldier would deny them a little sympathy. In front of them was the sea, behind them the flooded meadows. On the narrow strip of dunes between the two, the most concentrated bombardment of history had just fallen. Now the survivors, emerging dazed from the deepest of their shelters, saw the invaders storming up the beach, and behind them tanks rising from the sea, and behind them again the largest fleet which man had ever seen. They had been promised ample support, if this thing ever happened, from artillery and the air force and the secret weapons. But so far, the artillery had not fired, because its batteries were bombed or captured by the parachutists; the air force had not come, because what was left of it was busy defending Germany itself; and the secret weapons were not ready yet. The telephone lines to headquarters had gone dead in the early morning; nobody knew why. Men who had been sent with messages had never come back; nobody knew what had happened to them. It was impossible to ask for help or for orders.

In these circumstances, some of the defenders whose discipline was strongest fired their guns. Some tried to escape by running along the causeways through the floods, where they were quickly shot down by the parachutists lying in wait for them. Some saved their lives by surrendering; and these incurred the rage of Hitler himself, who called them traitors and deserters.

Mabry went down the ramp and felt the sand under his boots

in about four feet of water. Smoky David was on his left, and he saw him go over the side of the ramp and disappear entirely. Perhaps he had fallen in a shell-hole. Mabry had never wanted so badly to run, but of course he could only wade slowly forward. Looking back, he was glad to see Smoky David's head come up again. It was most of a hundred yards to the edge of the sea. Perhaps it took him two minutes to reach the shallow water where he could pick up his feet and splash on to the hard wet sand. But it seemed a long time, because he knew he was an unprotected target in the field of fire of the defences he had studied so carefully : and because he had gone a long way before he realised, to his astonishment, that there was far less shooting than anyone had expected.

Once on the beach, he only paused to see his companions close behind him with expressions of incredulous relief on their faces, and then he set off for the dune line. Even on the beach, he could not run. His sodden clothes were heavy, and his legs were cramped and numb from the coldness of the two hours' journey in the boat. There was a man lying on the sand. He went to him : a corporal he knew, wounded in both legs. He bent down to him and said he would drag him up to cover in the dunes. "No, I'm all right," the corporal said. "Keep going, captain." (But he died of his wounds, or was drowned when the tide rose.)

On the seaward face of the dunes there was a concrete sea-wall about four feet high, and there in the dry sand above the tidemark, among such familiar seaside holiday things as shells and seaweed and corks washed up from fishing nets, the leading two companies were pausing ; and there Mabry learned why he had not seen any of his landmarks. So far the battalion's landing had been easy ; but it had landed in the wrong place. General Roosevelt, who perhaps knew the terrain even better than Mabry, had already been up on the dunes to find out where they were, and had discovered they were over a mile too far south.

This mistake at the culmination of all the months of planning was the result of the series of mishaps which had started with the

rope round the screw of the radar boat. The sinking of the
patrol craft which Mabry had passed had left only two of four
guide boats in action. One of the two had turned back to help
tank landing craft which were delayed by the head sea ; and
that left only one. The off-shore wind had hidden landmarks
by blowing the smoke and dust to seaward ; and finally, no
allowance, or not enough, had been made for the tidal stream
which flows at two to three knots to the southward, into
the bay of the Seine, on the flood tide. It was this stream
which had carried the whole fleet of landing craft a mile off their
course.

But nobody on the beach was caring how the mistake had
been made. The urgent question was what should be done about
it : write off the first waves of troops, and allow the following
forces to land in the right place, or change the assault plans
and bring in the whole force to the wrong place. The mistake
might have led to totally disastrous confusion ; but the situation
was saved by the presence of General Roosevelt. He not only
had the quickness of mind to make the decision at once ; he
also had the authority to enforce it. In the lull so luckily caused
by the weakness of the German troops, he consulted the two
battalion commanders and for better or worse, he signalled the
navy to send in all the succeeding waves to the place where the
first had landed.

By then, heavy shells had started falling on the beach, and
desultory mortar fire was coming from somewhere beyond the
dunes. A man close in front of Mabry was blown out of existence
by a direct hit. Something small struck Mabry in the stomach.
It was a thumb. Some of the men thought the navy were shelling
them, and they were complaining furiously. Mabry watched a
few shell-bursts and guessed rightly that they were coming from
the south, from the heavy batteries five miles away on the other
side of the estuary of the Dives, but the men would not be
convinced and wanted him to fire another smoke signal. To
satisfy them he had a spare signal fired, but of course the shelling
went on. And then he saw the General, striding along the beach,

waving his cane in the air and roaring at everyone to get moving across the dunes.

Mabry went through a gap in the seawall which led to a track. His job, as he had no command of his own, was to join G company and keep them in touch with the battalion command post ; and G Company's job, in the plans he had worked on so carefully, was to turn left along the dunes and attack the defences to the southward till they came to a causeway which was known as Exit 1.

In the gap in the seawall there was a dead German, the first he had seen ; through the gap, on the left, the remains of a barbed-wire fence. A sergeant and three other men were scrambling through the fence, and the sergeant was from G Company— he knew him by his red hair. He followed them : a heavy explosion threw him off his feet, and he stood up again to see all four men lying dead or wounded. It had not been a shell : perhaps the sergeant had touched a trip wire and fired a mine. Rather shaken, he went through the fence himself and took off southwards through the dunes to try to catch up with the rest of the company.

Mabry's legs were working all right by then, but perhaps for the moment, after the explosion, his head was not very clear. At all events, he went on for a long way, scrambling up the hillocks of sand and sliding down them, before he noticed land-mines. As soon as he saw one, he saw dozens, lying about on the surface, uncovered perhaps by the bombing. He reckoned they must have been duds ; but he was certainly in a minefield, where there might be others, still covered and still alive. He wondered whether to go back or go on, and went on, hurrying because he thought he was left behind : and then there was another bang and he fell and rolled down a dune, and the sand rained down on him and he lay there and thought he was dead.

Far from being dead, he was not even hurt, except that the breath was knocked out of him ; but as his senses came back, he felt sick with mortification and rage at himself. All these years, he had meant to be out in front in combat, if only to prove to himself that he could do as well as anyone in spite of being small; and now, he thought, in his very first combat, he had got left far behind all alone, just following on the tail of the company. So he got up again and ran on; and went over the top of a dune and came face to face with five Germans. One had a grenade in his hand and raised his arm to throw it, so he shot him, and the others threw down their rifles and put their hands up.

This was queer and unexpected. He wondered why four of them should surrender to him alone; they could easily have got him before he got all of them. But glancing round, he saw what they had seen: through a gap in the dunes, there was a view of the sea, and almost all the horizon was hidden by ships. The sight was enough to make anyone glad to surrender. He did not want to be delayed by prisoners; but luckily, he saw an American soldier just then—the first he had seen since he started through the dunes. He called him over, and gave him the prisoners, and also asked him if he had seen G Company. The man said that so far as he knew they were still on the beach. Even then, Mabry went on believing they were still in front of him.

What brought him up in the end was a pillbox, from which a machine gun fired at him. By then he was through the dunes, in a flat meadow behind them. He took cover in a convenient drainage ditch and tried to crawl along it; but he was shot at again whenever he showed his head. At last, this personal attention convinced him that the company had not already passed that way.

Once he had made up his mind to that fact, Mabry began to enjoy himself. It was true that he had failed to do the job assigned to him in the battalion plan, but he was much happier to be in front of the company than behind it, and he never thought twice about going back to look for it. Instead, he lay in the ditch and studied the little tactical problem of the pillbox. While he was there, several other men came up behind him, and quickly dived into the ditch when they came under fire. But even with their support, he could not figure out any way of capturing the pillbox; so he sent one of them back to look for a tank.

Mabry had rather lost count of time by then. Probably it was after nine o'clock. At all events, the engineers, who landed in the third wave, must by then have blown a new gap in the seawall and bulldozed a track through the dunes; because Mabry's rather imperious demand for a tank was soon answered. One of the twenty-eight amphibious tanks which had reached the shore came roaring along at the back of the dunes, fired four shots at the pillbox and roared away again, leaving him and his followers to collect the two dozen Germans who had come out waving the white flag which the defending forces seemed always to find at short notice.

With them out of the way, Mabry went on a little farther; and after a while he was rewarded by the irresistible sight of a causeway across the floods which seemed to be intact and totally undefended. This was Exit 1, the most southerly of all the causeways, the one which led to Pouppeville, and thence to Sainte-Marie-du-Mont. There was a little bridge in the middle of it; and while he advanced towards it, a few Germans came running from the other end and jumped off the road by the bridge and disappeared beneath it. They might just be looking for a hide-out, he thought; but they might be laying charges to blow up the bridge. The sight of them decided him. He collected his followers—a dozen or so by then, stragglers like himself—and began to stalk the Germans. It was while he was crawling towards the bridge through the flat wet meadows that he heard shooting from Pouppeville, and rightly guessed that there could not possibly be any Americans there unless they were parachutists. He hoisted the small orange flag which he had been given to use in that very situation: the flag which Colonel Ewell's men saw and recognised when they finished their battle in the village school.

The parachutists came down the causeway, and Mabry and his men went up it, and the Germans at the bridge were caught between them. An airborne lieutenant greeted Mabry as if he

had not seen an American for years, and told him that General
Taylor was there and would certainly be glad to see him.

The whole thing had not been at all the sort of combat which
Mabry had always imagined. From a military point of view, he
had made rather a mess of it. But even though it had happened
by mistake, he had fulfilled an ambition : he was certainly out in
front.

The whole landing had been much easier than anyone had
anticipated. The confusion caused by landing too far south
had not lasted long ; the plans had been flexible enough to stand
the strain of this sudden change, and most of the infantrymen
had used their own common sense and initiative, like Mabry, and
made for their objectives as soon as they found where they were.
The battalion as a whole crossed the floods in safety and joined
up with the airborne men soon after midday ; and of all the
thousands who landed that morning on Utah, only twelve were
killed and just over a hundred wounded. For this comparatively
easy passage, the seaborne troops were indebted to the parachutists, and to the bombarding forces of the navy and the air force.

Many men on the ground on D-Day, American and British
and German, took it upon themselves to criticise their air force.
Some of them—the Germans in particular—had some reason to
be annoyed, but most had none at all. In retrospect, it is too easy
to accept the soldier's view ; few of the critics were pilots, and
few of them had any idea of the difficulties of flying on that day.
The weather and the anti-aircraft fire were obvious difficulties ;
but another, less obvious, was the unprecedented congestion
in the air. The crews of the Marauder bombers, which Mabry
had seen as he approached the beach, thought much less about
the German opposition than about the risk of collision with one
another.

These crews had not been briefed till two o'clock that morning. It is strange to reflect that even after the parachutists
were in action and the fleet was assembled off shore, men who
had such an important part to play were still in bed in England

and had never heard of that stretch of beach or been told that the invasion was beginning. But they had to be kept in the dark. They were flying every day over France, and any of them, any day, might have been shot down and captured; so they could not be told the secret. In its organisation, their part in the invasion was very much like any other raid.

However, the whole of the tactical air force had known since the previous day that something unusual was brewing, and had guessed pretty well what it was; because all their aircraft had suddenly been painted with black and white stripes of distemper. Someone had foreseen that when there was such an enormous number of aircraft in the sky, both the troops and the fighter pilots would need a very quick and infallible method of distinguishing enemy from friend. New identity marks were needed; and they had to appear for the very first time on the morning of D-Day, so that the Germans could not possibly have time to copy them. Broad stripes of distemper were a good answer; they could be put on quickly, and scraped off without much trouble when the need for them was over. But even this simple plan was not very easy to execute on the scale which was required. Ten thousand aircraft had to be painted in a single evening. To make sure of the job, one hundred thousand gallons of distemper were ordered. In the whole of Britain, there was nothing like that quantity. The distemper industry was mobilised, worked overtime, gave up its Whitsun week-end without ever knowing why its humble produce had suddenly become so important, and finally delivered the stuff in time. It was received without thanks on airfields where nobody, at that stage, knew what it was for. By comparison, the purchase and distribution of twenty thousand paint-brushes was a simple affair.

One of the Bomb Groups of Marauders destined for Utah Beach was briefed by its colonel, Wilson R. Wood, and his briefing made such a deep impression on his crews that many of them never forgot what he said. Colonel Wood was rather an impressive person at any time, partly perhaps because he was tall and remarkably handsome, partly because he was a Texan and had the distinctive charm of a southerner, and partly because he was only just twenty-five. He himself had known of his group's invasion mission for nearly a fortnight, and he had not been allowed to fly since he had been told it. That morning in the briefing-hut on his airfield in Essex, north-east of London, he stood up as usual and began to speak in his unemphatic sleepy Texan voice.

" This morning's mission," he said, " is the most important mission you've ever flown. Maybe the most important mission anyone has ever flown. This is the invasion. Our job is to bomb the beach, and right after our bombs go down, thousands of Americans just like us will be landing there from the sea."

This introduction had his crews on the edge of their seats. " I don't care if any of your aircraft are not a hundred per cent." he went on. " You'll fly them this morning, and you'll get over that beach whatever happens, and you'll take any risk to get right on your targets and give those boys in the boats every bit of help you can."

After that, he gave the crews his usual meticulous details of timing, targets, routes and tactics. The targets were seven of the centres of defence on the narrow strip of dunes. The timing was more critical than usual, because the whole operation had to start after dawn and end by the clock immediately before the landing craft reached the shore. When Wood sent his men out to their aircraft, they were certainly imbued with his own conviction that the safety of a few aircraft and even the lives of a few crews were of small importance beside the help they could give to their fellow-countrymen in the boats. In this spirit, they took off at 4 a.m.

Wood led his own group very low across the Thames below London, over Kent and Sussex and out across the Channel, flying all the way below the cloud base. As usual when he was flying, he was happy. One might say that he was a born airman. His father was an engineer, his home was four hundred acres of virgin land in Texas, and from his earliest boyhood in the era of

Lindbergh, flying had been his dream and his delight. He had joined the air force as soon as he left his university, when he was twenty, and had risen from enlisted man to colonel in five years simply because he was a natural leader and had a single-minded love of aircraft. Like most American bomber pilots, he did not particularly hate Germans, or particularly like dropping bombs; but he would have said that the only way out of a war was to fight your way out of it. Somehow, he had managed to combine his love of flying with being happily married. It was typical that when he was made a colonel, four months before the invasion, he sent his wife a cable saying " Promoted—Wilson," and forgot in his excitement to send her his love; but she was sufficiently sure of it to forgive him.

Now he was in the middle of a tour of fifty combat missions; and he felt that this morning, whatever the future might bring, was a climax in his flying career. Over the Channel, this feeling was strengthened when he saw the countless white wakes of ships all pointing like arrows towards the coast of France.

Visibility was supposed to be eight miles, but it seemed to be less. There was broken cloud from two thousand up to seven thousand feet, and a fairly solid layer of cloud above that. It was not very comfortable to fly just under clouds into an area where German fighters seemed sure to be around; but that was the best way, he thought, to find a difficult target on a bad day.

He saw the coast less than two minutes before he crossed it : the straight featureless line of shore, so long that it vanished in haze in both directions. In those minutes, he flew into the most congested bit of air he had ever seen. The area of each of the seven targets was very small—perhaps a hundred yards square —and the air space above them was limited by the clouds and the small-arms fire which came up from below. Two hundred and seventy-six aircraft converged on these areas, all flying within a couple of hundred feet of the cloud base. Some had to make more than one run; some, which had approached above the clouds, came down through gaps at unpredictable moments.

Wood had expected a crowd, but he found it distracting. The anti-aircraft fire was a danger he could easily dismiss from his mind, because there was nothing much he could do about it; on the other hand, the risk of a collision was much more of a worry, just because careful flying and a good lookout could have reduced the risk. But keeping a lookout for other aircraft was no help towards accurate bombing. Wood determined to concentrate his eyes and his mind on his target, and leave a collision to chance : but it needed all the self-control he had.

When his own bombs went down, he turned away towards the sea. He could not possibly have seen where they had fallen, the whole shore was smoking and flashing like a firework; but he was satisfied. As he cleared the coast, he saw the sight which justified the dramatic words he had used to his group that morning : the landing craft, heading towards the beach in an endless column which emerged from the glare on the sea in the east where the early sunlight filtered through the clouds. He wished them luck. He had done all that an airman could to help them through.

Before eleven o'clock, the time when Mabry saluted General Taylor in Pouppeville, and Wood had had breakfast in England and was preparing for his second flight to France, the landing on Utah Beach had become a routine. Among the men who were pouring ashore, an outstanding figure was that of Chaplain Luechinger, a Capuchin friar and a native New Yorker, who was better known to his Manhattan congregation as Father Bruno. He waded ashore in a lull in the German artillery, and so far as he could remember afterwards, he was on the beach for an hour before he heard a bang.

To be a friar from Manhattan suggests a contradiction, since friars are reputed unworldly and Manhattan is best known for its worldly splendours. Father Bruno's church was a couple of blocks off Broadway, within sight of all the glitter of Times Square, and its spire reached less than a quarter as far towards heaven as the roof of a big hotel across the street. But the contradiction was only superficial. The brown hood and habit of a Capuchin often hide a remarkable amount of worldly wisdom ; and Manhattan's famous façade, on the other hand, hides every kind of activity of the spirit and intellect. And for a Capuchin friar to wade ashore on D-Day was no contradiction at all, because the order has provided chaplains for armies since the Middle Ages.

Even if he had not been a friar, Luechinger would have been a remarkable person ; for he was not only a very learned man, but was also a master of the opulent slang which is the hallmark of the true New Yorker. Englishmen in Devon had been delighted by his combination of clerical appearance with Yankee wit, even when he used his wit to heap good-humoured scorn on everything English. His own troops found it easy to confide in a priest who naturally spoke their own language, and spoke it more fluently than they did.

In the past few months in England, the padre had listened to a great many personal troubles, mostly arising in one way or another from homesickness, and so he had learned even better than before to understand and appreciate his countrymen, with their strength and their weaknesses. He crossed the Channel with apprehension for the men on whom the burdens of pain and death were so likely to be laid. Their almost carefree landing was therefore a surprise and a pleasure to him, as it was to them.

His landing had a touch of drama in it, as well as a touch of farce. While the fifth wave of landing craft were circling round before setting course for the beach, his own craft rammed the one in front of it. It was a boat of a British design, and nobody but a Limey, the chaplain remarked, would have put the helmsman right at the back where he could not see out. They had to go back to the transport to change to another boat, and before they had done so the wave of craft had started and disappeared ; so they set off for the beach alone. The new helmsman had never been told that the landing was a mile too far south. The southerly tide had slackened, and he steered an accurate compass course according to his orders. Probably this craft was the only one

in the landing at Utah which arrived off the right stretch of
beach, where its passengers found, with no little consternation,
that there was not a soul in sight. But they saw some activity
to the southward, so they turned that way and cruised along the
coast ; and in doing so they passed the guns of a major German
strongpoint. It shook them to hear, when they landed, that
this strongpoint had not yet been captured. But by this time the
Germans on Utah Beach, whether captured or not, had given up
the fight.

On the beach, when he got there at last, the padre found a
scene which was humming with activity but showed little sign of
battle. The desolate shore had already been transformed.
Roads had been bulldozed through the dunes, and tanks, artillery
and supply trucks were rolling out of tank landing craft, assembling and roaring along the new roads towards the causeways,
as if the embarkation on the Devon coast had been reversed.
There were hundreds and hundreds of men on the beach,
infantry landing, waiting for orders and moving inland, signallers,
prisoners, naval units, medics : it was with these, in the aid
posts, that a padre's work was found. He went from post to
post, giving thanks in his heart that so few of his men were
lying in need of the service of a priest, and perfectly confident,
like every man on the beach, that the plan had succeeded and the
army was there to stay.

But twelve miles to the eastward, at this same hour, on
Omaha Beach, there was a man whose home was quite close to
Father Bruno's ; and he was crouching in a foxhole, bewildered
and leaderless, looking out on a scene of terror and utter confusion.

V

OMAHA BEACH

———————————

THE MAN in the foxhole was P.f.c. Henry Meyers. He felt he was looking at himself from outside himself, with sorrow and pity, as people sometimes do when events are almost too much for them. The real Henry Meyers, the I of his existence, the school-master from Brooklyn, the man who was loved by Molly his wife, did not seem the same person as the soldier crouching like an animal in the hole he had scraped in the sand, made numb by the concussion of explosions, and staring aghast at the sand spurting from the strikes of bullets and the bodies dead and half-dead on the shore. His emotions were in disorder and his only clear thoughts were why in hell am I here? What am I doing in this mad place?

The merely factual answers to those questions are easy enough to record, though of course they were not the answers which puzzled him. He had never wanted to be called up. The call-up had interrupted his vocation as a teacher of mathe-matics, and his marriage which was only a few months old, and the placid life he enjoyed among all the bustle and noise of an industrial part of New York. The army had wrenched him away from all that, and discovered he was a mathematician and made him, by army logic, into a signaller. Of course he knew the necessity for army service as well as anyone else. He would not have dodged it if he could, and he had done his best at it; but he had never pretended he had any ambitions in soldiering for its own sake, or that he wanted anything more than to get it over as quickly and efficiently as he could, and go home and start teaching again. In the army, he just made himself feel content to do what he was told. Whenever he was faced with some unpleasant chore he cheered himself up with the thought that if he did not do it, somebody else would have to. He had even made himself interested in the mechanics of signalling, but he could not help despising it as a mental exercise when he compared it with the beauty of pure mathematics.

When Meyers's small unit had been packed on board a troopship and told that this was really the invasion, he had been glad. He did not need to be told that invasion was the quickest way to end the war, or that any minute degree of help he could give would be help in the right direction. On the Channel crossing, this glad resolution had been almost swamped by seasickness—he was so sick that he wished he was dead—but he felt better again when he boarded the landing craft, where at least the air was fresh; and as it pitched and rolled on its way to the beach, he felt ready for anything. The companionship was encouraging: all his own unit grouped together joking and shouting, men he knew well, all very literally in the same boat together, all keyed up for the adventure.

Henry Meyers could not see much from his position in the boat, wedged in among other men who were taller than he was. He could not move much either. Apart from his equipment and his rifle, he was carrying a heavy coil of wire over his shoulder. It was telephone wire, and he and a couple of friends were supposed to lay it from the beach to some place inland which somebody would show them. But he could hear. There was a tremendous noise, and as the boat came nearer to the beach the noise grew louder. He had never heard such a noise before. It was infinitely worse than the practice runs with the live ammunition, but he supposed it was all right and was only what had to be expected. In the last few seconds, above the ramp of the boat, he had a glimpse of shell-bursts and of clouds of yellowish smoke and the crest of a green hill showing dimly through it:

and at that same moment he heard a different noise, alarming and very close : the unmistakable splatter of bullets on the ramp itself. And then the boat grounded, the ramp went down, the men in front ran forward.

Meyers knew he hesitated, but for such a short time that nobody would have seen it. It was not the danger which made him hesitate, because he still could not see very much and still had no real idea of what he was in for ; it was just an instinctive ridiculous reluctance to do anything so unnatural as to jump in the sea with his boots and trousers on. But then he was in, and it was warmer than he expected ; and he could see.

He could see men in front of him falling : and not just stumbling, but falling limp face-down in the water and making no effort to rise. On the edge of the sea where the waves were breaking, he could see bundles washing in and out, rolling over and over : bodies. Beyond, he could see the sandy beach, very wide, and bodies lying there too, and a tank burning, men clinging to its shelter like a cluster of bees ; and here and there, all the time, the beach was erupting in sprays of sand and debris where shells or mortar bombs fell, while small flicks of sand from machine-gun bullets ran across and across it like wicked living things. Far away up the beach was a bank of shingle, and behind that in the smoke the low hills, flashing with fire, but whether from shells bursting or guns firing he could not have told, because he had seldom seen either before. And the noise was so terrible that he could not think : his brain stopped dead.

They had told him to run. Instinct told him the same. But instinct would not allow him to run up the beach : he could not, simply could not run that way. He turned to the right and ran along the water's edge, splashing through the little rims of foam.

It was difficult to run in wet clothes, the rifle and the coil of wire jolting awkwardly on his shoulder. He had an impulse to throw the wire away. But that brought him up ; the wire. The wire was what he was there for. They would be stuck

without it. He had a job to do, and if he didn't do it somebody
else would have to. He stopped and stood still for a second,
every inch of his body expecting the horrible whack of a bullet :
and then he started to run up the beach.

He ran terribly slowly in spite of his utmost effort, like
another childhood dream, the one in which one runs and runs
to escape from a monster but cannot move at all ; and while he
was running he was only conscious of a little area of sand around
him, a yard or two on each side and ahead. It was such ordinary
sand, he thought. It was so like the sand on the beaches on
Long Island where children built castles and ran and shouted,
and he and Molly had sunbathed ; sand of bathing-dresses,
sun-tan lotion, ice creams, Coke in bottles with straws ; sand
that got into the picnic basket. Things came into the little
circle of his vision as he ran : a German obstacle, a mangled
body in uniform, blood, wreckage, rifles, torn equipment. He
ran over them or round them, and hardly knew they were there.

Then the high water mark, the line of sea-wrack, and then
the dry sand where he could not run any more but only drag his
feet forward ; and then the bank of shingle. They were big
stones, three or four inches, like cannon balls ; and men were
lying elbow to elbow, hugging the steep face of the shingle for
cover, or squatting in holes in the sand, some wounded. He
dropped down there, aware for the first time of the rasping of his
own breath and his heart thumping, and he peered at the men
near him, hoping to see his friends and his officer. But there
was nobody there that he had ever seen before.

What ought he to do ? Above the dreadful noise, he heard
thin screams, and shouts which might have been orders, but if
they were he could not understand them, and nobody moved.
What ought a good soldier to do ? With nobody to tell him,
the answer could only be : keep alive, if you can, till they need
you. So he started to dig. He was trembling from the shock of
what had happened ; and that is no wonder, because that same
shock, the shock of the instant transition from the companionship and shelter of the boats to the very whitest heat of war,

where every man is always alone in spirit, had strained every man who landed to the limit of what brain and will can stand. Some had run up the beach, as he had in the end, and they had a chance to survive; and some had been unable to make the decision, as he had at first, and they lingered on the edge of the water and died.

Desperately digging in the loose dry sand, Meyers threw down his coil of wire beside the hole. There it lay, half a mile of it, and something must have gone wrong, he thought, the landing could not have been meant to be like this; because he was meant to go on and lay the wire to some place inland, but nobody, so far as he could see, had even been able to cross the bank of shingle.

He was right; since the very beginning, an hour before he landed, almost everything had gone wrong, and at that moment the landing on Omaha was only being saved from total failure by blind tenacity and the last shreds of courage, and by the very impossibility of the idea that it could have failed. In calm analysis the causes which led to this situation can be listed and understood: the weather was bad, the bombardment had failed, the beach was naturally a good position for defence, the German forces manning it were better troops than had manned it when the attack was planned, and finally—though this may still be a matter of opinion—there were basic mistakes in the plans. But the men who were suffering on the beach that morning were only aware of two of these causes: the weather, and the formidable hills they were expected to assault.

Omaha Beach is five miles long, and very slightly curved, and like Utah Beach it has sand which is firm and yellow and slopes so gently that the tide runs out for three or four hundred yards. But that is its only resemblance to Utah. Behind it, instead of dunes and flat meadows, there is first the bank of shingle which Henry Meyers reached, and then a stretch of marshy land two hundred yards across, and then green grassy hills or bluffs, 150 feet high, which are easy to climb but too steep

for trucks or tanks. At each end of the beach, the bluffs run
out into vertical cliffs which extend for nearly ten miles in each
direction. There are four small valleys in the bluffs, with trees
and bushes in them. Before the invasion, one of them, the
most westerly, had a good road in it, which led down to a few
seaside villas on the flat strip behind the shingle, and the other
three had lanes. The military importance of these otherwise
insignificant little valleys was equally obvious to the attack and
the defence: except for one isolated gap at Port-en-Bessin, the
four valleys were the only possible ways for a mechanised army
to move inland on the whole of the stretch of twenty miles of
coast from the mouth of the River Vire to the village of Arromanches.

From almost anywhere on the bluffs, the whole length of the
beach can be seen. On flat beaches like Utah, the Germans
had to build their pillboxes and emplacements close to the edge
of the sand; attacking infantry did not have very far to go
before they could get to grips with them. But on Omaha, the
gun positions were built on the sides of the bluffs. Overlooking
the beach, they had an enormous field of fire, and to reach them,
infantry would have to cross not only the beach itself, but also
the shingle bank which had barbed wire on top, and the flat
strip behind it which was mined; and then they would have to
climb the slopes. For the whole of this journey of five or six
hundred yards, they would be plainly visible from the bluffs,
except in the couple of yards where they could hide behind the
shingle.

The Germans had grouped their defences mainly round the
mouths of the valleys, but the whole of the beach was covered
by their fire. The heavy guns were in concrete emplacements
from which they could only fire along the beach, not straight
out to sea, the seaward sides of them being protected by fifteen
to twenty feet of concrete which made them almost proof against
naval gunfire. Each group of emplacements was connected
by trenches and tunnels, with underground magazines and living
quarters. It was estimated that the beach was covered by over

sixty pieces of artillery, besides mortars and a very large number of machine guns.

In addition to these manned defences, the Germans had made great use on Omaha Beach of the underwater obstacles which had occupied so much of the energy of British and American reconnaissance. Aerial photographs had shown four different kinds. About two hundred and fifty yards out, not far from low water mark, there was a row of what the reconnaissance men had called Element C. These were like very large and heavy field gates of steel, facing the sea and buttressed behind by girders. Farther up the beach, there were rows of wooden ramps, with their pointed ends towards the sea, and of stout wooden posts driven into the sand with contact mines on top. Finally, on the upper part of the tidal flat, steel "hedgehogs" were scattered about. They were made of three lengths of angle iron or railway line, welded together in the middle so that they formed a kind of double tripod, with spikes sticking up which-ever side they lay on. These obstacles were laid so thickly that a landing craft which tried to go through them would stand perhaps a fifty-fifty chance of getting in, but a smaller chance of getting out again by turning or going astern. The first step in the plan of attack was to remove the obstacles before the tide rose over them.

The plan had been as follows. H Hour was 6.30, which was soon after low water. From 5.50 till 6.27, a tremendous naval bombardment had been arranged. From 6 o'clock till 6.25, over 400 bombers were to attack the shore defences. At 6.29, 64 amphibious tanks were due to land; at H Hour itself, 32 ordinary tanks and 16 armoured bulldozers; and one minute later, 8 companies of infantry, 1,450 men in 36 landing craft. Two minutes behind the infantry were a Special Demolition Task Force, to clear and mark lanes through the obstacles before the tide rose up and covered them.

After these demolition men, a pause of half an hour was left in the planned landings, to allow them to finish their work.

Then bigger waves of infantry were due to arrive, with the first artillery units beginning to come in at 8 o'clock.

The demolition men were really the crux of this plan. There were 270 of them; rather more than half of them were naval men. They would have a delicate and fiddling task in attaching explosive charges to the obstacles and connecting them with fuses and detonators, and they would be much too busy to protect themselves. For defence, and for conditions sufficiently quiet to allow them to work, they had to depend for the first half hour on the infantry and the tanks. But 1,450 men and 96 tanks were no match for the German defences, unless the bombardment had already largely destroyed them or stunned the men who manned them.

Not one of these plans was fulfilled. The air bombardment missed its targets. The naval shelling had little apparent effect on the defences. Most of the tanks were lost at sea or quickly destroyed on the beach, and the infantry were scattered and decimated. The demolition men lost nearly half their number almost at once, and the remainder struggled to carry out their orders under conditions which were all but impossible. The beach became a chaos; the programme of landing was abandoned. And the whole of this chain of disaster was started by the weather.

The conditions of cloud in the early morning varied from place to place, but there is no evidence that they were worse at Omaha than they were at Utah. The difference between the air bombing on the two beaches was a difference in policy and aircraft. At Utah, medium bombers, Marauders, carried out the last-minute bombardment; at Omaha, the job was done by heavy bombers, Liberators. These heavy bombers could either bomb visually or by instruments, which in those days was a much less accurate method. The decision was taken the night before, on the basis of the weather forecast, to use instruments, and this decision was endorsed by the Supreme Command.

The infantry men, who had hoped and expected to find the

defences in ruins, knew nothing of this decision, or of its im-
plications. Because of the inaccuracy of the instruments, there
was thought to be a risk that the bombing would hit the landing
craft. The aircrews were therefore ordered to delay their drop
after crossing the coast, the length of the delay to vary inversely
with the length of the time before H Hour until it reached as
long as 30 seconds. This meant inevitably that the centre of
the weight of bombs fell at first a few hundred yards inland, and
crept farther away until just before H Hour, when it was three
miles beyond the beach; and none of the bombs, except perhaps a few which were badly aimed, fell near enough to the beach
defences to do them the slightest harm.

The results of the naval bombardment were also meagre,
but this is not so simple to explain. The bombardment looked
heavy on paper. There were two American battleships, *Texas*
and *Arkansas*, three cruisers of which one was British and two
were Free French, and eight destroyers. They were to fire 3,500
rounds of calibres from 5 to 14 inches. Army artillery was
mounted on landing craft so that it could fire while it was waiting
to go in, and was scheduled to fire 9,000 rounds in the 30 minutes
before H Hour. Finally, nine rocket craft were each to fire a
thousand high-explosive rockets. What happened to 21,500
projectiles? There are many answers, and none of them are
certain. Only quite a small proportion of the volume of fire
was real naval gunnery. The rockets were notoriously inaccurate
at the best of times. The aiming of army guns in small landing
craft could only have been uncertain, because the sea was rough.
The morning was rather misty and the beach was soon covered
like Utah with smoke and dust, which made spotting difficult
for the larger ships. The Germans had taken care to make their
emplacements difficult to see and almost impregnable by fire
from seaward, and intelligence and reconnaissance had not
detected them all. Part of the naval effort, especially of the
battleship *Arkansas*, was directed against heavy German batteries
far out on the flanks which threatened the sea approaches but
did not affect the beach. A naval historian, summing it up,

believes the bombardment was simply too light and too short :
no more ships could be used, because there was no more room
for them in the sea, and the navy needed more time to do the
job thoroughly. It was the army, he implies, who restricted the
length of the shooting to 35 minutes.

Nobody can be certain either exactly how much damage the
shelling had done before H Hour, and the guesses vary. The only
certain thing is that it did not do nearly enough, and that when
the troops started to cross the beach the greater part of the
German defences was still intact and went into action against
them.

The weather which had rendered the aerial bombing useless
and distracted the gunners' aim caused its greatest havoc among
the infantry landing craft and the amphibious tanks. The conditions of cloud at Utah and Omaha were much the same, but
the conditions of sea were quite different. The wind was blowing at 10 to 18 knots from the north-west. At Utah, the wind
was off-shore, and the closer one went to the beach, the calmer
the sea became. At Omaha it was on-shore ; and the waves
were four feet high, and sometimes six feet. Neither the landing
craft nor the amphibious tanks were designed to work in such a
rough sea as that. The very first of the victims of the tragedy
at Omaha were the crews of the tanks.

Amphibious tanks were a new invention then, and were
used on all the beaches. Those for Omaha were carried across
the Channel in 16 landing craft commanded by a reserve lieutenant named Dean L. Rockwell. It could truly be said that Rockwell was in the navy, and found himself in this curious command,
and became the first man to put landing craft ashore on Omaha,
simply because he had been a professional wrestler : so unpredictable are cause and effect in war. He came from Detroit.
Before he joined the navy, he had never seen salt water except
on his honeymoon in Florida ; but many excellent naval men
had had even less experience of the sea. In Detroit, he heard

that Gene Tunney, the heavyweight boxer, was making a recruiting tour as a naval lieutenant-commander; and for admiration of Tunney, Rockwell hurried off and joined the navy as an instructor in physical education. But that was a disappointment. He did not approve of the way the navy ran its physical education, and his criticisms gave him a reputation as a bolshie. As a punishment, or as a fitting fate for bolshies, his senior officers managed to post him to landing craft, which they regarded as the navy's suicide squad. But there Rockwell found his vocation. Men brought up with ships might think that landing craft were ugly, or unseamanlike, or unhandy; but Rockwell loved them, and because he loved them he became exceptionally clever at handling them and understanding their sometimes strange behaviour. He was only a petty officer then, but he was soon given a craft of his own to command. By the time he reached England, destined, he knew, to take a front seat in the invasion of Europe, he was an officer and commanded a flotilla, and was perfectly happy about it. And then in March he was summoned to the naval base at Dartmouth and told he had been chosen for a new job in co-operation with the army. He was disgusted at first, but he soon changed his mind. He was let into the secret that amphibious tanks existed. His job was to study the technique of launching them from landing craft at sea. In good time for the invasion, he had made himself expert at that as well; and in doing so he had developed the deepest respect for the men who manned the tanks.

The idea of a tank which would float and propel itself in water, and yet still remain an efficient tank on land, had interested and baffled engineers in every army, mainly because tanks had grown in size and weight between the wars until they were too heavy to cross rivers by most of the ordinary bridges. The solution of the problem, the invention of the D.D. tank, is attributed to a Hungarian-born engineer called Nicholas Straussler who was working in Britain. The Admiralty condemned his design as unseaworthy; but the War Office, caring less about standards of seaworthiness, saw the possibilities of the tank as a weapon of surprise in invasion. They took up the idea, and as soon as Eisenhower and Montgomery saw it demonstrated, orders were given for hundreds of Shermans to be converted.

Straussler's basic idea had the simplicity of many great inventions. A kind of canvas screen was fastened round an ordinary tank. Tubes in the canvas could be blown up like an air mattress; and when that was done, the canvas stood up to make a primitive sort of open boat, of which the canvas formed the sides and the tank itself formed the bottom. The tank's own engine was connected by extra clutches to two propellers. D.D. stood for Duplex Drive, and not, as many tank men surmised, for Donald Duck.

The beauty of this invention, from a tactician's point of view, was that when the tank was swimming it was a small and insignificant target which looked like a boat and not like a tank at all; but at the very moment when it touched shore, the air could be let out of the tubes and the canvas collapsed, and within a couple of seconds the tank was in action. The sight of full-sized tanks rising out of the sea was expected, quite rightly, to surprise and alarm the opposition. A second advantage was that if tanks could swim ashore themselves, there would be no need to risk the large vulnerable tank landing craft in the first waves of landing. But beautiful as the D.D. tank appeared to tacticians, from the point of view of the men inside it, no more unpleasant means of going into battle could easily be imagined. Even the top of the tank was several feet below water level. The tank commander could stand on a platform behind the turret, and from there he could see out above the canvas gunwales; but the rest of the crew were down inside the tank. The driver had a periscope, but the others—the co-driver, radio operator and gunner—could neither see nor hear what was going on outside. They did know, however, that their 30-ton tank was suspended from a flimsy structure which would collapse if it was punctured or be swamped by a moderate wave, and that if that happened the tank would sink as quickly as a stone, with them inside it. They also knew, because they had tried it in training, that it was

possible to get out of a sunken tank, using submarine escape
apparatus; but that a good many people, in emergencies, had
failed to do so. And they learned, from Rockwell's experiments
with his landing craft, that once they were in the water there was
no going back. The tanks could go down the ramps of the landing craft, but they could not go up. Once launched, they had to
reach land or founder.

When the experiments in launching these tanks were completed, Rockwell's flotilla assembled in Portland Harbour in
Dorset; and while they were waiting there for the day, an
incident occurred which perhaps deserves a place in history.
The King came to inspect them, escorted by Admiral Stark, the
senior American naval officer in Europe, and a formidable
array of brass. On one of the craft, the King asked the ensign
in command if he was all ready for sea.

" No, sir," the ensign replied, to everybody's stupefaction.

The King asked him why not.

" Well, I've asked time and again for an extra fresh-water
tank, but I've never got it and I know what'll happen, it was the
same in the Mediterranean, sir, the army drink you dry and
you're left out there for days——"

The King suggested to Admiral Stark that he might look into
the matter. Admiral Stark told a vice-admiral to investigate.
The vice-admiral told a commodore to see to it, and the commodore told a commander, and the commander told a supply
officer, and the ensign, no doubt, thought his water tank was as
good as installed. But he was wrong. Too much brass can be as
bad as too little. They all forgot.

The crossing was hard for the landing craft crews; perhaps
harder for the tank crews. After the false start on the previous
day, they finally sailed from Portland at 9.15 in the morning
with a voyage of 20 hours in front of them. The farther they
went, the rougher the sea became. The tank landing craft were
built in three sections, bolted together, with all their heavy
machinery in the after end. Loaded with four tanks, they worked
in the seaway and gave an ominous impression of being liable to

buckle in the middle. The decks where the tanks were lashed were often awash. Even Rockwell had to admit that they were showing their worst behaviour. Steering a course was difficult, and keeping station in close convoy was worse. There were a good many collisions. None of them was serious, but every now and then a craft which was trying to avoid a crash would be caught by the sea, and yaw, and career off the course of the convoy all by itself, the helmsman wildly spinning its wheel.

Most of the tank crews and many of the naval men were sick all the way. Between their bouts of sickness, the tank men speculated endlessly about the prospect of the weather in the morning, wondering whether they would be able to launch their tanks at all, or whether all their amphibious training would be wasted.

This worry was on Rockwell's mind as well. Everyone knew the tanks could not swim in rough water. It was so obvious that nobody had ever risked a tank and his life by trying it. Rockwell's orders were that if the sea was too rough for the tanks to swim, the landing craft should take them right in to the beach and land them. The decision had been left to the men on board, but the orders about it were vague. The sixteen craft were to divide, before they reached the area for launching, into two groups of eight craft each. The senior naval officer and senior army officer in each group were to consult and make a joint decision whether to launch or not. It is unusual for any military decision to be left to two officers of equal authority, and nobody had told them what they were to do if they disagreed.

Nightfall on the stormy sea threw the convoy into even worse confusion, and offered no chance of rest to Rockwell and his skippers who had been on their bridges all day. At dawn, Rockwell was pleased and secretly rather surprised to find all his sixteen ships still afloat and still in sight. He led them through the lines of the infantry transports, anchored ten miles off shore, along the lane of buoys which had been laid by the minesweepers, and past the heavy ships which were waiting to open their bombardment. The groups divided, his own eight craft towards the western end of the beach, the others towards the east.

From the first moment when it was light enough to see the waves, Rockwell himself had no doubt in his mind that the tanks would never make it. It could not be anything more than a hunch, but he was sure he had never seen a tank launched in such a sea, and he did not believe it could be done. The senior army officer of his group was in another craft. Prepared to argue, Rockwell went down to one of the tanks and called him on the tank's radio. He was thankful to hear him echo his own thoughts : " I don't think we can make it. Will you take us right in ? " Rockwell said he would. It meant that his eight large, unarmoured, vulnerable craft would be in exactly the position of danger which the D.D. tanks had been meant to obviate ; but of course he had been prepared in his mind for that ever since he had handled a landing craft, and the prospect did not dismay him. The important thing was to get the tanks ashore ; what happened to the landing craft was of minor consequence. At that moment, in the early dawn, his ships were steaming in line ahead to the eastward, waiting to launch. He signalled them to prepare to turn 90 degrees to starboard in line abreast and beach. At 5.30 he gave the executive signal, and saw them all turn together with perfect precision towards the shore, the van of the landing on Omaha. It seemed a proud sight to him.

The other group decided to launch. At the crucial moment, the extraordinary order that the army and navy should share the decision caused the confusion which might have been foreseen. The result was terrible. Each of the landing craft dropped its ramp, and on each of them the four tanks moved forward to enter the water from which they could not possibly return. Some of them went off the ramps successfully and travelled a hundred yards or so before they abruptly vanished below the waves. Some never floated at all. There was a certain gallantry, however unwise, in the way they went. Commanders of the second, third and fourth tanks in each craft could see the leaders founder ; but the order had been given to launch, and they launched, one by one, each of them hoping perhaps for better luck ; and once they had started, the navy could not stop them, but only watch each one till the moment when a wave broke over it, or the canvas collapsed, and the tank instantly disappeared and nothing was left on the sea but one man swimming, perhaps two, but seldom more. Within two or three minutes, twenty-seven of the thirty-two tanks were at the bottom of the Channel : one hundred and thirty-five men were drowned, or swimming for their lives. It was difficult, in the large tank landing craft, to rescue survivors, the best that most of the crews could do was to throw out extra lifebelts and leave the swimmers to wait for smaller craft.

On one of the landing craft, the fourth tank tore its canvas on a gun mounting as it moved along the deck. Its commander was a sergeant called Sertell. He stopped to see what damage had been done, and while he was stopped everybody on the landing craft, including him, watched the three tanks in front of him go under. The naval officer on the bridge advised him to stay on board, and told him that his orders had been that if the last tank was damaged he should land it later in the day. But Sertell insisted on going. He said he thought his bilge pump could keep down the water from the leak. He drove down the ramp and sank. Later in the day, the same landing craft was hailed by a small patrol-boat which handed over a body to be taken back to England, and the body was Sertell's.

Two of the tanks reached the beach under their own power. Three more were saved by an accident. One craft launched its first tank and watched the tank commander and gunner desperately bracing their backs against the bulging canvas to try to stop it collapsing under the pressure of the waves. Their struggle only lasted half a minute. But the landing craft had lurched when the first tank went off it, and the second ran backwards into the third and fourth and all three of them tore their canvas so badly that they could not possibly have floated. The ensign commanding the landing craft decided on his own responsibility to make for the shore : and he fought his way in all alone, and landed the three last tanks.

The infantry on the eastern half of the beach thus had the support of five D.D. tanks, out of the thirty-two they had expected.

Rockwell did not see this tragic proof that his own decision had been right. His own eight craft were some distance to the westward, and he was intent on watching the beach ahead, and the clock, and the crowds of other craft all round him. The clock was important. If he was two minutes too early, he would run into the tail end of the bombardment. If he was two minutes too late, the infantry would not have the help of the tanks at the moment they needed it most. The time and position for launching had been decided to suit the speed of the tanks ; but the landing craft were faster, so they had to waste time. It was a navigational problem which was elementary enough, but it needed concentration because so many things were happening. The battleships and cruisers behind him were shooting over his head. On each side of the aisle reserved for the landing craft, the destroyers and army artillery were banging away. Threaded through the racket of guns, there was a continuous noise of aircraft engines, although the bombers were hidden by clouds. And as he approached the shore, the rocket ships began to let loose their own particularly horrifying roar, and the tanks on his own craft started up their engines.

From far at sea, the shore had been dim in the early morning haze. Now, as he came nearer, it almost disappeared in smoke, and only the level top of the bluffs could be seen against the sky. For a time, Rockwell and his skippers lost sight of their landmarks. But a shift of wind rolled back the smoke for a minute from the mouth of one of the valleys and the group of villas underneath the bluffs, and Rockwell saw they were being set to the eastward by the tide. All of them changed course to starboard and increased their speed. At exactly the time when the barrage lifted, all of them were exactly opposite the points for their landings, ready to run the last six hundred yards to the water's edge.

This was precisely the scene which Rockwell had always

imagined, ever since he had been thrown out of physical education and steered his first landing craft. It was the moment for
which a landing craft existed. But he had always expected, and
been trained to expect, to land under heavy fire. So far, he had
not been aware of any opposition. With all the noise and the
smoke, he had not been certain whether German guns were
firing at all. The only missiles anywhere near him were rockets
falling short. Even when the close barrage stopped, there was
plenty of noise; but it came from the revving engines of his
own four tanks and the gun of the first which was firing over the
ramp; and the wide beach, covered with obstacles, looked
quiet. The villas were ruined, the bluffs deserted, smoke rising
here and there from burning grass. Within his view, there
was no human being alive or dead, and the whole desolate scene
had the air of a place deserted in the face of disaster. In those
last two minutes, from 6.27 to 6.29, while the tank landing
craft approached the breakers, stopped engines and grazed the
sand of Omaha, there was a fleeting hope that the bombardment
had done its work and the defences had been destroyed.

The ramp of Rockwell's craft went down, the first of the
tanks lurched forward, dipped its nose to the slope, crawled into
five feet of water and ahead through the breakers to the sands
fifty yards away, the water washing over its back and pouring
off again. In that same moment the Germans came to life.
Perhaps they had waited on purpose: more probably, their
gunners had just come up from their shell-proof shelters of
which the strength had been so badly underestimated. Rockwell
saw the muzzle flashes from casemates on the bluffs. For the
first few seconds their shooting was ill-directed. His second tank
got away. Then three of the landing craft on his right were hit
in quick succession: an 88-mm. gun was enfilading the beach
from an emplacement at that end. He watched his third tank
go out, and waited with an interest which was almost detached
for the German gun to raise its sights to him: for the landing
craft, lying still and almost broadside to the gun, was a target
which it could not possibly have missed. But the last of his

tanks went into the water, and the moment it was clear the ramp was raised and the engines put astern.

The work of a landing craft was dangerous but short. Rockwell's own job was finished on the stroke of H Hour. The tanks were ashore, and his only duty then was to get his craft away in safety, if he could. Seven of the eight backed out from the beach, two burning ; one was left there wrecked. But the German fire which had concentrated on them for the first few seconds seemed now to be random. Many more guns on the bluffs had begun to shoot, but they had shifted their targets. Rockwell saw the first of his tanks start to pick its way between the obstacles on the beach. Before it had gone ten yards from the water, it burst into flames. And looking astern as his craft got under way, he saw the new targets which had drawn the German fire : the infantry landing craft, ploughing their way towards the breakers, running the gauntlet through the spray of shell-bursts.

The first of these landing craft should have been carrying infantry, with the Navy-Army Demolition Force close behind them ; but on some parts of the beach they all arrived together, and on some the demolition men were in the lead. This letter was written by a demolition man.

". . . We stood looking over the side at the beach we were to go in at soon. We were all happy and smiling, telling jokes and yelling. Six o'clock came and we went in. . . . There hadn't been a shot fired from the enemy yet. But soon as we dropped our ramp, an 88-mm. came tearing in, killing almost half our men right there, the officer being the first one. We all thought him the best officer the navy ever had. . . . From then on things got hazy to me. I remember the Chief starting to take over, but then another one hit and that did it. I thought my body torn apart. When I woke I seen a big hole in the bulkhead between the sergeant and me. He was dead, it must have been instant. I was blood from head to foot but didn't know it at the time. Later I found the shrapnel

had got me in the left leg and arm. I looked round and seen
no one else alive. The explosive was on fire and was burning
fast, so I went overboard and headed for the beach. The surf
was filled with soldiers trying to get ashore. But the bullets
in the surf from the enemy were thick. They were getting
killed fast. I reached the obstacles and got behind one to
shelter. Just then the landing craft blew up, that got me,
not caring whether I lived or not I started to run, through the
fire up the beach. Which was plenty far to run, it probably
seemed longer at that time. That's when I found my leg and
arm stiff. After a while the soldiers were pouring in thick.
I did a little rifle firing with them. . . ."

A great many of the 1,450 men of the eight companies of
infantry also suffered this kind of experience. One company,
landing on the western end of the beach, a little to the right of
Rockwell's tanks, had one of its six craft sunk half a mile from
shore; men were seen jumping overboard and being dragged
down by their equipment, which was too heavy to allow them
to swim. A second craft was blown to pieces by mortar fire.
The other four grounded and the men scrambled out, but the
beach had deep runnels there, and some men were out of their
depth. Intense machine gun and mortar fire enveloped them.
Many were wounded in the water, and fell down and were
drowned. Those who struggled to land took refuge behind the
German obstacles, or went back into the sea for cover. A few
formed a firing line on the water's edge; but soon all the officers
of the company and most of the sergeants were killed or wounded,
and the men, without leaders, gave up any hope of advancing
across the beach. Within fifteen minutes, the company was out
of action. Some of its survivors stayed in the water all the
morning, and succeeded in reaching safety in the end by crawling
up the beach as the tide came in.

This company had landed in the right place. The only other
infantry who did so were a small company of Rangers, who had
a special mission on the right hand end of the beach. All the

rest of the eight companies were carried eastward by the same tidal stream that had upset the landing at Utah. It had not mattered at Utah; the infantry had landed at the wrong place but in good order, and the weakness of the opposition had given them time to organise. But here at Omaha, all order was lost before the soldiers reached the shore at all. Some craft were only two hundred yards to the east of the places where they should have been; some were a mile. One company, after two of its craft were swamped, approached the shore two miles away, and had to come back against the wind and tide, and landed ninety minutes late. All the others were mixed up together. Two stretches of the beach, both half a mile long, had no infantry at all; other parts had too many. Men found themselves pitched on to the shore in single boatloads, cut off from their officers, faced with defences which were not the ones they had studied in their briefing, under a terrible gunfire which they had never been warned to expect, and with nobody to tell them where they were or what they ought to do. Almost all the heavier weapons were lost in the struggle through the surf; and most of the men who succeeded in crossing the beach and reaching the temporary safety of the shingle were so shaken by the ordeal that, for the time being, no organised action was possible.

Not even the heaviest gunfire puts such a strain on a soldier's morale as not being told what to do. In this respect, the demolition men were better off than the infantry. They had a specific job to do, and they could do it, or try to do it, wherever they landed. There were the obstacles in front of them; and each team of them, one officer and a dozen men, had to clear a fifty-yard gap right through to high water mark; and they had to do it quickly, because the tide was rising. To move and work on that beach would have seemed impossible if they had stopped to think; but none of them had time to stop or think.

The training of the demolition force, on the sandy shores near Barnstaple in Devon, had been hurried and incomplete. It was hurried because obstacles on Omaha Beach had only been seen in reconnaissance photographs for the first time in April, and then, under Rommel's pressure, had multiplied very quickly. It was incomplete because nobody knew exactly what the obstacles were like. They could not tell from the photographs what the things were made of, or how they were put together, or whether they were mined. Perhaps the American demolition men were not well served by their liaison with the British; for British commandos had landed on different parts of the coast of France and inspected at least three kinds of obstacles—steel hedgehogs, and wooden ramps and stakes—and had taken measurements of them at their leisure. But only part of this information filtered through to the Americans, and their plans for getting rid of the obstacles had to include an element of guesswork.

Even the organisation of their teams was rather an improvisation. They had started as a naval force, divided into teams of one officer and seven enlisted men: sixteen teams, to blow sixteen gaps in the defences. But whenever new photographs were taken of Omaha Beach, the belt of obstacles was seen to have grown more complex; and not long before D-Day, the naval command concluded that a team of eight men was too small to blow a gap during the half hour which the plan allowed them. The navy had no more explosives men to spare, so the army lent them some. Five army men were added to each of the naval teams.

The commander of this peculiar composite force was a naval reserve officer called Joseph H. Gibbons, and in their six weeks of training, Gibbons had managed to make his men sure that nothing could stop them doing the job they had been assigned to do. He himself was prepared for the job to be tough, but a tough job suited him well; and indeed he had probably been chosen more for his character than for his knowledge of demolition, which was small. He was a powerfully built man of moderate height with a bulldog's tenacity and a habit of saying exactly what he thought no matter who was listening: strict, outspoken, fair, a man to whom right was right and wrong was

wrong, and no shades of rightness existed in between. He was
very much aware of his responsibility to the navy and especially
to his men, whom he treated like a very stern, old-fashioned
and yet affectionate father. These qualities probably dated back
to his upbringing in the woods and the blue grass country of
Kentucky, and perhaps they owed something to his training at the
Naval Academy at Annapolis; for he had graduated there in the
twenties but then had left the service, which seemed a dead end
to him, and taken a job in a telephone company. Whoever
discovered Gibbons and appointed him to his command had
made a clever choice. He was exactly the man to give his forces
the moral impetus they needed to carry them through the ordeal
on the beach.

Gibbons himself landed exactly in the middle of the beach.
As he was in charge of all sixteen teams, the job he had planned
for himself was simply to walk along the beach and see how they
got on and help them when help was needed; and that is what he
did. He was absorbed by his technical problems. The thought was
certainly there in the back of his mind that something must have
gone wrong and that conditions were very much worse than anyone had expected; but the gunfire tearing down the beach
worried him first and foremost for the effect it might have on
the job.

The first two of his men he met told him the whole of the
rest of their team had been killed while they were landing. He
told them to take cover behind the shingle bank till he found a
job for them. Next he found a team which had landed intact
and started already to fasten its charges to the obstacles. Each
man had landed with a string of two-pound blocks of explosive
round his waist, and each team had an extra supply in a rubber
boat which it was supposed to haul ashore from its landing
craft. Gibbons had always expected the best of his men: watching this team, he was very proud to see how well they justified his
confidence. He saw them moving methodically from one obstacle
to another, taping the charges on to the stakes and angle-irons
quickly but not hastily. One of them was running out the

instantaneous fuse which was to connect all the charges together. One had laid out the two buoys which were to mark the gap, and was going up the beach carrying posts with triangles on them which he had to set up as additional markers in line at the top of the beach. None of them was showing any visible sign of fear.

Gibbons moved on. Absorbed as he was, his walk had some incidents. Once, suddenly aware of shells bursting all round him, he dived into a hole in the sand. Another man, a moment later, dived in on top of him shouting furiously : " Get the hell out of my foxhole." Gibbons got out, ashamed of himself, and did not go to ground again. Somewhere along the beach, another thing penetrated his consciousness : a scream, a long terrible dying scream which seemed to express not only fear and pain, but amazement, consternation, and disbelief.

He found other teams at work, and other teams decimated on the water's edge ; and he found a gap blown, and the bodies of the men who had blown it scattered among the wreckage of the obstacles. He watched the tide rising. At half tide, it rose a foot in eight minutes, and within the first few minutes of the landing it was among the outer obstacles, swirling into the runnels and advancing at an average of a yard a minute up the gentle slope of yellow sand.

On the beach, he only gained a rough impression of his men working against time under conditions which he vaguely knew were terrible. It was not till later in the day, when the tide put an end to their efforts, and their survivors took refuge at last behind the shingle, that he began to learn the extent of their successes, and heard of the accidents which had overwhelmed the teams which had failed.

Five gaps had been blown, and two partially blown, out of the sixteen which had been planned. Two or three teams had been lost before they landed, or been landed so late that the tide was up before they got to work. At least two had been slaughtered in landing. One had had its rubber boat hit by a shell while the whole team was gathered round it dragging it ashore. It blew most of them to pieces. One team had laid all its charges and connected them, and the men were still standing by them preparing to fire them when a shell hit the fuse and ignited it and set off all the charges prematurely and wounded or killed them all except the man with the markers. One team had everything ready when some tanks, arriving late, drove over the fuses and cut them to pieces so that the charges could not be fired at all.

The remaining teams were all delayed by a humanitarian consideration which nobody could possibly have thought of: the infantry, desperate for cover, who huddled in groups behind the slenderest obstacles. One of the warrant officers, his charges laid and ready at the cost of the lives of two of his own twelve men, ran round frenziedly kicking the soldiers to try to make them move so that he could fire the charges. Another team leader, when every persuasion had failed, lit his fuse and then ran round from one obstacle to another shouting to the men that it was burning and they had half a minute to get out. For some teams, the difficulty was worse, because wounded men had been dragged into the imaginary shelter of the obstacles, and they could not move. Some teams wasted so much time in trying to clear men off the beach that the tide rose and drowned their charges and their gaps were never blown. None of them could bring themselves to do what the logic of war demanded: blow the gap and kill their own countrymen.

In the face of all these difficulties, the blowing of five gaps was a wonderful achievement, although it was only a third of the number planned. Gibbons might say he had never been brave himself, but his unit action might well be judged the most gallant of all on D-Day. Of his 272 engineers, 111 were killed or wounded, almost all in the first half hour. Yet their gallantry was largely wasted, by hastiness in planning. The fault lay with the markers they had been given. Some of the buoys and posts they had brought to mark the gaps were lost or broken in the landing. The posts which they set up at the top of the beach were easily knocked down, and were not conspicuous enough to be seen through the smoke from seaward. The buoys, which they laid on each side of each gap, were ordinary metal dan buoys with a spar and a flag on top ; but they could be punctured and sunk by a single rifle bullet, and instead of being port and starboard buoys they were all the same colour, so that when one was sunk, nobody could tell which side of the gap was marked by the one which remained.

So when the tide had risen and covered the obstacles, the gaps which had been made by such sacrifice were practically impossible to find. All the morning, landing craft skippers milled around off-shore looking for buoys and posts, and most of them, knowing that gaps had been planned, hesitated to trust to luck and charge the obstacles.

Two other cumulative disasters helped to deprive the stricken infantry of the support which they had the right to expect. A large proportion of the artillery intended to land in the first few hours had been loaded in the amphibious trucks called Dukws. This plan had simply not made enough allowance for the rough sea which can be found in the English Channel even in June. With guns, ammunition, sandbags and men on board, the Dukws were top-heavy and the great majority were swamped or rolled over in the sea.

Secondly, it was a long time before army engineers succeeded in making any gaps in the bank of shingle, which was too steep for vehicles or even tanks to cross ; and so the tanks were not able to lead the infantry in any advance beyond the beach itself. The reasons for this delay again were losses of equipment. Explosives had been lost in the surf. Sixteen bulldozers had been provided, but only three survived, and one of those was unable to manœuvre because of the infantrymen who clung to its shelter. No gaps were made in the bank until ten o'clock. By then, high tide was approaching. The tanks which were still in action had been penned into a strip of beach which was only a few yards wide. Other kinds of vehicles, jeeps, trucks and half-tracks, had started to land, and as the tide rolled up to the shingle all of them were caught in a dense jam of vehicles, men and wreckage, from which nothing could escape towards the gaps. This concentration of material was still under fire from German guns at close range; and an order had to be sent, by a naval radio which had been landed in working order, to suspend all landings of vehicles till something could be done to clear the beach.

Into this scene of confusion and death, just before the landings were halted, a landing craft disgorged a unit of anti-aircraft guns mounted on half-tracks, of which one section was commanded by a sergeant called Hyman Haas; and Haas's experience was typical of that stage of the battle except for the very unusual fact that he brought his whole section and his guns and vehicles through it with hardly a scratch on the paint.

Hyman Haas's job was making frames for ladies' handbags. He was Jewish, and came from the Bronx, and was cheerful, friendly and efficient. This was his first combat.

Haas's unit were principally trained as anti-aircraft, but they had also practised on surface targets; and that was just as well. Even while they were still out at sea, he knew they were out of a job as anti-aircraft gunners, because the sky was full of planes with black and white stripes of distemper, and there was never a single German to be seen. But the moment they hit the beach they found a job which was very much more important; to help to take the place of the artillery which had foundered in the Dukws.

Like everybody else, Haas was shocked and amazed at his first close sight of the beach; and like everybody else, he found that his orders were impossible to fulfil as they had been planned. He was supposed to drive his half-tracks straight across the beach and up one of the valleys to the village of St. Laurent at its head, and then set up his guns on the top of the bluffs. He was landed in the right place. The water was deep. It came up to his waist in the cab where he was sitting with his driver. But his waterproofing held, and the half-track wallowed through the water to the sand. There was the valley, just where he had expected

it to be; but there also, only a few yards ahead of him, was
the shingle bank, still intact and impassible, and between him
and it were the debris, the wrecks of tanks, the corpses and the
hundreds of crouching men. There was no room to go forward
at all. To let the rest of his unit squeeze on to the beach behind
him, he had to tell his driver to turn to the right and try to move
out of the way between the wreckage and the water.

The sight of a 37-mm. gun coming ashore just behind them
must have appeared as a godsend to the infantry, some of whom
had been there for two hours without any artillery at all. An
officer ran towards Haas before he had even stopped, shouting
and pointing out a pillbox on the side of the bluff about three
hundred yards away. Haas looked at it and saw it fire. His own
gun was mounted so that it could not fire forward on low eleva-
tion. There was no room to turn round on the beach. He told
his driver to turn to the right again, and drive back into the sea.
That brought the half-track stern on to the bluffs; and there,
half submerged in the surf again, Haas trained his gun and laid
it on the pillbox. He fired ten rounds. So far as he could see,
they all went through the aperture and exploded inside. Anyhow,
the German gun was silent after that.

By then, the whole of the unit was ashore, and for a long time
nobody showed Haas another target. There was nothing for
him to do but to sit and wait, and hope that somebody somewhere
would punch a hole in the shingle bank and let him move before
his gun was destroyed.

Few people had the opportunity that morning to see the
landing at Omaha as a whole; but to all who did, it seemed
for several hours that the attack was going to fail. A German
officer in the fortifications on the cliffs at the west end of the beach
counted ten tanks and a great many other vehicles burning, and
saw the American troops taking cover behind the shingle and the
dead and wounded lying on the sand; and he reported that he
believed the invasion had been halted on the shore. The German
divisional commander, receiving this and similar reports, was so

confident of the outcome that he sent a part of his reserves to counter-attack the British farther east. General Bradley, out on the cruiser *Augusta*, could do nothing at that stage to influence events ; the battle, he wrote later, " had run beyond the reach of its admirals and generals." All the morning, he was extremely anxious at the alarming and confused reports which came in by radio. About nine o'clock, he sent an observer close inshore in a fast patrol boat ; but his first-hand report was no more re-assuring. He had been able to see the shambles on the beach, and another staff officer who was very close in at the same time reported landing craft milling around " like a stampeded herd of cattle." At noon, a further radio report told Bradley that the situation was still critical, and he began then to contemplate diverting his follow-up forces from Omaha to Utah and to the British beaches : a decision which would presumably have meant writing off the landing at Omaha as a failure, and abandon-ing most of the forces already ashore to be killed or captured. For the next hour and a half, this terrible prospect remained in the General's mind : so near did Omaha come to defeat. And then, at 1.30, seven hours after the landing, he received the message : " Troops formerly pinned down . . . advancing up heights behind beaches."

Something had tipped the balance which had been swinging towards defeat, and inclined it slightly at last towards victory.

It was partly the slow effect of the almost irresistible weight of American arms. The American forces could lose all the tanks and all the artillery in the first waves of their attack : there were still enormous quantities of tanks and artillery to follow in later waves. They could even lose their infantry : man-power was no problem, for tens of thousands more men were waiting and ready to go in. But the German defences, strong though they were, were limited and immobile. From time to time, a lucky shot like Haas's wrote off a pillbox, and nothing could replace it. Time was bound to wear the static defences down.

This process was certainly quickened by the navy's interven-tion. The naval bombardment had been scheduled to stop three minutes before the troops landed, for fear, of course, of hitting them while they advanced. But when it became obvious that the soldiers were not advancing at all, but were penned on the beach, and that the situation was desperate, destroyers were ordered in as close as they could go, to shell whatever targets they could see. Some of them went in till they scraped their keels on the sandy bottom.

So, by naval fire aided by the remnants of artillery on the beach, German guns were silenced one by one, and German fire against the beach must slowly have been slackening. But none of the men on the beach were aware of any slackening. It is nearly as bad to be shot at by ten guns as by twenty.

What really turned the balance was a final stubborn reserve of human courage. It came to the surface quite independently, at several different places on the beach. The shock of the landing had numbed the will-power of a great many men, not because their morale or their courage was particularly weak, but simply because the shock was too great for any ordinary man. The loss of leaders and lack of orders had created a feeling of hopelessness and lethargy. But here and there during the morning, officers and N.C.O.s of more than ordinary moral strength, recovering more quickly than others from the shock, began to take stock of the situation and to rally whatever men they happened to find around them.

It is impossible to say how many of these natural leaders were discovered by the very horror of the position on the beach : perhaps there were a score, perhaps a hundred. None of them had any example to follow, or knew that anyone else was even trying to break the deadlock, because in general nobody knew what was happening beyond the very limited distance he could see. Sometimes a single man's action inspired others ; sometimes men had to be bullied or persuaded ; sometimes a single concise remark stuck in men's minds long afterwards as the turning point, and was repeated in recollection after the battle was over, and so found its way into official records. On one bit of the beach, a lieutenant and a wounded sergeant quite suddenly stood up among the men who were lurking behind the shingle, and walked over the top of it : the very thing which nobody had dared to do. They looked at the wire entanglement just beyond the bank, and then the lieutenant came back and stood on top and looked down at the cowering men and said to nobody in particular : " Are you going to lay there and get killed, or get up and do something about it ? " Nobody moved, so he and the sergeant found explosives and blew a hole in the wire ; and then men began to stir. An infantry colonel, on another part of the beach in the same situation, expressed the same thought : " Two kinds of people are staying on this beach, the dead and those who are going to die. Now let's get the hell out of here."

In the largest and most effective advance which was made from the beach that morning, it was actually a private soldier who was the first to go over the bank and set a Bangalore torpedo in the wire. Before he could fire it, he was killed. A lieutenant went over next, and fired it and blew a gap. The first man to try the gap was shot ; but others made it, in twos and threes, and found shelter in some empty German trenches ; and little by little the numbers increased till the remnants of a whole company were following.

In this way, several small groups of men, mostly ill-armed and mostly unsupported, began to creep inland behind a leader. The groups varied in size, from half-a-dozen men to a company, and each of them, so far as its members knew, was alone in trying to penetrate inland. Nobody will ever know how many groups started and failed. Roughly a dozen succeeded. None of those which succeeded were opposite the strongly defended valleys ; they were all in between them. There, they began to find that there was really more cover beyond the beach than on it. There were ruins, and bushes, and small folds and hollows in the face of the bluffs. Once they were clear of the beach, they found the German fire less dangerous than the minefields. None of them had time to clear the mines, and few of them had the knowledge or apparatus. One engineer lieutenant, who was trained in mines but had no mine detector, led men through a minefield in the marsh below the bluffs by crawling on his stomach and probing with a hunting-knife. Most of these tentative advances were made in single file, each man treading in the footsteps of the man in front, stepping over the bodies of men whom the mines had killed. In some minefields, wounded men were left lying where they fell while a column walked over them, because the column could not be stopped and there was no room, on the narrow track which was proved to be safe, to carry them back to the beach. It was through these hesitant columns of shocked and weary men that the advance from Omaha began. The landing there, one-fourth of the whole invasion, had stood on the verge of failure; but a few brave men, mostly of junior rank, had refused to believe it had failed, and had begun to lead their companions to success.

But for the whole of the day, success remained uncertain. By noon, a few of the infantry were up the bluffs, and began to attack the defences from behind. But no tanks or artillery could follow them, because the valleys were still being strongly held. Sergeant Haas saw soldiers on the skyline of the bluffs above him but he still had to wait for a gap in the shingle through which he could drive his half-track, and until he could move he could not find any targets for his guns. Almost all the beach obstacles were still intact and were still a menace to the landing of reinforcements. Gibbons was still waiting impatiently for the tide to go down again so that he could renew his attack on them. Communications hardly existed at all. Most of the radios which had been landed were full of salt water, and it was long after nightfall before anyone had any use for the telephone wire which Henry Meyers, the mathematician from Brooklyn, had carried ashore and was waiting to lay inland. Through all these hours, a strong counter-attack could have pushed the whole of the American forces off Omaha Beach and back into the sea again.

But no counter-attack was made, and for this reprieve, as

for so much else, the thanks of the troops on the ground were
due to the air forces which had won complete supremacy in
Western Europe. Allied aircraft that day were delaying the
movement of German reserves far and wide over France; and
before that day, they had already played their part in disrupting
communications and in sowing confusion in the minds of the
German commanders.

From the first moment when parachute landings had been
reported, the German command had been reluctant to believe
a real invasion was beginning, because of the weather. The
Germans were far less well equipped than the British and
Americans with weather stations in the North Atlantic area.
This was partly, of course, a matter of geography, but partly
also because their air force had been worn down to a point
at which it could hardly risk long-range aircraft on weather
reconnaissance. As a result, their meteorologists failed to forecast the temporary break in the weather which had been spotted
by Eisenhower's advisers. They predicted nothing but bad
weather, and on the strength of a forecast which seemed to offer
safety from invasion for several days, Field-Marshal Rommel
had gone to Germany to spend a day at home and then to report
to Hitler; and in the invasion area itself, all the divisional commanders had been summoned to a meeting in Brittany which
was to take place on the morning of the sixth. Even when the
landings had started, it seemed unlikely to the German High
Command that the Allies would have launched a full-scale attack
with such a forecast.

To this unwillingness to believe the truth, the Allied air
forces had added uncertainty, by keeping German reconnaissance
aircraft away and by successfully attacking German radar stations.
German reconnaissance flights in the previous week had reached
the Dover area and reported the dummy fleet which was lying
there, but had not been able to penetrate to the English harbours
farther west where the real fleet was waiting. The early warning
radar stations along the coast of France were sufficient, in theory,
to detect ships or aircraft over most of the English Channel;

but in that same week, the stations had been bombed, and on the night of the landing those which remained were jammed. However, enough of them were deliberately left in working order in the eastern part of the Channel to ensure that the dummy fleets approaching the Calais area were detected.

To the High Command, a full-scale landing anywhere that morning therefore seemed unlikely; the information which reached von Rundstedt's and Rommel's headquarters was meagre; and what there was of it seemed on the whole to confirm von Rundstedt's belief that the main attack would come in Calais, and to suggest that the action in Normandy was a mere diversion. At the crucial moment, they hesitated to throw in the whole weight of their reserves.

Their reaction was also delayed by the fact that their command was divided between the army and the Nazi party. The army had one armoured division close to the invasion shore. It was stationed near Caen, and was in action against the British early in the day. There were two more first-class armoured divisions between Normandy and Paris; but they were S.S. divisions, Nazi party units which were not under the army's direct command, and von Runstedt had been forbidden by Hitler to commit them to battle without consulting him. Before dawn, von Runstedt's chief of staff asked for Hitler's permission to move them up; but Hitler, at home in Berchtesgaden, refused to let them move to the west, in case it should be true that the main attack was still to come in the east. Having made this decision, Hitler took a sleeping draught (according to Chester Wilmot) and went to bed, and his decision was not reversed till the afternoon. By then, it was much too late for the two divisions to play any part in opposing the first assault; and when they did begin to move, they found movement by daylight made almost impossible by Allied fighter-bombers which patrolled the roads and even hunted out tanks which tried to advance across country.

These armoured divisions were the nearest strategic reserves. The tactical reserves close to Omaha Beach had already been dissipated. There were two infantry brigades; but before the landing at Omaha had been reported, part of this force had been dispatched to the west to tackle the American airborne landing, and during the morning most of the rest of it was moved east, to a point where the British were quickly advancing inland. The Atlantic Wall at Omaha was tough, but it was thin.

VI

THE BRITISH BEACHES
Gold—Juno—Sword

As THE tide came up the Channel from west to east, the British
army, half an hour later than the Americans, began its assault
on the three beaches which had been given the code-names
Gold, Juno and Sword; and on Gold beach, fifteen miles east
of Omaha, the experience of a captain of the Westminster
Dragoons, called Roger Bell, provided a contrast in character and
technique with the Americans and their landings.

Bell was like a good many young officers in the British
wartime army, at least in his attitude to the army and to the
war. He had been twenty when the war started, articled to a
chartered accountant in Sheffield; and he had joined up at
once, partly in a fit of patriotism, but partly also because he was
afraid he was going to fail his next examination in accountancy,
which was due in a month or two. What had followed had not
been at all what he expected; not gallant action, neither death
nor glory, but four and a half years of solid training and exercises,
and less contact with the enemy, on the whole, than was experienced by the women and children of his native town.

The reversal of the rôles of civilians and soldiers in Britain
in the four years between Dunkirk and Normandy had affected
the outlook of everyone in the army who had had the misfortune

to be stationed there all the time. Throughout history, armies had gone to the wars with bands playing and the population lining the streets and cheering. Physical courage had been the soldier's pride. The bombing of Britain had exploded an age-long myth by showing that courage was not confined to soldiers but, on the contrary, was a virtue which almost everybody had when it was needed. Courage did not need bands, or uniforms or traditions or drill, or any of the pomp and ceremoniousness of armies. It was not even an exclusively manly virtue any more. Most soldiers who had been in Britain all through the war must have had the experience of feeling rather foolish, when they went home on leave from a secure and well-sheltered camp in the depths of the country and saw what had been happening in the towns, or found themselves secretly alarmed in an air-raid which their mothers and wives and neighbours and even daughters took as a matter of course.

This upheaval of the fundamental hypothesis of war may have been the cause of the widespread fashion in the armed forces to make light of courage and pretend to be a coward. During his training, Roger Bell had never been able to bring himself to take the army quite seriously, and he would not have known whether to feel flattered or not if anyone had ever told him he was a good soldier; but probably no one ever did. When their divisional commander told the Westminster Dragoons they were to have the honour of being among the first to land in France, Bell and most of the other junior wartime-only officers agreed it was an honour they would gladly have done without. But that was not much more than a pose. Bell was glad, at a rather deeper level, that he was going to have a chance at last to do something really dangerous. Apart from the patriotic feelings which he would hardly have dared to confess, he was tired of feeling faintly ridiculous. Having joined the army, it would have been a final blow to his pride to have gone right through the war in safety.

So on the whole, he had been perfectly happy when the years of training ended with the final embarkation in a landing craft in Southampton Water : an embarkation not just for another practice landing round the corner in Studland Bay, but for the real thing at last. The landing craft carried a team of six tanks, and he was second-in-command of the team and had a tank of his own. When the tanks had been reversed on board and the small ship backed off from the shore, there was a holiday atmosphere which lasted all through the extra day of waiting. Bell sighed with relief to think that all the worries and annoyances of preparing were over, and that if he had forgotten anything there was nothing anyone could do about it. He and all his men knew exactly what they were supposed to do, and they were sure they could do it, or at least have a bash. Meanwhile, it was up to the navy : the army could relax.

What Bell was going to try to do was something which the Americans did not try at all. His tank was a flail, specially designed to open tracks through minefields, and his team, which was a mixture of Westminster Dragoons and Royal Engineers, included three different kinds of the peculiar tanks which were officially known as Specialised Armour, and less officially but more usually as Funnies.

These tanks were the products of a tremendous fund of ingenuity, and of a study of the problems of invasion which went back to the raid on Dieppe in August, 1942. They were developed by the 79th Armoured Division under the command of Major-General Sir Percy Hobart, a pioneer of armoured warfare who had retired and become a corporal in the Home Guard but was dragged back into active service by Churchill.

The experience of Dieppe had persuaded the British—and Churchill in particular—that army engineers, in a seaborne assault on prepared defences, could not efficiently demolish obstacles, lay roads, clear minefields, fill anti-tank ditches, or destroy fortifications while they themselves were under heavy fire. The Funnies were designed to provide the engineers in the forefront of the landing with armoured protection and mechanical means for carrying out their tasks.

The D.D. tank was one product of the 79th Division. Others

were flails, such as Bell commanded, bobbins, fascines, roly-polys, petards, crocodiles, self-propelled ramps, and tanks which carried bridges. The whole of the British plan of assault was based on the use of these tanks, and a description of the British landings must start with an explanation of what was hidden by their code-names.

The flail tanks were designed to supersede the slow and dangerous process of clearing landmines by hand. A flail was an ordinary Sherman tank with two arms in front of it which carried a revolving drum. On the drum, there were short lengths of chain, and when the drum revolved the chains flew round and flailed the ground in front of the tank, exploding mines before the tank had reached them. The tank left a wide visible track which other tanks or infantry could follow.

Bobbins and roly-polys unrolled various kinds of matting or steel mesh, drove over it and left it behind them to form a temporary roadway. They had been designed for laying roads across dunes, or over the patches of clay which reconnaissance had revealed in some of the British beaches.

Fascines each carried an enormous bundle of logs which they could drop into an anti-tank ditch so that they themselves, and other tanks, could cross it. Self-propelled ramps were tanks without turrets, which could lay themselves against a sea-wall or an anti-tank wall so that other tanks could climb up them and get over. The bridging tanks carried thirty-foot bridges for the wider ditches or craters ; they laid their bridges and then drove over them. Most of these machines reverted to the functions of ordinary tanks as soon as they had finished their special missions.

Petards and crocodiles were tanks for destroying gun positions. The petard threw an enormous bomb from a short-muzzled mortar, sufficient to blow a large hole in a concrete emplacement ; and the crocodile threw flame, much more and hotter and farther than the flame-throwers which were carried by infantry.

For the invasion, these products of inventive flair applied

to destruction were assembled in teams to suit the terrain and defences they were expected to have to face. Each team fitted into one landing craft. Bell's piece of beach, for example, was not complicated by dunes or a seawall, and it was defended by mines and gun emplacements, and wire and obstacles on the sand. It also had a patch of soft clay on it. The first tank in Bell's team was therefore a bobbin, to lay a track across the clay. Then there were three flails to clear the minefields. The fifth was a fascine, in case of craters on the roads which led inland, and the last was an armoured bulldozer to push the beach obstacles out of the way. Other teams, to land on each side of him, included armour to deal with the gun emplacements. There was no need for ramps or bridges on his sector.

All these gadgets had been offered by the British to the American High Command, but they had politely refused them excepting the D.D. tanks, which unfortunately, when the day came, were the least successful of all because they were dependent on the weather. It has puzzled military historians that Americans, usually regarded as the most mechanically-minded people, should have preferred to try to do by hand the work which the specialised armour could do by machinery. Possibly there was an element of national pride involved in accepting British inventions. By the time the offer was made, which was after Eisenhower and Montgomery were appointed, the American engineers had made up their minds how they were going to tackle their problems and had started to train their men ; and they could not bring themselves to scrap the planning and training they had done and start again. It was also characteristic of American military planning to be more spendthrift with the lives of their soldiers than the British, perhaps because they had a much bigger population behind them, and perhaps because the British still remembered more vividly the loss of a generation in World War I. But whatever the reason, American instinct, confronted with defences like those at Omaha, was to go for them bald-headed with their bare hands, and to support the action with the argument that this was the quickest way to achieve success, so that although it might cost more lives at the time, it would save them in the long run.

It would have been difficult to support this argument after Omaha. It is usually uncertain in military affairs to say what might have been ; but it does seem likely that if the American commanders had accepted the British equipment and used it on Omaha in sufficient force, it would have punched gaps at once in the shingle bank, and cut the wire and rolled up the minefields, and so let the infantry and tanks get off the beach without the lethal and paralysing delay which they suffered. The outcome of the battle would never have been in such doubt, and many of the three thousand men who were killed or wounded there would have been saved.

As soon as the landing craft which carried Bell and his tanks got under way on the morning of the 5th, and out of the lee of the Isle of Wight, the rough weather took the edge off the party feeling. Most of the thirty men on board were sick, in spite of the pills of hyoscine they had taken. There was nothing for them to do, and not very much to see. Peering out over the high wet bulwarks, the tank crews saw the other landing craft of their own flotilla, but no other shipping at all, and some of them wondered gloomily whether there had been a ghastly muddle. Perhaps, they thought, the whole thing had been postponed again and the naval types who were running the flotilla had missed the signal. Nothing seemed more likely. Perhaps they were crossing the Channel all alone. As dusk began to fall that evening, they were a little cheered up by the sight of two cruisers. They were a long way off, but they were going in the right direction : south.

Bell was a fairly good sailor, and managed not to be sick. He did not feel the slightest apprehension either, or fear for what was coming in the morning. He had never seen battle. He had never even seen a dead man. But as darkness fell, and the landing craft plunged onwards, he felt a tremendous elation at taking part in such a great adventure. It never crossed his

mind that the invasion might fail. He had read the personal
message which Montgomery had circulated; and Monty said he
had complete confidence, and so that was that. It had never
occurred to him either to think very much about the cause he
was going to fight for. If he had ever paused to think of it at all,
he would certainly have thought the battle was right and just.

At nightfall, he encouraged his men to lie down on the steel
decks and get what sleep they could. There was only one army
officer on board besides himself; and the skipper of the landing
craft, who had to be on the bridge all night, had offered them
his cabin. There was that much to be said for being an officer.
At midnight, two-thirds of the way across the Channel, with
a clear conscience and no worries in the world, Roger Bell was
fast asleep.

At that same hour, in a gun battery on a hill behind the exact
part of the coast which was Bell's objective, a young man called
Friedrich Wurster was on duty as a sentry; and his thoughts
were wandering, as the thoughts of sentries do. He was listening
to heavy bombers going over, on their way, he imagined, to bomb
the towns of Germany; and he was thinking of the air-raid sirens
sounding at home, and his mother waking and having to get up
and go down alone to the shelter again; alone, because his
father was stationed as a soldier in the north of Norway, and
his brother was in the air force. The thought of it made him both
sad and angry, exactly as similar thoughts of home made British
soldiers in outposts sad and angry.

Wurster, however, was spared the feeling which Bell had
found so hurtful to his pride; the feeling that while the civilians
suffered, he was safe in the army. His army career had been far
from safe. He was twenty-one, and he had been a soldier for
four years. At seventeen, he had marched into France with the
conquering army. At eighteen, he had marched into Russia.
At nineteen, he had been wounded within a hundred miles of
Moscow. Before he was twenty, he had been patched up and
sent back to Russia and witnessed advances and then retreats;

and he had been wounded a second time, so badly that they could not make him fit for Russia again but sent him to the Atlantic Wall instead, a semi-invalid at twenty-one.

So he knew a lot about war ; and in fact, as he sometimes admitted to himself, he had not had much time to learn about anything else. On his solitary nights as a sentry, he often wondered how it would end, whether it would ever end, whether he would survive it, whether he would ever live at home with his family again ; and he dreamed of all the things he would like to do, now that he was grown up, and if there was peace and he was free.

But although he longed for the war to end, he had never so far imagined its end as anything but a German victory. He was the son of a farmer, and he had been ten when Hitler came to power. Like every boy and girl he knew, he had automatically joined the Hitler Youth ; and practically the whole of his education had been at the hands of Nazis or under the control of Nazism. It would be inaccurate to say that he believed in Nazi doctrine ; it was not a question of belief or disbelief. Nazism was truth. It was the only social system and the only philosophy he knew ; for he had not learned anything of democracy in France or communism in Russia, except that he was told they were decadent and almost laughably inferior. Even in Russia, he had never had to consider the idea that Nazism and the German army might fail to win the war.

But still, Wurster was fundamentally a simple, decent peasant, with normal feelings of charity. So far, what little he had come to know of the dreadful degradation and cruelty of the system he represented had always been explained away to him, either as something right and necessary, or as a lie invented by enemies. The character he had inherited from generations of hard-working and God-fearing country people was quite different from the character driven into him by his upbringing, and it may be that he was doomed, whatever happened, to a revulsion sooner or later, when he grew up enough to discover that these parts of him were irreconcilable. When the revulsion came, it was bound to be painful for him, and to turn upside down the whole of the world he knew; but the sooner it happened, the better for him, and for the world. That night, he was on the verge of the first spasm of the revulsion, as he stood unsuspecting and bored at his post in the dark, looking out towards the glimmer of the sea.

At two o'clock he was relieved, and he went back to his quarters to turn in; but before he had finished undressing, the alarm bell rang and the battery loudspeakers called everyone to the first state of alert. His companions crawled out of bed grumbling sleepily, and slowly began to grope about for their clothes. There had been so many false alarms in the last few weeks that they were fed up with them and did not take them seriously any more. Before any of them were ready, the second state of alert was sounded, and through the loudspeakers an officer told them that parachutists and gliders had landed beyond the River Orne and attacked the battery at Merville, which all of them knew at least by name because it was manned by their own regiment.

But still they did not worry or feel that things were urgent. They had been told by their leaders time and again that the Atlantic Wall was impregnable, and they believed it. The artillery had more reason to believe it than the static divisions of infantry. Their own positions and armament were good, and so was their morale, and they did not know of the doubts and inefficiency of some of the infantry units on whose co-operation they depended.

So they went on dressing in a leisurely manner, discussing the news. Merville was twenty miles away, and the general opinion was that this was a local raid. Wurster's companions had been told it would be crazy for the British or Americans to make a serious attack on the Atlantic Wall, and they did not believe they would try.

When Roger Bell woke up and looked out at the break of dawn, what he saw was astonishingly different from the scene of the evening before : the same grey turbulent sea, but full of ships from horizon to horizon. Bell had been cynical—or pretended to be—when General Hobart had talked of the honour of being among the first to land. Now he began to see for the first time exactly what the General had meant. It was the first time he and his tank crews had ever seen a fleet prepared for action, and the first time they had had any real impression of the fantastic size and power of the force which had been assembled to support them. As their flotilla steamed through the lines of battleships and cruisers and destroyers towards the smudge of the shore-line of France, they did feel proud at last of being among the star performers in such a drama.

On board the landing craft itself, as it passed inshore of the fleet, the scene was almost domestic : the tank men finishing breakfast, stowing away their blankets, washing their faces, some trying to shave. Some, after a miserable night, had not been able to face the British army compo tea—a ready-made mixture of tea and sugar and powdered milk which made a fairly nauseating drink at the best of times. Bell, as part of the pretence that he would be scared out of his wits, had stowed a bottle of navy rum in his tank to give himself dutch courage for the landing ; but now that the moment had come, he was so excited that he forgot all about it and swallowed his tea with enjoyment. Everyone was cheerful, now that the crossing was nearly over. Whatever was going to happen on the beach, they looked forward to being on land again.

Bell saw to the clearing of the chains and chocks which held his tank, and then from his turret he looked out at the shore ahead—the shore which he knew, from maps and photographs, almost as well as Friedrich Wurster knew it. This was Gold Beach. It was a straight stretch of sand about three miles long, which has a small village at each end of it : at the west end, Le Hamel, and at the east, La Rivière. Beyond Le Hamel, a line of hills runs out to the coast and ends in cliffs which separate the beach from the little town of Arromanches. Beyond La Rivière, at the other end, the shore was protected in 1944 by a very high seawall of concrete, with a road on top of it ; an obstacle which was even beyond the powers of the specialised armour.

But between the two villages, there were only dunes behind the beach, with a few holiday houses and wooden bungalows. Beyond the dunes there was a narrow strip of marshy ground, and a road which joined the villages, and then a line of gentle grassy hills. The hills are not so steep as the bluffs of Omaha, and they presented no obstacle for tanks ; but they command a view of the whole of the beach, and Wurster's battery, among others, was built on top of them.

Bell was to land at the eastern end of the beach, just clear of the seawall of La Rivière, and one of the landmarks he had been told to look out for was a large emplacement on the top of the seawall, which was believed to contain an 88-mm. gun which was sited to enfilade the beach.

So far, as Bell advanced like Rockwell at Omaha under the arch of the gunfire from the heavy ships behind him, he had not seen any activity from the German batteries. The smoke of the bombardment hid the hills and hung over the village ; but as the craft drew in, the beach itself was clearly visible. It looked dead and perfectly deserted, as if nobody had set foot on it for years ; and that was no wonder, because La Rivière itself, which was no more than a score of houses defended by a single platoon of Germans, had just been bombed by six squadrons of heavy bombers and was now being shelled by the sixteen five-inch guns of four destroyers, and by twenty-four 25-pounders of the Royal Artillery in landing craft, and by two thousand rockets.

The bombardment, striking just before dawn, was the first warning Frederick Wurster had that anything really serious was happening. It did very little structural damage to the battery, but while it lasted the artillery was paralysed. Not even the veterans like himself from the Russian front had ever known anything like it, and not even the best trained soldiers could stand up and keep a look-out or lay a gun. Even after dawn, they could not have seen anything through the smoke and flame, and they could not have heard an order. Wurster dived into an armoured emplacement, and so did everybody else who could; and in the only glimpse he had outside in the whole of that awful hour, he saw cows and horses in the meadow beside the battery felled by the high explosives and set on fire, some still alive, by incendiary bombs.

Before it stopped, the trained hearing of the artillery men had detected the sound of shells among the other noise, and shellfire could only have come from a ship, improbable though that seemed; and so, when suddenly there was silence, or what seemed by comparison like silence, and Wurster stood up and looked out, he was partially prepared for what he saw. But it was still an overwhelming shock. He had half expected ships, but he had never expected or even dreamed of six hundred ships, and at least that number must have been in sight from his battery at dawn. Nor had he ever heard of landing craft; yet there they were, already in the surf, and men and tanks were pouring out of them and advancing across the beach to the foot of the hill.

Bell's was among them. Still surprised that he was not being shot at, he had spotted the end of the seawall and the 88-mm. emplacement on top of it, and he knew his skipper was going to succeed in putting him down at exactly the right place and the right time. The map of the shore was clear in his mind's eye and his job was simple: to flail a track through the mine-fields, across the road, and straight on up the hill. He was intensely excited. The supreme moment of all his training was approaching; and like Mabry, like Gibbons, like thousands of other men, he knew it was a moment he would remember all his life.

The crews of the other tanks, the bobbin ahead of him and the other flails astern, were starting up their engines. Bell gave the order to start up too: and then something terrible and quite ridiculous happened. The starter motor whined, and whined

again. He shouted to his driver. They tried again and again;
no good. At the moment of moments, his engine would not
start.

No motorist stalled in a busy city street ever felt such a fool
as Bell. He had to move, to let out the four tanks behind him.
The line of breakers and the beach were just ahead. There was
only one hope : a tow. He jumped down and seized the towing
cable from the bobbin tank ahead of him and shackled it on to his
own. The Royal Engineers in the bobbin were not at all pleased
at the idea of entering battle towing a derelict 30-ton tank of the
Dragoons. In the excitement and argument, Bell had no time
to look around him and before he expected it the landing craft
was aground and the ramp banged down into the water. The
bobbin lurched forward and jerked the cable taut.

Bell's tank moved a few yards along the deck, and that
did it. The engine started. Bell signalled O.K. to the bobbin
and cast off the tow. As he climbed back to his turret, the
bobbin roared down the ramp and almost vanished into deep
water. His turn had come. Thinking of nothing but his engine
he followed, and in a few seconds waves were breaking against
the turret and splashing over him, and the tank was crawling
towards the shore. For the minute or so while he had fumbled
with the tow, he and the bobbin had been easy targets ; but if
anyone had fired at them, he had been too busy to notice it.

As the tank rose up from the sea and the water streamed off
its hull, Bell in the turret had an impression of stakes on each
side of him with landmines fastened on top of them : and he
glanced along the beach to his right, and saw through the eddying
smoke that the beach was no longer deserted : all along it, as far
as he could see, tanks were rolling out of the water and making
for the dunes. Even in that momentary glance he saw two of
them hit : two of the flails of his own regiment which had
landed a little to his right. And then a petard tank of the Royal
Engineers a few yards ahead of him exploded with a sudden
appalling crash and a gush of flame. At almost the same instant,
Bell felt his own tank shudder and felt rather than heard an

explosion just behind him. He looked round. Flames were
pouring from the stern, just behind his head.

A tank only starts to burn if its petrol is alight. Shermans
had the reputation of burning often and quickly : British tank
men called it brewing up—the phrase also means making tea.
The Germans grimly but aptly called them Tommy Cookers.
When they brewed up, the crew had a matter of split seconds to
get out before they were burnt alive. Seeing the flames, Bell
ordered his crew out and began to get out of the turret himself.
Then a large lump of flaming twisted steel fell off the stern
of the tank and lay blazing on the sand, and he realised that he had
not been hit at all : a piece of the exploded tank ahead of him
had landed on him still burning and then rolled off again. He
shouted to his crew, above the din, that it was all right : but
what, he wondered, had hit the three tanks ahead ? Accurate and
powerful fire was coming from somewhere, but he did not
know where it was. And then he saw a small puff of smoke :
it was the 88-mm. gun in the emplacement a hundred yards
away which was still in action in spite of the bombardment and
was enfilading the beach and picking off the advancing tanks
at point-blank range.

The emplacement at La Rivière, like many others, was built so
that it could only fire along the beach, and not out to sea. On its
seaward side it was protected by 17 feet of concrete, as defence
against naval gunfire ; and the concrete had held. Bell, landing
almost in front of it, was out of its field of fire, but to advance
anywhere he had to cross almost under the muzzle of the gun.
Indeed, all the armour on the beach was having to run the
gauntlet of its fire, and the outcome of the whole of the first assault
in that sector was likely to depend upon somebody doing something about that gun.

At the sight of it, Bell's reaction was immediate ; an instinctive reaction much deeper than all the superficial talk about being
frightened. He might have paused to think that it was somebody
else's job, but that did not cross his mind. He drove on full
speed to the place where the others had been hit, so that he could

see the embrasure in the side of the emplacement and the muzzle of the 88 sticking out of it towards him. There was a steel shield over it. He stopped, and brought his own gun to bear. He was a sitting target, and he knew it, a hundred yards in front of a gun which could knock him out at twenty times that distance. He fired the two rounds of H.E. which were in his gun, but they seemed to have no effect. The German gun fired again, but it fired past him at one of the dozens of other targets down the beach. He fired three more shots with armour-piercing shells. He could not have missed, but he could not see whether his shots had gone through the shield. Before he could fire again, another tank which had not seen what was happening drove up from the beach between him and the gun and masked his fire : he watched it fascinated, waiting to see it brew up, as it crossed the field of fire within fifty yards of the emplacement. Nothing happened. The 88 was dead. He and his tank and his crew had done what all the bombardment that morning had failed to do.

Ahead of him now was the wire and the first of the mine-fields. He crashed through the wire, and started his flail and began to flog his way across the minefield towards the road, the whirling chains churning the soft sandy earth like a gigantic cultivator. At this point he had been ordered to light a green smoke grenade and throw it overboard as a signal to somebody—he could not remember whom—who was coming in behind him. It was the kind of grenade which is lit by a striker like a matchbox, and he lit it ; and at that moment the tank gave a lurch and he dropped the grenade and it fell inside the turret. Immediately, the tank was filled with a lurid green smoke. As it flogged on across the mine-field, he was grovelling in the bottom of it for the grenade and smoke was pouring out of the turret top. He found it at last and came up gasping and dropped it over the side. The flail did not seem to be exploding any mines. The ground was very wet, and it got worse towards the road ; and just before the tank reached the road, it stuck in the mud.

While the tracks of his own tank dug themselves deeper, the two other flails of his team went past him on luckier patches of ground, and climbed the embankment on to the road, hesitated, and then turned left and roared off into the ruins of La Rivière. Annoyed with himself, Bell got out of his tank and climbed carefully down into the minefield. His gunner laughed, and he looked at himself and found the grenade had dyed him bright green all over. He looked back at the beach. The infantry were pouring ashore, and crossing the tidemark where the German gun would have decimated them a few minutes before. All kinds of tanks were following the tracks of the flails through the minefield. Bell began to laugh too; and still beautifully green, he walked back to the beach, down the path which he had flailed, to find a tank recovery vehicle, or somebody else who had time to pull him out.

Almost everything, he thought, had gone ridiculously wrong with his landing. Well, what could they expect? He had always said he was no good as a soldier. It simply never occurred to him, till they gave him a medal long afterwards, that he had gone and done something brave at the very first opportunity he had had in all his five years in the army. But he had; and his moment of blind courage, and his five unerring shots, had been worth the best part of a battalion.

The flail tanks on this end of Gold beach had not had much to do in their primary task of cutting paths through minefields. The first minefield, in which Bell and several others were stuck, turned out to have been sown with Belgian mines which did not explode, either because they had been badly made to begin with, or else because they had lain too long in the wet earth. The second minefield, beyond the road, was much wetter than air photography had suggested. There were reeds and standing water in it. Only one of the flail tanks tried it, and that one was damaged immediately by a mine because the ground was too soft for the flail to work. The commanders of all the other flails which reached the road decided at a glance that the bog was impassable, whether it was effectively mined or not; and they turned left, towards the ruins of La Rivière, and began to drive inland by road. One minefield had been too easy, and the other too difficult for the flails.

Nevertheless, in their secondary rôle as ordinary tanks, the flails and the other Funnies had largely cleared this beach for the infantry, by many such actions as Bell's, and made up to a great extent for the absence of the D.D. tanks, which had not been launched because of the weather and were brought ashore behind the infantry ; and as soon as the flails were safely on the road, they set to work to force the exits from the beach inland.

Beyond the minefields, there was an anti-tank ditch ; and soon the first of the flails, rumbling down the road which led inland from La Rivière, came to the point where the road crossed over the ditch, and the tank commander saw to his surprise that the crossing had not been blown up. He reported by radio to his squadron that he was going to try to cross. " If you hear a loud bang," he said, " you'll know what's happened." But there was no bang : the tank crawled safely over. A little farther on, the road was blocked by an enormous bomb crater. One of the R.E.'s bridge-carrying tanks was called up, and quickly laid a bridge across it. The flails went on and flogged a track for half a mile further. Within half an hour of the landing, the specialised armour had broken a route right through the Atlantic Wall ; and other tanks and the infantry—the Green Howards—began to pour along it into the open country, while the East Yorks cleared out the village.

Further west, in the centre of Gold beach, out of the point-blank range of the gun at La Rivière, the attack went in with even more precision ; but at the opposite end of the beach there was serious trouble in front of the village of Le Hamel. The Germans there had fortified a sanatorium on the sea-front, and the bombardment had left this strong-point still in good working order. The aerial bombing had missed it, and the shelling from the sea, though it had wrecked the sanatorium, had not done any important damage to the guns because they were heavily protected, like La Rivière, on the seaward side. But, again like La Rivière, the main guns of Le Hamel could not fire straight out to sea. They were sited to cover the high water mark along the beach, and so at low tide, close under the strong-point itself, there was a small area of beach which was almost safe but was surrounded by other areas almost impossible for a man to cross alive.

Here other teams of the Royal Engineers and Westminster Dragoons went first, followed seven minutes later by the infantry of the 1st Battalion, the Hampshire Regiment. Among the veterans of the Hampshires was Company Sergeant-Major H. W. Bowers, and his landing may be taken as an example of the experience of the foremost companies, or at least of their survivors.

C.S.M. Bowers was the opposite kind of soldier to Captain Bell: a Cornishman, a regular with seventeen years' service, the son of a soldier, whose army service was both his profession and his pride. At the age of thirty-six, he was not only an old soldier, he was almost an old hand at assault landings, for the landing in Normandy was his fourth. His first had been the invasion of Sicily, and the next two were on the Italian coast. He had won the Military Medal in one of them, and been men-tioned in dispatches in another. So, unlike the great majority who crossed the Channel, he had known what he was in for. It had scared him, more than it had scared Bell who knew so much less about it. All the way over, his stomach had been doing what he called the Butterfly Hop. He had felt the same on his way to the other landings. The trouble was having too much time to think. He knew he would be all right when he got his two feet on dry land, because then there would be no time to think at all, and because he was quite convinced that man for man, and hand to hand, a British soldier was more than a match for a German; but meanwhile, on the landing craft, being a sergeant-major, he had to take care to look much tougher than he felt.

Beside that lurking fear, there had been another private thought at the back of Bowers's mind all through the crossing, a somewhat less sombre one. His British army boots were killing him. Whatever else happened in the invasion, what he meant to win was a nice soft pair of German boots to give his feet a rest.

In the last mile towards the beach, Bowers and his boat-load of men had been encouraged and roused from the lethargy of seasickness, like so many others, by the majestic scope of the bombardment. Above the roar of the shells and rockets going overhead, somebody shouted : " Fancy having that lot on your breakfast plate." It was hard to imagine that anyone could still be alive on the receiving end : so the shock was all the greater when the Hampshires ran ashore straight into a deadly counter-fire.

On the beach, as Bowers waded ashore with his company, the noise and concussion were so stunning that he was uncon-scious—like Henry Meyers on Omaha—of anything more than the few men close beside him and the few yards of sand ahead. But he knew exactly what he had to do, and so he did it. He ran blindly up the beach to the first of the rolls of concertina wire above high water mark, together with other men carrying Bangalore torpedoes. They thrust these into the wire and fired them, and Bowers went through the first of the gaps which they blew and reached the low concrete seawall which lay beyond it. Breathless in the illusory shelter of the wall, he looked round and saw that desperately few of the company had made it : most of them were lying far back towards the water's edge, dead, or wounded, or shocked into immobility. But his company commander, Major D. J. Warren, had got through. The two of them could see their company being slaughtered, but time passed before they saw that the bulk of the fire was sweeping along the beach from right to left, and more time before they spotted its source in a pillbox built on the seaward end of the sanatorium. An attack on the pillbox was imperative, but only four men close to Bowers were fit to move : the major and himself, and his runner, who carried a walkie-talkie radio, and one other soldier.

These four crawled along below the wall towards the pillbox ; but a hundred yards away from it the wall petered out, and they found themselves pinned down on open ground, looking into the muzzles of three or four machine guns and an 88-mm. which was firing close over their heads at the tanks along the beach. While they searched for a way of moving nearer, the radio operator received a message for Major Warren to take over command of the battalion. The major began to crawl back. The radio operator shuddered in the sand and died without a sound. At this, the other soldier turned back and followed the major, and Bowers was left all alone. He was not feeling too good himself. But there was no way forward, so he also crawled back to where he had started; and there he found his colonel with a badly smashed arm.

" What, Bowers, you still alive ? " the Colonel said.

" Just about, sir," Bowers said; and he told him about the pillbox.

The Colonel listened, and then Bowers understood him to say, " Well, go and see what you can do about it."

" Very good, sir," Bowers replied: and he thought, " Christ, he expects me to take on the whole bloody Jerry army."

Bowers had lost his sense of time by then, but a lot had happened while he had been alone. More of the Hampshires had made their way across the beach, but he did not recognise any of his company. For the moment, in fact, the situation was the same as at Omaha, the infantry being shocked and shot to pieces; but the specialised armour had broken the deadlock. The armoured force had lost its commander, who was killed by a sniper very soon after he landed, but the petard tanks had blown breaches in the sea-wall. At least one of the flails, though Bowers had not seen it, had turned along the beach to fight a duel with the pillbox and had got the worst of the encounter; but several more had gone through the gaps in the wall just to the left of the village and started to clear lanes through the minefields up to the coastal road. In the first of these flails was the second-in-command of the armour, Captain B. Taylor. The second was commanded by a sergeant called Lindsay. Captain Taylor's tank was damaged in the minefield, but Sergeant Lindsay reached the road and turned right towards the centre of the village where, according to his orders, he was to find the command post of the Hampshires. Captain Taylor knew the Hampshires were not yet in the village, and with consternation he saw Lindsay accelerate and charge into the village street. He tried to warn him, but his radio was out of action; and Lindsay disappeared into the enemy village and was seen no more that day.

Lindsay, in fact, had soon discovered he was out on his own, ahead of anybody else, but he went on methodically with his business. Finding no infantry at the rendezvous, he shot his way right through the village and round the back of the sanatorium and began the second task in his orders: to clear the road which led out of the village to the westward. He was foiled in that by a tank trap of steel rails planted in the road, and by an anti-tank ditch on the inland side of it; so he turned round and went back into the village, and found a place where he could cross the ditch, and started his third task of flailing a lane through a minefield beyond it. Slowly flogging his way across open country, he was an easy target, and before he had gone far his tank was hit twice by an 88-mm. gun on the cliffs above Arromanches, half a mile away. On the second hit it brewed up, and Lindsay and his crew baled out, all more or less burned, and hid in a cornfield. Lindsay and two of them waited there till midnight, and then rejoined the British forces. The other two had the experience, unusual on that morning on the sea-front, of being taken prisoner by the Germans, but they escaped a few days later and joined the Americans.

This solitary escapade behind the santorium distracted the Germans' attention for a time and probably diverted some of their fire from the Hampshires. It probably also helped Bowers as he started to carry out the order which he thought he had been given.

Bowers was armed with a Sten gun, some British hand-grenades, and a haversack full of Italian grenades, for which he had formed affection and respect in Italy. With this equipment, the only way to " do something about " a pillbox was to get within arm's length of it, and that was impossible head-on along the beach; so he went through the gap which the tanks had made in the seawall, and plotted a possible course through an open space which might have been a garden or a playground.

In the gap he met two sailors of the R.N. Commandos. They had been with him on the landing craft, and he knew them as Paddy and Taffy. " Hey, Harry," they shouted. " Where are you going ? Can we come and have a bit of fun ? "

" Some people have a queer idea of fun," he said, glad of their company and of their tommy guns.

The three men worked their way across the devastated space behind the seawall, fighting it out with some Germans who threatened to take them in the rear, and won a position behind the pillbox, close to the ruins of the sanatorium. A grenade was thrown at them there. It rolled along the ground, rolled so long that Bowers shouted " All right, it's a dud " : whereupon it exploded and wounded Paddy in the leg. The others patched him up. Bowers put the two sailors in a position to cover the pillbox with their tommy guns, because he had spotted a way to get to grips with it. They poured a continuous fire at the openings they could see, and under the protection of their fire he climbed into the ruins, and through them, and found an empty window above the pillbox and jumped down on to the roof of it. He ran across the roof, and lay down on his stomach and leaned over the edge with a grenade in his hand. Through the firing slit below him, somebody was pushing a white sheet of surrender, but he thought " Hell with you, mate, after all this trouble," and he dropped his grenade through the slit.

After the explosion, the door of the pillbox was opened and the survivors ran out. They had their hands up. From his perch on the roof, he looked down at them with interest, partly because they seemed to be shouting that they were Russian, and also because some of them were wearing nice soft German army boots.

As soon as Friedrich Wurster and his companions in the battery on the top of the hill had recovered from the bombardment and the shock of seeing the fleet and the landing craft, they started to fire, with their 105-mm. French guns, against the beach; but the firing was interrupted again and again by low-flying aircraft which drove the gunners to shelter with machine guns and cannon shells. Several men had been killed by the bombing: now the number of casualties grew till the aid post overflowed. It was not very long either till they lost their forward observation post, which was down by the shore. The battery commander was down there, and everyone in the battery heard his last call on the communication system.

"They're coming right in the post," he cried with a frantic note in his voice; and he added "*Lebt wohl, Kamaraden*," and the line was silent. Soon after, the last call came also from regimental headquarters, which was near Merville. It said that Merville had fallen, and headquarters itself was under fire from tanks and infantry. Then that line went dead too, and the battery was isolated.

But Wurster could see the British tanks still coming ashore in what seemed to be limitless numbers, and disappearing into the folds of the hills and the countryside around; and one after another, the neighbouring German strongpoints were falling silent. Wurster knew the battery must be surrounded by tanks already, and that an attack was sure to be made on it very soon; and he heard somebody say there were only three anti-tank grenades left in the battery because they had used the rest in an exercise three days before and they had never been replaced. On the verge of despair, the men looked up for help; but the sky was full of enemy aircraft, and not a single German could be seen. The position was terrible and hopeless; the only choice, if it was a choice, was death or surrender. It had happened so quickly that Wurster could hardly believe it, and yet there was the proof in front of his very eyes: the Atlantic Wall had crumbled away into ruin as soon as it had been tested, and the air force had abandoned them to their fate.

The attack soon came, but it was short. The gunners managed to bring three of their 105's to bear against the tanks and hit two of them, and then the rest broke off the fight and disappeared inland ; and Wurster knew what that meant. The battery was so securely trapped that the British would not waste time in fighting it, but would leave it to be captured at their leisure : the technique which the Germans had taught them in 1940.

It was Bell's squadron of the Westminster Dragoons which captured Wurster's battery in the end, though Bell and Wurster probably never saw each other and certainly never heard each other's name. It did not happen till the next morning, and it happened in a rather peculiar way. After an exciting day, made even more exciting by a totally false report that forty German Tiger tanks were about to attack them, Bell and the squadron of flails settled down for the night in an orchard. Their resting place was within a couple of hundred yards of an outpost of the battery, but neither side knew the other was there and both spent a quiet night. At dawn, the German gunners saw the tanks, and defiantly opened fire. The Dragoons, with two of the flame-throwing tanks of the Engineers, then roused themselves and quickly over-ran the battery and took a hundred prisoners.

A squadron of flail tanks did not expect to take prisoners, and these—after nearly five years of war against Germany—were the first German soldiers that Bell and his men had ever seen on a field of battle. Naturally, they regarded them with tremendous interest and considerable pride, and finding themselves so unexpectedly in the rôle of victor, they treated their fallen enemies with old-fashioned courtesy and honour. This made a deep impression on Wurster, who would have been much less surprised to be bullied or even shot ; and he remembered this first impression a few days later, when he heard of Hitler's denunciation of him and his fellow-prisoners as traitors. This contrast, between the off-hand chivalry of his enemies and the shocking injustice of his own leader's accusation, was often in Wurster's mind in his imprisonment. It forced him to face the bitter alternative : that his own High Command had either been deceived itself about the strength of the Atlantic Wall and the air force, or else had deliberately deceived its own troops. So he began to think critically about the German conduct of the war, and to question the cause for which he and his family had suffered and so many of his friends had died. It was the events of D-Day which started the revulsion in Friedrich Wurster's mind, the revulsion of the man he had been born, against the man that Nazism had made him ; and the same could be said of very many Germans.

Long before Wurster's battery fired its last despairing shots against the tanks, the issue on Gold beach had passed beyond any doubt. The Germans in Le Hamel had held out till the afternoon, and the Hampshires had suffered badly ; but already, in the middle of the morning, seven exits from the beach had been cleared by the armour, the follow-up forces were pouring through them, and the advance had carried over three miles inland and was going strong.

Bell and Bowers, and probably everyone else who fought his way ashore on Gold beach, believed they were the first Britons to set foot on it in the past four years, but they were not. Two soldiers had been there, on New Year's Eve. They went ashore at precisely the spot where Bell landed and made a survey of the beach in the dark ; and although this escapade happened five months before D Day, it had an influence on what happened that day ; and so it deserves to be mentioned. The men were two Commandos called Logan Scott-Bowden and Bruce Ogden Smith ; the first was a major and the second a sergeant, and they were the chief exponents of the curious art of swimming ashore by night and crawling out of the water unobserved.

A small unit for the reconnaissance of the beaches had existed for years. Like many odd little fighting units, it owed its existence to the passionate belief of one man. The man was a naval navigator, Lt.-Cdr. Nigel Willmott ; and his belief was that it was stupid to land an army anywhere on a hostile shore using only charts and photographs, because there were so many things which neither charts nor photographs could show. One of these things was the hardness of the sand : a matter of obvious interest in landing tanks and trucks.

Willmott had always said that the only way to find out such important details was to go and see, and that this was not nearly so difficult or dangerous as it sounded ; but he had had a hard time persuading anyone to let him do it. He himself had swum ashore and reconnoitred Rhodes in 1942 ; but then the projected invasion of Rhodes had been cancelled and the value of his observation had never been tested. Before the invasion of North Africa, his men had been forbidden to land for fear that they would be captured and the plans of the landing would be compromised. In Sicily and Italy, they had had some success ; but his unit, and his theories, only came into their own at the end of 1943, when photographs of the beaches of Northern France showed dark strips here and there, which might have been mud or soft clay. The plan of the whole invasion was suddenly seen to depend upon whether these strips would carry tanks or not, and none of the usual sources of intelligence could answer this question. After years of half-hearted support, Willmott found his ideas received with enthusiasm in the highest quarters. Although it was mid-winter, he was told to go ahead and get samples of the material of certain French beaches as quickly as possible. Now that his chance had come, he himself was ill and not fit for winter swimming ; but he had trained other swimmers. Scott-Bowden and Ogden Smith were two of them.

Sergeant Ogden Smith was the son of a family which had made fishing tackle for nearly two hundred years and sold it in a formidably dignified shop among the hatters and bootmakers in the neighbourhood of St. James's Palace. He had had the kind of education which makes it easy, in the British army, to become an officer. When people asked him why he was not one, he explained that he was quite happy as a sergeant. This was an attitude which had been fashionable, in the first year of the war, among the intelligentsia of the territorial army, of which he had been a member ; but few men stuck to it as a principle, as he did, and resisted the comfort and prestige of being an officer right through the war. Once, he had given in to temptation and started an officers' training course, but he had only been half-hearted and had been returned to unit when he wrote rude words on an intelligence test which he thought was a waste of time. When he was asked why he made a practice of swimming ashore on hostile beaches, he simply said that he liked it—it was not too blood-thirsty, and yet was quite exciting. In short, Ogden Smith was one of those brave but eccentric soldiers who can be a great asset to an army if it does not have too many of them : a square peg who had luckily found a square hole. Very few people knew of the job he had made his speciality. He had not even told his wife, who only knew that he sometimes got week-end leave when he had been on an expedition somewhere, and that she could expect a summons any moment, at the factory in Wales where she was working as welfare supervisor, to join him for a night out in London.

Through most of the winter and spring before the invasion, whenever there were moonless nights, Scott-Bowden and Ogden Smith were taken across the Channel to within a few hundred yards of the shore of France by small landing craft or midget submarines, usually navigated by Willmott. The equipment they took was simple : a lot of thought had been needed to make it so simple. They wore loose-fitting waterproof suits, and each of them carried a torch, compass and watch, an under-water writing tablet, an auger with which to bore holes in the beach and bring up cores of the material it was made of, receptacles for carrying the cores, some meat skewers, and a reel of fine sand-coloured fishing line with a bead on it at every ten yards. The fishing line and the reel, of course, had been made in Ogden Smith's father's workshops. They also took a fighting knife and a .45 Colt, which they had found to be one of the few fire-arms which still work when they are full of salt water and sand ; but they relied more for their safety on the hypothesis that only an exceptionally wakeful sentry would see a man swimming in surf or crawling on a beach at night.

When the shore was in sight on these expeditions, and Will-mott had fixed their exact position, they slipped over the side of their boat and struck out for the breakers together. It was always extremely cold. When they felt bottom, they waded to the edge of the surf and lay there to get their bearings and study the skyline till they were sure of the movements of the sentries ; and then, if everything was reasonably quiet, they stuck a skewer in the sand with the end of the fishing line tied to it, and started to crawl on their stomachs up the beach, probing for mines and unwinding the line as they went. At each bead on the line, they bored a hole and took a sample, and skewered the line again and crawled on, on a compass bearing.

In this way, they made passably accurate surveys of a great many beaches. A large proportion of the places they visited were not in the invasion plans at all, but they were sent to them to ensure that if they were captured they would not be able to tell from their own experience where the invasion was going to be. They found it difficult, after several months, to remember which beach was which ; but they did remember their landing at La Rivière because it was there that Ogden Smith had suddenly remembered the date, and noticed that it was midnight, and had taken it into his head to crawl to where the major was lying listening to the conversation of two sentries on the sea wall, and in a stage whisper had wished him a happy and prosperous New Year.

Sometimes they did other work beside looking for mud and clay. They measured the gradients of the beaches, and charted sand bars off shore where landing craft might have stranded ; and here and there they went inland to measure and investigate obstacles beyond the beaches. They crossed the minefield and the road where Bell's tank stuck, and had a good look at the gun emplacement there. In the middle of January, they were on the top of the fatal shingle bank at Omaha. They made an entirely uneventful tour of Utah ; but on a second visit to Omaha, a sentry came along the beach between them and the sea and tripped over their fishing line. It was through this accident, exciting at the time, that the American army was able to land with the assurance that the beach had not been mined ; because if it had, the sentry would not have been there. The two men bore a charmed life. They were not only never seen, but every time, when they had finished their probing, they waded out through the waves again and swam three hundred yards to sea and flashed their torches away from the land and waited ; and every time, before cold and cramp and exhaustion crippled them, their boat came in and picked them up again. In the quest for mud, they swam ashore on thirty beaches.

The result of this unique performance was to be seen in the plans of the specialised armour : in Bell's landing craft, for one. The tank in front of Bell's was a bobbin, placed there to lay a track across a patch of mud on the beach. Probably the bobbin's crew never guessed how anyone knew the patch of mud was there. On many other parts of the British beaches, track-laying tanks were sent in first on the evidence gouged out by Willmott's swimmers.

This was the final vindication of the ideas which Willmott had pressed forward so long. But even before the invasion, an event occurred which must have given him the greatest satisfaction. General Bradley had been worried by a suspicious patch on photographs of Omaha. He had never heard of beach reconnaissance, but he asked British Intelligence whether anything was known about the texture of the beach. The inquiry was passed to Willmott. Without telling the General, he sailed across and landed Scott-Bowden and Ogden Smith ; and the next day he attended an American conference and produced a sample of sand from his pocket, with an elaborately casual air, explaining that his unit had fetched it the night before, and that the beach was firm and would carry tanks all right. This achievement amazed General Bradley, and he generously said so. Perhaps he perceived the pride which Willmott believed he was hiding.

As for Ogden Smith, his wife received an invitation to an investiture at Buckingham Palace, where he was to receive the

Military Medal, though nobody had told her what he had done to earn it. The date of the investiture was June 6th. On June 5th, she had already put on her best hat and was on her way to the railway station in Wales when she had a telephone message to say that her husband was unavoidably detained and would not be turning up to meet the King. Nothing surprised her by then. She went home, and sadly put the hat away again, hoping she would need it to go to the Palace one day.

It would have been quite in character for this curious soldier to have been late for his own investiture, but in fact it was hardly his fault. He and Scott-Bowden were on Omaha Beach again : this time not alone. The American army had taken them there as guides. They were the only people in England, so far as anyone knew, who had ever been there before.

Others of Willmott's men were playing an important and peculiar part in the invasion. They were lying about a mile off-shore in midget submarines, one at each end of the British sector ; and at H Hour they had already been there for three nights and two days and were not far from being dead of suffocation.

These submarines had the distinction of being the first of the whole invasion fleet. The code name of their operation was Gambit. Their crews, uneasy about this name, had looked up the word in the dictionary, and found it meant an opening move in a game of chess in which the player deliberately sacrifices a pawn. As they suspected, the name was shrewdly chosen. They were the pawn.

The submarines were the type called X Craft, about fifty feet long and five and a half feet in diameter. Each of them was commanded by a lieutenant R.N.V.R. with a crew of two, and each of them carried two of Willmott's specialised navigators ; and their job was to place themselves as lightships. It was a simple and common-sense idea, because in the light of dawn on D-Day, and in the heat of battle, it was expected to be difficult for the first landing craft or their escorts to fix their exact positions

from observations of the shore, and mist or an off-shore wind
which blew the smoke of the bombardment out to sea might
make the shore invisible, as it did in fact at Utah. The X Craft,
on the other hand, were meant to arrive off the shore 36 hours
before anyone else, so that they would have a whole day, if they
needed it, to put themselves exactly in position by periscope
bearings and anchor there. The fleet could then home on them.
The American navy rejected the idea. If it had not, it might have
succeeded in landing the troops at Utah and Omaha in the right
places ; but still, its decision may have been wise. The reason
for turning down the idea was that the X Craft might be spotted
and draw attention to the beaches, and there certainly was such
a risk. On the British sector, the X Craft mission was successful
and useful ; but the bad weather and the postponement made
it far more risky than the British themselves had foreseen.

Of these two humble vanguards of the fleet, X23, commanded
by Lt. George Honour, R.N.V.R., had the more easterly position,
a mile off the port of Ouistreham. His craft was unarmed, and
was fitted with a radio beacon, a flashing light on an 18-foot
telescopic mast, and an underwater signalling device, as well as
extra navigational equipment and marked charts. It could not
have been anything but a lightship. If the Germans had captured
it, or its sister ship at the other end of the beaches, they could
not possibly have missed the implication. These two obvious
clues to the exact position of the British assault lay for 56 hours
within a mile of the Germany army—and lay there in an on-
shore wind and in weather worse than any they were designed
or built to stand.

But the responsibility of his job had not weighed too heavily
on Lt. Honour before he sailed ; it was only afterwards that the
risk he had run began to make him lie awake at night. He knew
all about X Craft. Two years before, when he was skipper of a
landing craft running stores into Tobruk, he had impulsively
put his name down for a job which was only described as
hazardous ; and ever since then, he had been training with X
Craft at Rothesay on the Clyde, and in the deserted sea lochs in

the west of Scotland. At Rothesay, he had mainly distinguished himself by marrying one of the Wren drivers at the base, and on the evening of June 3rd, when he sailed his small ship out of Portsmouth harbour and through the fleet which was waiting off Spithead, his wife was working as a censor officer in H.M.S. *Victory*, the naval base ashore ; and she guessed, although he had never told her, exactly what he was doing.

All through the night of June 3rd, X23 and her sister ship X20 were towed by trawlers southward across the empty Channel. At 4.15 the next morning, Saturday, the trawlers slipped them and went home, and an hour later, in the dawn, the submarines submerged and each set course alone towards its assigned position.

Inside an X Craft there was not much room to move. A short man could stand upright in the control position ; elsewhere, there was less than five feet of headroom. There were two bunks, one amidships and the other on top of the batteries. The crew breathed oxygen, but after a time, especially with five men on board, the atmosphere became almost unbearable, and the smell of diesel oil, although it was harmless, gave a feeling of suffocation. There was no conning tower, and at sea, even when the submarine was surfaced, waves often washed right over it. At sea, therefore, the hatches could not be opened, and the only way out was for one man at a time to enter a watertight compartment, shut the door behind him, and then open a hatch above his head. If the compartment flooded, it had to be pumped out before the next man could use it. Many of the men who volunteered for X Craft had to give up because they could not stand the sensation of being shut in.

From five in the morning on Saturday till half past ten at night, Honour and his crew, shut down in the darkness below the surface, drove slowly on towards the coast of France. At dusk, they had reached the edge of a German minefield. They surfaced, and crossed it in the dark ; and at four o'clock on Sunday morning the echo sounder showed only ten fathoms below them, and they could see the coast as a shadow in the night. They went down to the bottom then, and lay there to wait for daybreak.

At 8 they came up to periscope depth, and the navigator, who was a regular naval lieutenant called Lyne, roughly fixed their position from landmarks ashore. They set course to the east for two hours, and lay on the bottom again until five in the evening, when they came up a mile off shore for a final fix. This was easier said than done. One of the submarine's pumps had gone wrong, and so had the gyro compass. It was two hours before Lyne was perfectly satisfied that he had identified marks ashore and taken accurate bearings of Ouistreham lighthouse, and the church towers of Ouistreham, Langrunes and La Delivrande ; and all that time Honour and his crew, short of one pump, were in the utmost difficulty in holding the craft four feet below the surface. None of them had much doubt of what would happen if she broke surface : for through the periscope Lyne could see German soldiers bathing and playing with a ball on the beach below their artillery observation tower.

At about this time, Honour's wife, back in Portsmouth, heard another Wren officer say, " We've lost those two midget subs." But she was not supposed to know anything about them, so she could not ask questions.

After dark on Sunday night they surfaced, thankful to be able to breathe fresh air and blow out the submarine, and they anchored in a position which Lyne was confident was within fifty yards of the spot assigned to them. By then, a considerable sea and swell were running, and waves were breaking over the submarine all the time. All the men were tired and dizzy from breathing the artificial atmosphere, and several of them were washed overboard ; but they were wearing frogmen's suits and had made themselves fast with lifelines, so that did not matter very much. Their weariness was overcome by the thought that there was not much longer to wait ; and so it was a bitter blow when at one a.m. they heard the radio signal which meant a day's postponement. That morning at dawn they were all extremely gloomy as they battened themselves down again and sank to the bottom for another nineteen hours' incarceration.

All day, they lay and sat around, moving and talking as little as they could, because they were listless and because they had to save oxygen. Even at sixty feet, the submarine began to rock and bump gently on the bottom. That implied a rough sea above, and each of them, lost in his own thoughts and depressed by semi-suffocation, wondered whether there would be a second postponement and, if there was, whether they could get back to England before their oxygen failed. Two or three times during the day they heard propellers : always an ominous sound in a submarine submerged in enemy waters. By evening, their third evening off the invasion shore, they felt that their luck had been too good to last, and when they surfaced it was with more than the usual apprehension that an E boat would be waiting for them there. Honour crawled into the watertight compartment, and shut himself in and opened the hatch above. A deluge of water fell on him, and filled the whole compartment. He clambered out, and hanging on to the casing he shut the hatch, and waited alone until the pumps could clear it. There was nothing to be seen on the darkening stormy sea : but the ship was pitching and rolling heavily and tugging the anchor rope. Every sailor knows the fear of being anchored off a lee shore in worsening weather. That was Honour's fear that night; and no lee shore was ever so menacing. If X23 had been wrecked, no shipwreck would ever have had such terrible consequences.

That night, they heard the signal that the invasion was on, and they went to the bottom again where they could lie more safely. At 4.45 in the morning they came up, started the radio beacon and the underwater signal, and raised the mast and flashed their light to seaward ; and at dawn, in the last extremity of exhaustion, they saw the sight which was ample reward for sixty-four hours' submersion : the host of ships converging towards their light. They had the Germans' view of the fleet approaching, and it was terrifying, even before the start of the shelling over their heads. At 6.55 the first wave of landing craft, led by a launch equipped to receive the sound and radio signals, passed by the solitary submarine, and its job was done. At 8, Honour cut the anchor rope because he and his crew were much too weak to raise it; and twenty-four hours later, he was back in Portsmouth, to explain to his wife exactly what he had been doing and—which was much more difficult—to explain to his base ship why he had lost the anchor.

Among the ships which bore down on Honour's submarine at dawn, the only naval engagement of D-Day was fought, and was quickly ended.

The bombardment fleet for the eastern beaches had been led, in the latter part of the crossing, by two Norwegian destroyers, *Stord* and *Svenner*. This position had been meant as a compliment by the British naval authorities, and the Norwegian crews appreciated the honour, uncomfortable though the position might have been.

The captain of *Svenner* had particular reason to be proud of the place which his ship had been given, for she was brand-new. He was a 30-year-old Lieutenant-Commander from Trondheim called Tore Holthe; and he had been in the Norwegian navy before the war and had seen it grow, from the humiliatingly feeble state in which the country's neutrality had kept it, to a force which had sailed and fought its destroyers in British flotillas all over the North Atlantic. His own story had run parallel to his navy's development.

When the Germans invaded Norway in 1940, Holthe was captain of a torpedo boat. At that time, the Norwegian merchant fleet was one of the largest and most modern in the world; but Holthe's torpedo boat, a vessel of about 100 tons, was coal-fired and had been built before the first world war: a museum piece among warships. The German invasion caught him, as completely surprised as all Norwegians, in Arendal on the south coast of the country. Before anyone knew what had happened, the Germans were in all the south and west coast ports, and as the torpedo boat could only steam a negligible distance before it needed more coal, there was absolutely nowhere that Holthe could take it to keep it out of the hands of the Germans. So he sent his crew home, and scuttled his pathetic ship, and set off to look for some more efficient means of fighting against the Germans. He made his way to the west coast, and requisitioned a fishing boat and set sail for Britain, with three even younger naval officers, to an exile which was to last for exactly five years.

His first command in Britain was better, but not much better : a Norwegian destroyer, so called, of the vintage of 1909. But that was just after Dunkirk, when the British were glad of the help of anything that would float, to help to repel the invasion which they in their turn expected every night ; and for eighteen months, Holthe coaxed his ancient vessel up and down the east coast of England.

But his next appointment was a big step forward : first lieutenant of a new Hunt Class destroyer, the first modern ship of its size which the Norwegian navy had ever owned. After that he became first lieutenant of *Stord*, when she was also new ; and he sailed with her as far south as Gibraltar and as far north as Murmansk, and was serving aboard her when she played her distinguished part in the sinking of the German cruiser *Scharnhorst*.

And finally, after nearly four years in Britain, he got a new ship of his own : *Svenner*, straight out of the builder's yard, a fleet destroyer of 1,800 tons, four 4.7 inch guns, eight torpedo tubes and a complement of over 200 men. No captain can ever have had more pride in a new command : Holthe's pride in *Svenner* was national as well as personal.

By then, it was already the spring of 1944, and even while *Svenner* was working up, it was clear she was destined for a part in the invasion. Most of her practice shoots, up in Scapa Flow, were at targets ashore, and most of her fleet exercises were rehearsals of landings. In May, she sailed to the Clyde ; and there Holthe received the orders for her first action, and his own

first action in command of a modern ship. *Svenner* and the flotilla
to which she was joined were to escort the capital ships to the
area off Ouistreham where they would anchor to start the
bombardment; and then she was to go farther inshore, to
3,000 yards if necessary, to engage the coastal defences at short
range.

The fleet sailed on June 2nd : the battleships *Warspite* and
Ramillies, the old monitor *Roberts*, the cruisers *Mauritius*,
Arethusa, *Danae*, *Dragon* and *Frobisher*. Holthe was free then to
tell his crew what they were going to do. Most of them, like himself, had been completely cut off for years from their own country
and their homes and families. The only thing they really wanted
in life was to help to win the war and get home again ; and the
scope of the plan he described elated them because, indirect
though it was as a route to Norway, it was so clearly a positive
step in that direction. The sight of the fleet of which they were
part had inspired them too, and their excitement increased as they
steamed down the Irish Sea, and were joined by American,
British, French, Dutch and Polish warships, and by the scores
of old merchant ships whose fate was to be scuttled to form the
first breakwaters of the artificial harbours off Arromanches and
Omaha.

This was the force which turned round, on Eisenhower's
postponement, and steamed north for twelve hours to waste
the extra day ; and so it was on their third day at sea that they
rounded Lands End, and steamed up Channel, and reached the
area south of the Isle of Wight which the navy called Piccadilly
Circus, where all the convoy routes converged to turn south
through the ten channels which minesweepers had already
cleared ahead.

At 11 p.m. they entered the easternmost channel, between
the lines of lighted buoys which the minesweeper flotillas had
laid like street-lamps across to France. *Mauritius*, the flagship
of the eastern bombardment fleet, was in the van, with *Svenner*
30 degrees on her port bow at a range of 1,000 yards. At midnight, Holthe ordered his crew to action stations, and felt for the

first time in *Svenner* the intense aliveness which pervades a ship before an important action. A little after midnight, the force moved into line ahead, with *Stord* leading and *Svenner* second. A stream of reports was reaching Holthe from the radar and hydrophone watches : the sea was full of the sound of propellers, and the ether full of echoes ; so full that Holthe could only assume that all the ships were friendly and that the worst risk he was running was the risk of collision. The air also was full of sound ; the sound which had already woken England of the endless fleets of aircraft overhead. Towards dawn, from *Svenner's* bridge, Holthe and his look-outs saw the flashes of bombs on the coast ahead, and the flicker of fires reflected by the clouds.

At 5.30, in the grey of dawn, the battleships and cruisers anchored. By then, the shore could be seen, and certainly the fleet could be seen from the shore, but the Germans were silent. The fleet was not only in range of the shore ahead, but also of heavy batteries at Le Havre, which was seven or eight miles away to the east ; and to protect the ships from that direction, aircraft began to lay a smoke screen. *Svenner* and the other destroyers stopped to the west of the capital ships, to wait for the minesweepers to open a channel even closer towards the shore. This moment was a climax of the first ten years of Holthe's career : the fleet poised for action, the scene set for a battle of supreme importance to his country, and he with the most perfect of modern ships and a well-tried crew at his command. It was in that moment that he saw, three hundred yards away, the unmistakable track of a torpedo.

Three German torpedo boats had emerged from the smoke screen on the far side of the fleet.

At that stage of the war, the German navy had only three ships larger than destroyers that were fit to go to sea ; its U-boats were fighting a losing battle, and its coastal forces that night had failed even to detect the invasion fleet until it was within gunshot of the shore. The navy, in fact, was a spent and ruined force ; but its regular officers would not have admitted that, even to themselves, and when the commander of the torpedo boats was ordered to sea that morning, he acted as any good officer of any navy would have acted. His name was Heinrich Hoffman; his ship was of 1,400 tons, the size of a small destroyer; and perhaps no other officer of any navy has ever found himself facing such odds or offered such a target.

Hoffman had been in the Channel since 1940, except for occasional sorties to Norway and the Bay of Biscay, and he had been in action against the British raids on Dieppe and St. Nazaire. After those four years, there was not very much he had still to learn about quick night battles between naval forces. He felt respect and a kind of sporting affection for the British navy. But experience of the last year or so had taught him to care more about air than surface opposition, and he believed it was a useless risk to go to sea on moonlit nights, when aircraft had the advantage over ships. So on the night of the 5th of June, he had decided to keep his flotilla in harbour at Le Havre, not because of the roughness of the sea, but because of the moon.

It was about two a.m. when the first warning of enemy forces reached him from the naval operations staff ashore. The report was of six large ships in the Bay of the Seine, steering a southerly course. It probably originated from a naval radar station at Cherbourg which had not yet been put entirely out of action by the bombing and jamming which had destroyed the army's radar chain. Hoffman had six ships in his flotilla, and he called his captains together at once. Only three of the six, including his own ship, were ready for sea. At about half past three, he led this half-flotilla out of harbour.

So far, Hoffman had no idea that his three small ships alone were challenging the greatest force which Britain and America had ever put to sea. But as he left harbour and set a westerly course, he heard the fleets of aircraft. He did not bother about them, because he knew that if they had been out for attacks on shipping, they would not have flown so high; but the quantity of aircraft, together with the report of ships, soon made him

suspect that the invasion was beginning. In spite of that suspicion, he held his course and speed. He personally believed
at that time that if the invasion could be held off, the war might
yet be won, but that if the invasion succeeded, nothing then
could save Germany. So he was perfectly ready to sacrifice
himself and his flotilla if he could help to defeat the invading
forces.

When he first saw the smoke screen, he thought it was a
natural bank of fog; but then he saw an aircraft dropping
smoke floats, and he suddenly recognised that the whole mass of
it across his course was artificial. That finally confirmed his
belief that a major operation was under way. His ships had no
radar, and so he had no means of knowing what he might find
beyond the wall of smoke; but he went into it, at 28 knots in
line ahead.

The sight which he saw when he came through the smoke
amazed him, prepared though he was for something extraordinary.
Straight ahead of him, in the early light of dawn, he saw six
battleships or heavy cruisers, and so many minor warships that
he had no time to count them; and yet, to his further surprise,
not one of them opened fire. He signalled his base that he was
going to attack, set course to present the smallest silhouette,
and had time to manœuvre his ships into a text-book approach.
Between them, they fired seventeen torpedoes.

When Holthe saw the torpedo, he instantly gave the order
for full ahead and full port rudder, and the telegraph rang and
the engine room acknowledged the order; then time seemed to
stop. He stood on the bridge and watched the wake of the
torpedo tearing through the choppy sea towards him, and knew
it was going to hit his ship, because she was lying stopped and
there was never a chance to get steerage way on her. And he had
a moment's astonishment because the torpedo was coming from
the port side, right out of the middle of the fleet of friendly
ships. And then for a fraction of a second his heart lifted because
the wake always follows behind a torpedo, and the wake came

so near that he thought the torpedo had gone under her. Then it hit. It hit her amidships, and oil went up in a great fountain and covered the whole ship from bow to stern.

For Holthe himself on the bridge the physical shock of the explosion was small. His emotions were numb. Immediately, *Svenner* was visibly buckling amidships : he knew she was doomed. Probably less than two minutes passed before he gave the order to abandon ship. The boats were wrecked : the crew got some rafts overboard, and began to jump. She broke in two and sank, and as she went down Holthe jumped from the bridge itself.

When he came up and began to swim, men of his crew were scattered all round him in the water as far as he could see, and he was confident most of them had got clear except for the engine room watch who must have been instantly killed. He saw the canopy of his motor boat floating, and he swam to it and held on, and then looked back at the beautiful ship which had been his pride. To seamen, the sinking of a ship is like a death, and the death-throes of *Svenner* were grotesque. Her bow and stern rose high out of the water, and her broken midships section stuck on the bottom of the shallow sea ; and there she stood, a gigantic ironic V for victory. Holthe watched her with the most intensely bitter disappointment that she had not lived to fire a single shot.

At the moment when Hoffman fired his torpedoes, the first British salvo of shells fell in front of his bows, so close that his ship, still moving at 28 knots, steamed into the spouts of water before they fell. The concussion put out all the lights on board, and cut off the radio. He altered course abruptly to avoid the fire, and returned it impudently with his four-inch guns. By vigorous evasive tactics, all three of his ships got back into the smoke screen, and not one of them was hit.

Emerging again on the homeward side of the smoke, Hoffman met a forlorn and almost pathetic sight. Three armed fishing boats, the only other German naval units which had reacted to the report of enemy ships, were steaming purposefully at eight knots towards the sounds of battle. He could not tell them what they were up against, because his radio was gone; but his sudden appearance was sufficient warning. The British gunfire, controlled by radar, followed him through the smoke, and then transferred to the leading fishing boat. All three turned back, and he crossed their bows to try to draw the fire back on himself; but one fishing boat was hit and sank. British fighter bombers appeared then, and escorted Hoffmann's flotilla back to port.

From Hoffmann's point of view, it was the most extraordinarily bad luck that *Svenner* was the only ship he hit. His seventeen torpedoes went right through the close-packed British fleet. Two of them passed between the battleships *Warspite* and *Ramillies*. A third headed straight for *Largs*, the headquarters ship of the area, which only avoided it by going full speed astern. The destroyer *Virago* reported a near miss. The torpedo which hit *Svenner* had already gone through the fleet from one side to the other; *Svenner* was on the west of it, and Hoffmann on the east, and they were never in sight of each other.

Nobody would have denied that the spirit and execution of Hoffman's attack would have been a credit to any navy. He succeeded because the British smoke screen protected him, and because the British radar was confused by the enormous number of echoes from British ships. But his was the only action of any kind whatever that the German navy took on D-Day, and *Svenner* and the American destroyer *Corry*, which was hit by a shore battery north of Utah, were the only warships of their size which were lost that day.

Thirty-two of Holthe's crew were killed, and two of the British liaison men who had been on board with him. After half an hour, the stern of *Svenner* rolled over and disappeared, but the bow stood there for a long time, and thousands of troops on their way to the beach saw it projecting above the surface, like a tombstone. Holthe was picked up, while the bombardment in which he had hoped to take his part roared overhead towards the beach and the town of Ouistreham.

The bombardment was an ordeal for the French people in the towns and villages on the coast. It was short, but it was far more intense than any air raid, and every house which was close to the shore was destroyed or badly damaged; but the number of civilians injured or killed was smaller than might have been expected. All of them, of course, had been warned for at least a year, by the Germans and by the B.B.C., to go away from the coast, and more than half of the original population had left. Some areas had been forcibly cleared by the Germans; and many of the houses were seaside villas which had only been used in peacetime in the summer. So most of the ruins which lined the shore by the morning of D-Day had already been empty, or full of German soldiers, before the bombardment started. Far greater numbers of French people were killed in the towns inland—Caen, Montebourg, Valognes, Pont l'Abbé—which remained on the perimeter of the bridgehead for several weeks.

On Utah and Omaha, there were not many houses, because the coastal villages were a mile or more inland. Probably no Frenchman witnessed the landing on Omaha, and very few on Utah. One of the few on Utah had a nightmarish experience which yet—since it ended happily—had some comedy in it too. He lived in a cottage just behind the dunes, and his wife had just had her first baby. Early in the morning of D-Day, he heard things going on outside, and went out to see what was happening. While he was out, his cottage was hit by a shell, and he saw it collapse, with his wife and the baby inside it. Distraught, he ran back and began to drag away the wreckage with his hands, but before he had moved very much of it the first American troops came storming over the dunes and he was seized and marched over the beach and hustled into a landing craft. He protested and shouted and tried to tell everyone about his wife and baby; but nobody understood a word he said, and before he knew what had happened he was hoisted into a troopship and

taken across to England. Perhaps the Americans took him away
for his own safety. Perhaps they thought anyone so near the
beach was either a collaborator or a German. He never knew.

Later in the day, some other Americans passed the ruined
cottage and heard the baby crying, and paused long enough
in the battle to dig out the mother and child, both of them still
alive; but by then, of course, the first lot had moved on, and
nobody knew what had become of the father. It was a long time
before either the man or his wife discovered that the other was still
alive, and much longer still before anyone could spare the time
and transport to send the outraged Frenchman back to France.

But in contrast with the deserted dunes of Omaha and Utah,
the British and Canadian beaches were on a stretch of coast
with small towns and villages, almost continuously joined
together by a line of villas and hotels and boarding-houses
where middle-class French families, in summers before the war,
had taken their children to play on the beautiful sands. The
names of these insignificant seaside resorts are famous now,
with the peculiar immortality which wars confer on the places
which they ruin: Le Hamel and La Rivière, the two small ham-
lets at the ends of Gold beach; the oyster port of Courseulles
and the town of St. Aubin, where the Canadians landed; Langrune and Luc-sur-Mer, where the Royal Marine Commandos
fought from house to house; and Lion, and the port of Ouistreham, with its seaside resort called Riva Bella. In all these places,
the French people who still remained suffered like the people
of Coventry and Rotterdam and Hamburg; and yet on the
whole, through the worst of the bombardment, they were
buoyed up by the thought that the four years of German rule
were ending. Perhaps they did not think very clearly about the
liberation of their country; if they had, it might have seemed
bad luck that the process of liberation had begun on their door-
steps, instead of somebody else's. But for most of them, liberation
had some more personal importance. To mention a single
example, Mme. Sustendal, who lived on the sea front at Luc,
ran to the garage of her house when the shelling started, and

pushed her two small boys underneath her husband's car, and got her own head and shoulders underneath it too, and she lay there quite happily and almost without any fear, illogically certain that British bombs and shells would never harm her. The reason for her happiness was this : her husband, the village doctor, had made plans of the local defences and sent them to England, and he had been arrested and sent to a concentration camp. To her, liberation meant simply that she could begin to hope she might see him again alive.

It was in Ouistreham that people suffered most, because it was the largest of all the towns along the invasion coast, and because the defences of its little port at the mouth of the Caen Canal were right in amongst its houses. Ouistreham and its smart beach of Riva Bella had a population of four thousand before the war began, and something like twenty thousand in the summer holiday seasons. All of these had moved inland except four hundred ; but of the four hundred, one third were killed on D-Day and another third were seriously injured.

A young man called Raoul Mousset was a native of Ouistreham. As it happened, he was in Caen on the night of June 5th, but his wife Odette was in Ouistreham where they had bought a small hotel six months before. The sound of the bombing and shelling woke him, and soon after dawn Caen was full of rumours of what was happening on the coast. Mousset had a truck, and he set off to join his wife. But only a little way beyond the town, the road was blocked, and he heard the sounds of battle close at hand. German soldiers stopped him and told him he could not go any farther, and one of them said that Ouistreham was burning.

"Did you see the Hotel de Normandie ? " Mousset asked.

"No, I didn't," the German said. "It isn't there any more. It's gone."

Odette had looked out when the anti-aircraft fire had started just about midnight and she saw the parachutes coming down, beyond the River Orne. She thought at first it was a German exercise ; but the town was awake, the firing was very heavy, and rather than go to bed, she stayed downstairs with one or two late customers in her café, uneasily discussing what was happening. About two o'clock two German army truck drivers rushed in. They had been in for drinks earlier in the evening, and their trucks were still parked outside. Perhaps they had been impressed by Odette, who was a remarkably pretty young woman. Now they had come to urge her breathlessly to get away while she could. The English were coming, they said, and they were getting out. But of course she refused to leave her hotel. She heard the trucks drive away towards Caen.

She was still in the hotel when it was hit by a British bomb about four o'clock in the morning. But she ran out through the back door unhurt and crossed the yard and took refuge in a little wood on a patch of waste ground between the houses. From there, distraught and shocked, she watched the hotel begin to burn, and flare up till the roof crashed in, and then die down till only the walls remained.

About twenty of her neighbours had joined her in the wood. At seven o'clock a naval shell fell on this group of anxious women and killed thirteen of them. Odette was appallingly wounded.

The carnage in the wood was discovered by Leon Tribolet, the local barber, and a young civil servant called Pierre Desoubeaux, who were both wardens in the Ouistreham civil defence force. They sorted out the wounded and the dead, and carried Odette away to the first aid post.

The civil defence had been on the alert since the previous evening, because Pierre Desoubeaux, for one, was connected with the resistance movement and knew a code message which the B.B.C. was to broadcast when the invasion was coming. He had listened in secret for months, and among the hundreds of code sentences on the evening of 5th June, he had heard it at last : the arrow pierces steel. He had gone round the town warning the rest of the civil defence men to stand by ; and so when the bombing started, they were as ready as they could be.

But there were only ten men in the first aid squads, and the size of their disaster overwhelmed them.

The post was in the village square, next door to the Mairie and the eleventh-century church. The only French doctor in Ouistreham was Dr. Poulenc, who was 73 years old. He was still an efficient doctor in spite of his age, but early in the day a bullet went through the palm of his right hand, and after that Pierre Desoubeaux and others who had a little first aid experience had to take a share of the heaviest jobs, like amputations. Early in the day also, the chemist's shop was destroyed, and the only reserve of drugs and dressings was lost; but mercifully, there was plenty of morphine. It was Pierre who gave Odette an injection and silenced her screams, but there was not much more they could do for her.

From five o'clock onwards the rows of injured grew on the floor of the first aid post, and so did the rows of dead in the yard outside. More and more people brought in their wounded relatives, and the uninjured stayed to help, or to pray with the curé, or just to lament. At eight o'clock the mayor of the town, Charles Lefauconnier, a civil defence man himself, burst in on this terrible scene, and people noticed an expression of joy on his face. " They're landing," he shouted. " They're landing." The shout was taken up all through the post. Dr. Poulenc was told, in the middle of an operation. People murmured it into the ear of wounded men on the edge of unconsciousness. It lifted their hearts.

Pierre Desoubeaux went out again soon after this, on his search for more wounded, and as he passed through the square, in a lull in the thunder of battle, he heard an unexpected sound : men whistling the Marseillaise, rather badly. And round the corner, in single file, came a dozen British soldiers. Pierre did not think he was an emotional man, but after the tension of the night, at the sight and sound of this symbol of liberty, he burst into tears. Ashamed of himself, he shook hands with the first of the soldiers ; and the soldier, perhaps feeling that this was a moment in the Frenchman's life which called for a souvenir, felt in his battledress pockets, and took out his pipe, and presented it to Pierre, who cherished it for years.

The first Allied soldiers to come to the first aid post caused even more surprise. People greeted them with joyous shouts of " Tommy ! " The Tommies, however, answered in the dialect of Brittany, for they were men of the Free French troop of No. 4 Commando—the first French soldiers to land that day in France.

Towards the evening of D-Day, the Royal Army Medical Corps got through to the first aid post in Ouistreham, and helped Dr. Poulenc to repair the damage which British shells had caused. They brought penicillin, which was still unknown in France. For many of the patients, this help had come too late ; but Odette Mousset was still alive, and sometimes conscious. A British medical officer examined her and told her she would have to go to England, because her wounds were far too bad to be treated on the battlefield itself. But she refused to go, because her husband Raoul, so far as she knew, was still in Caen and would not know where she was.

But Raoul, after hearing that their hotel had been destroyed, was quite determined to get home to see if his wife was all right. By the time he had reached the front line, on the German side, the battle was raging with its full fury between Caen and Ouistreham. Naturally, the Germans were ready to shoot any Frenchman who tried to cross to the British side, on suspicion of being a spy. All day on D-Day, Raoul prowled round unhappily, turned back whichever way he tried to go, either by German patrols or by British artillery fire. By nightfall, anxiety drove him to desperation. He came on a dead German soldier, and beside him a bicycle. He stole the bicycle, and pedalled furiously down the main road to the coast ; and by the kind of miracle which is sometimes the reward of determination, he went right through the German front, and the no-man's land, and the British perimeter, and nobody tried to stop him. At length, he found Odette. By then, the English doctor had said she would be dead the next day if she still would not go to England.

Few of the stories of Ouistreham had a happy ending, but

this one had ; for Odette was put in a dukw, and taken out to a landing craft which was full of wounded soldiers ; and the British army let Raoul go with her. She was in hospital in England for eleven months ; but then they both went home to the ruins of Ouistreham.

At the village of Graye-sur-Mer, at the present day, there is a bridge where the road from the village to the beach goes over a stream in the marshy land behind the dunes. Families on holiday use the bridge to go down to the beach to bathe, and carts drive over it to bring up sand and seaweed ; but many of the local people have forgotten its history and do not know that a British tank is buried underneath it.

Graye is three miles east of La Rivière, where Bell landed. Graye and the oyster port of Courseulles, and the villages of Bernières and Saint Aubin, all lie close together on the next stretch of shore which was attacked : Juno Beach, where Canadian infantry and tanks made the first assault with the help of the British specialised armour. The bridge, or most of it, was built between 8 o'clock and 9.15 on D-Day, and it was a masterpiece of improvisation under fire, and also a good example of the use of the specialised armour. To put its story in perspective, one must look back beyond that day at the lives of some of the humble British sappers who were there when it was built.

One of them was a coalminer from Sunderland whose real name was William Dunn ; but as he was a North Country man in a mainly southern unit, his army friends all called him George or Geordie, and most of them never knew he had another name. George was 20. His 21st birthday was on 9th June, and for two or three weeks it had been a matter of argument whether he and his tank crew would celebrate it in an English pub or a continental café.

George Dunn, for his age, was a resourceful, adaptable, well-balanced kind of man ; he had been trained to that in a fairly hard school. He had been born and lived all his life in a cottage in a row in a mining village. All the men he knew at home were miners. His father had been a miner; but when George was thirteen, he had been killed by a fall of roof. Naturally, the very day when George left school, when he was fourteen, he went to the mine and asked for a job and got it. He had never thought of being anything but a miner, and expected to be a miner all his life.

But the job had not lasted long. The mine exported most of its coal to France and when France fell to the Germans in 1940, the mine was simply shut down and almost the whole of the village was suddenly thrown out of work. George was seventeen then. He had to go on the dole, like all his friends and neighbours; and then of course he had to take whatever job was offered him by the labour exchange. They drafted him to an oil refinery far away. It was strange work and a strange place, and he was unhappy; and so, although he had never had any dreams of being a soldier, he was not at all sorry when his army call-up came.

An outsider, looking at George's village and the life which the British social system had given him so far, might have thought he had not very much to be grateful for, and less reason than most men to fight for his King and country. But it was not in George's nature to think that way. The outsider would only have seen the blackness and bleakness of the village; but George had only seen the friendliness and kindness and good humour of its people. It was home; and although he may sometimes have felt that society had given his family a raw deal between the wars, he was just as ready to fight to defend his home as anyone else: more so than many men who had far more material possessions but had never been taught to value them.

Anyhow, the army struck George as a very lazy life compared with mining, and he set himself to get as much out of it as he could. He soon found there was plenty of fun to be had in it, and plenty to learn. With that attitude, of course, he made a good job of it. By D-Day, he was driver of a Churchill tank. But he still did not want to do anything when the war was over except to go home and start in the mine again.

The radio operator of George's tank was even younger than he was. His name was Roy Manley. His father had also died when he was young. But apart from that coincidence, the two men were almost as different as two Englishmen could have been. Roy came from the opposite end of England, from Devonshire. When he left school, he had got a job with a builder's merchant in Exeter; and when he first met George, the two of them could hardly understand each other's language.

George's first impression of Roy was that he was rather a mother's boy; and perhaps by George's hard standards, there was some truth in that. Roy had more youthful interests: cricket and football and speedway racing, and collecting records of Bing Crosby. His ambition was to save enough money to buy a motor bike. He had been miserable on the day his army call-up came; he had dreaded leaving home.

For the first few weeks, he went on being miserable, while the army roughly shook him out of his shyness and forced him to stand on his own feet. But then he began to make friends who had nothing to do with the narrow circle of his life in Exeter, and he began to discover new pleasures and interests. Radio began to interest him; learning about it was much harder than any job he had had to do before, and finding that he could do it gave him self-confidence. The tank fulfilled some of his wish for the motor bike. People like George gave him a new masculine view of life. In the army, he suddenly began to grow up.

The rest of the crew of the tank were not much older than these two, except the commander, who was a sergeant called Jim Ashton. Sergeant Ashton seemed almost middle-aged to his crew: he was nearly thirty. Most of the time, except when they misbehaved, he treated them with fatherly benevolence, and he succeeded in making them proud of themselves and of the job they had to do together.

Their tank was a fascine: it carried a bundle of logs eight feet in diameter. Before D-Day, all the crew had studied the photographs and models of their beach, and they had seen the obstacles on the beach, and a gap in the sand dunes behind it, and the marshy ground two hundred yards wide at the back of the dunes. In the gap, they had seen a tank trap, and in the marsh a winding stream and a place where a culvert across it had been destroyed. Sergeant Ashton and George and Roy and the others all understood exactly what they had to do : to follow the flail tanks through the dunes and along the road to the culvert, drop their fascine in the gap where the culvert had been, drive over it, and hold a road junction just beyond it while the Canadian infantry followed across the open ground. That was just the kind of thing they had done over and over again on exercises, and they were sure they could do it again. Each of them knew his own job and a good bit of the jobs of the others as well, and each of them knew he could depend on the others whatever happened; for they had not only worked together but lived and slept and eaten together for eighteen months in getting ready for this day. Sometimes their friendly arguments on the tank's intercom. sounded more like a family party than a tank crew, except for the language. They argued about a lot of different things, but more than anything else perhaps about the sergeant's singing. Jim Ashton was always singing, and the microphone in the turret seemed to inspire him. His star turns were " Kiss me, kiss me again," and a sad Australian ballad with the refrain, " Why do I weep, why do I cry? My love's asleep, so far away." George and Roy used to beg him, not always as respectfully as they should, to sing something new if he had to sing at all; but he took the view that a tank commander could sing what the hell he liked on his own intercom., and if the crew didn't appreciate it they were just an ungrateful unmusical lot of bastards.

Sergeant Ashton was singing as the landing craft went into the beach. As soon as Roy had netted in the radio and switched on the intercom., the familiar tune came out of the headphones. To the crew, it seemed no more beautiful than usual, but this time they did appreciate it, because they knew he was doing it to remind them of all they had done together and to make them feel less alone down in the bowels of the tank where none of them except George could see any daylight at all; and absurd though it may have been, it did pull them together.

George's first impression of the beach, when he peered at it through his narrow visor, was the impression shared by everyone else who landed on the eastern beaches in the early hours: it was much narrower than it ought to have been. This was true. The tide was higher than the British Admiralty had predicted, either because the prediction was wrong or because the wind had piled the water into the Bay of the Seine, or perhaps from a combination of both these causes. His second impression was of dead or wounded men lying so thickly on the beach that he wondered how he would manage to drive between them. But there right in front of him was the gap in the dunes which he had seen so clearly on the photographs; and beyond it, he knew he would see the road and the tank trap and the broken culvert.

Jim Ashton had stopped singing and opened the turret and put his head out, and he guided George up the beach, avoiding the corpses as best he could. There was much less shooting than they had expected; and that was because one of the landing craft of their troop had had engine trouble and had made them all late, and the Canadian infantry and the D.D. tanks had already been there for twenty minutes and had crossed the beach as far as the edge of the dunes and decimated the first line of the German defenders. The flails which had landed ahead went up through the gap, churning a track which was easy to see and follow, and George went after them till he could see over the marsh to the crossroads and the houses beyond it. The tank trap barred the way, a ditch fifteen feet wide and nine feet deep. That was not their job, and George pulled aside while another fascine tank which should have been in front came past, and paused on the edge of the ditch, and released its great bundle of logs which fell with a crash in the hole, and then immediately crawled on again across its own logs. The flails queued up and followed it over the tank trap which, far from trapping the tanks, had hardly delayed them a second.

There on the back of the dunes it was not so quiet. There was no artillery, but mortars and machine guns were firing from the houses on the crossroad ; safe enough for tanks, but not for infantry. George drove across the logs, and followed the flails which flogged the road to the broken culvert fifty yards beyond ; and then they drew aside, and let him take the lead, with the tank of the troop commander close behind him.

The last twenty or thirty feet of the road surface before the culvert had been destroyed. Beyond the broken end of the road, George saw through the visor a few yards of sand and weeds, and then a narrow strip of water where the stream flowed through.

" Crater's filled up," he said.

" Looks all right," he heard Ashton say ; and on the radio, the troop commander told them to carry on.

George eased the tank forward on to the patch of weeds ; her nose dipped, and he saw the weeds part, and water gleaming through, and she started to slide. He had stopped the tracks, but she went on sliding, and then she fell, and the daylight through the visor was cut off, and she stopped with a crash. Water fell on top of him, and before he could catch his breath it was over his head, and with the gasp that he gave it went down in his lungs and choked him. He struggled to get out of his seat, and somebody, Ashton or Roy, grabbed him by the back of his neck and hauled him up : and then he was on top of the turret, lying on his stomach being sick, and the turret was only just over the surface and it was still sinking. Ashton got him on to the bank and shouted, " Run for the dunes," but he hardly had the power to run. The troop commander turned his tank to give cover from the machine-gun fire, and the crew made for the dunes, and got over the top of the first of them, and threw themselves down on the sheltered seaward side ; and before they were there, the tank had disappeared except for the top of its fascine.

The crew never saw what happened after that. The weeds on the top of the water had looked so solid—like those on the floods where the American parachutists fell—that nobody who saw them from the tanks had doubted there was dry land underneath. Blown sand had been lying on top of them. But after the tank had fallen in and broken the surface, it was seen that the gap in the road was sixty feet wide. The bridges which the specialised armour carried were only thirty feet long. Perhaps nobody would have thought of sinking a tank in the middle of the gap if George had not already done it by mistake, but that was the only possible way to bridge the gap. A bridge-carrying tank was ordered up, and it dropped the far end of its bridge on top of the sunken tank. The troop commander and two other men scrambled out to it, still under fire, and stood on the turret which was under water, and blew off the wire strop which held the fascine, so that it dropped in the water ahead. There was still a gap beyond it. More fascines were put into place ; more tanks were brought up to give covering fire, and troops from the beach carried up some logs which the Germans had left there and threw them in as well ; and at 9.15, an hour and a quarter after the troop had landed, the first tanks and infantry crossed the bridge and rushed the houses by the crossroads from which the machine guns and mortars had covered the whole operation.

Jim Ashton and his crew, not knowing the use which was being made of their derelict tank, were lying close together on the back of the dunes, fed up with themselves for having lost the tank when the battle had hardly started, and thinking of the eighteen months of training which had culminated in less than eighteen minutes of action. George blamed himself. Ashton reassured him. Roy, from his radio position, had not seen anything at all till the water poured in. Ashton, of course, was the first to get over the shock ; he was the only one of them who was really quite grown up, or had been more than a small boy when the war started. He began singing again to cheer them up a bit, not very loudly, against the sound of the machine guns and mortar bombs :

" Why do I weep, why do I cry?
My love's asleep, so far away."

He was singing it when he died. A mortar bomb fell right among them. George did not know what happened : something terrible happened, that was all he knew, and cut a few seconds out of his life in utter oblivion. Roy was lying on top of him. He pushed him off, and saw he was dead, and glanced and saw Jim Ashton was dead and the others were lying half-buried and still. He stood up, and fell, and rolled down the steep face of the dune, and opened his eyes again in agony and saw a rough board above his head with a skull on it and " ACHTUNG—MINEN " and he got up again and ran, like a desperately wounded animal can run, till he fell again with his left leg crumpled under him.

The doctors would never believe he had run on it, it was so badly shattered, but he knew he had. His other leg was wounded too, and he lost his left arm. So he never became a miner, but he got a good job in the mine which a one-armed man can do.

In Graye-sur-Mer, at the present day, they talk of the famous people who landed there in the first days of the liberation, and entered France by way of the bridge when it had been tidied up at leisure. Some say Churchill came that way, some say Montgomery, and others claim King George VI and Eisenhower and General de Gaulle. But of course nobody there has heard of Jim Ashton or Roy Manley, and underneath the bridge, even when the stream is low in summer, only a few inches of metal, red with rust, can be seen above the surface of the mud.

The pattern of the assault on the Canadian beach had been different, in its successes and failures, from any of the beaches farther west. In one respect, it resembled Omaha : the bombardment, owing to the poor visibility, mostly fell inland and left the beach defences intact and the men who manned them shocked but still alive. The weather, on the other hand, had a different effect on the landing. The troops were put in at the right places, but the rough sea delayed the landing craft ; the first waves of infantry were up to half an hour late, and some of the specialised armour was even later. As the tide was higher than had been predicted, and was still rising, the outer lines of obstacles on the beach were under water before anyone arrived at all. There was no chance for the demolition teams to get to work on them before the tide fell in the afternoon, and meanwhile the landing craft had to take their chance and drive blindly into them or through them. Most of the craft succeeded in reaching the shore, but many were damaged or sunk when they tried to go out, and the accumulation of wreckage added to the difficulties of the later waves.

The delay had given the defenders extra time to recover from the moral effects of the bombardment, and the Canadian infantry crossed the beach under very heavy fire. On some parts of it, the slaughter in the dash across the sand was as terrible as at Omaha. But here there were no hills behind the shores; the defences were close to the back of the beach, among the dunes or the houses of the villages; and once the Canadians reached them, they very quickly fell. Fifteen minutes after the first attack, the first line of defenders had been killed or disarmed in short furious hand-to-hand battles, and the firing on the beach, as Jim Ashton had found, had died away to mere sniping, and mortars fired at random.

The tanks and infantry tore through Courseulles and Bernières, and only met the first long check to their progress in the meadows and orchards beyond the villages. They were held up there for a couple of hours before they broke out and continued an advance which carried them farther than anyone else on D-Day; and during this delay, more armour and trucks had piled ashore behind them, and a tremendous traffic jam built up in the village streets and on the narrow beach above high water mark.

Right on the left hand end of the beach, at St. Aubin, a force of the Royal Marine Commandos landed a few minutes behind the Canadian infantry. Among them was a man called Anthony Rubinstein. He was 19. He was the son of a distinguished family of lawyers, and his childhood in England in the 1930's had been carefree and comfortable and sheltered. When the war began, he was in his second year at Cheltenham College. For three more years, he had led the cloistered life of an English public school, and when he was 17 he had gone straight from the sixth form to the army, because it was the accepted thing to do. By the pure chance which governs most people's fate in wartime, he was transferred to 48 Royal Marine Commando, and on June 5th he sailed as a second lieutenant in command of a section of thirty men. In some ways, he was still young for his age.

The Royal Marines, sea-going soldiers, have a tradition as a disciplined force which is older than the navy's and more continuous than the army's. Their commandos were new formations of the second world war, but they inherited the marines' strict standards of discipline and toughness. They were small élite forces of three to four hundred men: six troops in each commando, and two sections in each troop.

A social theorist might have expected that Rubinstein's thirty men would resent their section commander's youth and his privileged upbringing; nearly all of them were older than he was, and most of them had more experience, not only of war but also of life in general. But it did not work out that way. During their training in Scotland and in the bombed streets of south-east London, he had found them very easy to get on with. He liked them, and enjoyed their company. On their side, they must have felt that his liking was sincere, because all of them, and especially the N.C.O.s, helped him to avoid mistakes which he might have made through his lack of experience. Far from being cut off from his men by wealth and youth and education, he became more friendly with them than the convention of the Royal Marines allowed. In the end, he was reprimanded for being too friendly, but he was not in the least repentant. The reprimand might have been more severe if anyone had known that while they were in training his sergeant, whose name was Blyth, had given him lessons in ballroom dancing, and that he and another young officer called Yates and the N.C.O.s and men of the section had all frequented the same local palais-de-dance. That was shocking behaviour, but they had all enjoyed themselves; and it is hard to believe that friendliness was anything but a help to Rubinstein and his section in the events which awaited them in Normandy.

The Royal Marine Commandos, true to their independent spirit, crossed the Channel all by themselves in vessels called Landing Craft, Infantry, Small; and these were, in fact, the smallest landing craft to carry troops across under their own steam. Each of them was crammed with a troop of sixty to seventy men. Rubinstein's boat had a cabin like a hutch for officers, and he spent most of the night inside it, taking a drink from time to time to keep the cold out, with Captain Perry, the troop commander, Lieutenant Curtis, the second-in-command, and one or two others. He thought it was absurd that the officers should be segregated in a cabin of their own and he felt he ought to be out on deck or squatting in the forepeak with Sergeant Blyth and the rest of the section, but he had the good sense not to say so. Otherwise, he was quite content. The briefing before they sailed had given him a fairly clear idea of what the commando was meant to do. It was to land at St. Aubin, on the left of the Canadians, and capture the coastal defences in the four-mile gap between the Canadians and the British beach to the eastward. Half-way along, it would meet another commando which was to land on the British right and come up the coast in the opposite direction. The toughest obstacle in the gap was expected to be a German strongpoint on the sea-front in the village of Langrune-sur-Mer.

So far, his idea of the impending battle was right enough; but he had also understood from the briefing that everything was going to be easy. The commando would not be landing till half an hour after the first of the infantry and armour. By then, the underwater obstacles would be cleared away and the beach would be under control. The whole coast would have been bombed and shelled so heavily as to crush the defence and leave nothing much for the marines to do except to clear up the mess.

It is hard to say how much of this impossibly rosy picture was due to over-optimistic briefing, and how much to Rubinstein's own misunderstanding. Of course he had never seen a battle, and he had never even seen anyone die except in western movies. He had no conception at all of what it would be like, and very little of what it was all about, except that he firmly believed what everyone had told him since he was a child: that the Germans were a menace to the world and had to be beaten. So he did not worry. The chain of command protects a second lieutenant from worry ; and he knew he was in good company. His dependable Sergeant Blyth was in the same boat with him, and his friend Yates was in another just astern. He felt that his section trusted him, and he and all of them trusted and admired Captain Perry. If he had worried at all, he would have reassured himself with the thought that Captain Perry would tell him what to do, and Sergeant Blyth would help him to do it ; and if he did it wrong, he could depend on Yates for sympathy. So he crossed the Channel and approached his first battle in cheerful and youthful ignorance, still very much like the sixth form schoolboy he had been two years before.

The spectacle of the bombardment did nothing to disillusion him : it seemed unreal. The first shock of reality only came when the landing craft was a few hundred yards from the beach : and then, for a few dreadful minutes, reality crowded in upon him in quick impressions of horror after horror. Machine guns opened fire from the shore. Shells and mortar bombs began to fall in the sea all round. The briefing had been wrong : the defences were far from crushed. He saw that the beach ahead was covered with wreckage. Then, one by one, he saw the commando's other landing craft on either side hit hidden obstacles and explode or stop, impaled on the spikes below the water. But the one which he was in sailed on and on undamaged, into the chaos among the breakers, and grounded under the flying tracers and the gunfire.

" Don't stop to help anyone : get ashore." That was what they had all been told. The ramps were lowered, narrow gangways which men could only go down in single file. Waiting in the queue, Rubinstein had a glimpse of one of the sailors of the crew, standing right up in the open on the foredeck, blazing away with the boat's gun at the houses opposite. He admired him. Then his turn came ; and on the ramp, the man in front of him was shot straight through the head, and fell back against him and blocked the way. Without a thought, he shoved the body over the side of the gangway into the sea, but as it splashed in he felt revulsion at what he had done : had the man been dead ? But the men behind were pushing him on, and he got to the water and waded ashore and ran across the narrow beach to a seawall and a low earthy cliff where men were taking shelter. He dropped down among them, and looked back.

The beach was dreadful : dead and dying men, and vehicles packed together, some wrecked, some burning, some trying to find a way through. It was much narrower than the briefing had said it would be : where he had come in, the waves were not ten yards from the wall. Beyond, in the sea, half the commando's other craft were still stuck two hundred yards off shore. Some of them were sinking. Some of the men who had been on board them were trying to swim in : but the tide was running strongly and carrying them off to the east, to the beaches in the gap where nobody had landed. Sickened and yet fascinated, Rubinstein saw them struggling for their lives ; and then he saw his friend Yates out there among them, and he knew at a glance that Yates was going to drown. Human impulse conflicted with his duty. All his own instinct told him to throw off his equipment and swim out to help his friend : but orders had been to help nobody, and his duty still lay with his section. Fear and shock had confused him, and the moment when he could have decided passed. While he watched, his friend gave up the struggle and went under. He averted his eyes : and there, closer at hand, he saw the body of the man he had pushed off the gangway, washing limply backwards and forwards in the

breakers. Reason said that he must have been dead before he
fell, yet he felt he had murdered him.

While he crouched below the seawall at the end of those
terrible minutes, Rubinstein was very frightened and his feelings
were in chaos ; but as he began to take a grip on himself,
his thoughts began to crystallise into unanswerable questions
which were to remain with him for years. What possible use
could there be in such destruction ? What good could ever
come of such wanton slaughter ?

The commonest cure for fear is action. Rubinstein and his
men were not left long to brood on the disasters of their landing.
Somebody came along below the wall to say that a route off the
beach had been found, and the survivors crept out through a gap
in a minefield, away from the stricken beach to a quieter place
inland.

When the commando assembled there, it could count its
losses. So many men were missing that two troops were combined to form one. Many were shot, and many more were
drowned ; but fifty of the missing men who were assumed to be
dead were really still alive, for in the middle of all the stark
tragedy they had suffered a fate which was ludicrous and humilia-
ting. A tank landing craft had picked them up two hundred
yards off shore, but its skipper had insisted, in spite of furious
arguments, that his orders were to go straight back to England :
and straight back to England they went.

As soon as it seemed that all the men who had landed alive
had been collected, the commando set to its work of clearing
the defences to the eastward, and for a little way it advanced
along lanes without opposition. There were still a few Frenchmen lurking in their houses, and when the troops passed a café,
Captain Perry told Rubinstein, as the last out of school, to go
in and ask where the Germans were. There was a crowd of
elderly men and women inside, and Rubinstein brought forth
the best of his public school French : " *Ou sont les Boches ?* "
The answer was a torrent of Norman dialect which he did not
understand at all. But this was an incident more like normal

life; it was the sort of thing he had imagined might happen, and it helped to bring him back to a more normal state of mind. So did the sight of a cow, standing perfectly calmly in a meadow chewing the cud. It must have been deaf, he thought.

But the lull of relief and normality ended soon. A barrage of gunfire came down on the troop, and it was British, not German fire. Someone had made a mistake, and the Royal Navy shelled the Royal Marines. The troop was forced to retreat, angry and frustrated, and the misunderstanding cost the life of Lieutenant Curtis, the second-in-command and Rubinstein's immediate senior. He was cruelly wounded by a British shell, and there was nothing they could do but give him morphine. When the barrage stopped and the troop advanced again and left him behind, he was still conscious enough to tell Rubinstein he would see him soon in London. But Rubinstein knew he was dying, and wondered again at the uselessness of such agony. With this further tragedy, the troop came to Langrune-sur-Mer.

The Commando's fight for the strongpoint there was the most prolonged street battle in the whole of the assault on Normandy. The strongpoint, as the briefing had said, was a complete block of houses on the seafront, with the seawall on one side and streets on the other three. The houses were reinforced and their windows were blocked up, and they were surrounded by trenches, minefields, barbed wire and machine-gun posts which were connected to the houses by underground passages.

At about 11 o'clock, Captain Perry's troop, with Rubinstein now acting as second-in-command, began to advance up one street while another troop attacked the other end of the block. As they dodged from doorway to doorway, a stream of bullets came down the street from a machine gun in a pit with a concrete cupola over it, in the middle of the crossroads by the strong-point. Perry took the troops through the deserted houses into the back yards behind them; they climbed over or knocked down the walls between one yard or garden and the next, and quite quickly reached the house on the crossroads itself. So far, they had got on well; but the next step had still to be decided.

Perry left Rubinstein in the house, saying he was going to have a look round; and only a minute later a man ran in saying: " Captain Perry's killed, sir."

The men in the house were shocked that the man in whom they had put their trust was dead. The news went round among them of how it had happened: he had been shot by a sniper in a gateway beside the house. It was a shock to Rubinstein too, but he hardly realised the effect of it till somebody asked him: " What do we do now, sir?" It was a situation he had never remotely imagined. There was nobody senior left. The troop was isolated, a long way from headquarters, and he was in command of it, because he was the only one of its officers left alive. The survivors of sixty-five men were waiting for his orders.

When a boy is so suddenly forced to behave like a man, what he does is a matter of chance—the chance of heredity and up-bringing. Rubinstein was lucky. He was not consciously pre-pared for responsibility, but when it came, something made him able to accept it. It took him a few minutes. His first reaction was natural bu tineffective: he collected all his N.C.O.s because he felt he needed their support. But that had a result which only made matters worse. They assembled in the porch of a house, and while they were discussing the situation a mortar bomb came through the roof. It blew Rubinstein down the cellar steps. He was not hurt, but when he got up again he found two of the sergeants wounded. That finally showed him that if life was to be so cheap, it was foolish and cowardly to depend on anyone else for moral support: while he was still alive and unhurt, the least he could do for the troop was to stand on his own feet and make his own decisions. Action had pushed his first fear into the background: responsibility killed it.

For the next nine hours, the troop fought a solitary battle under Rubinstein's command. Later on, when he had learned a bit more about soldiering, he saw for himself some mistakes which he made that day. He might have sent back for help and for more explosives; but communication with headquarters was tenuous, and he did not think of it. Instead of that, the troop doggedly hammered away at the strongpoint, hunting for an opening they could take with the weapons they carried. It was a battle of wits against an enemy they hardly ever saw; an affair of advances from house to house and from room to room, and of retreats when the way was impassable, of snipers' shots and mortar bombs which fell unpredictably from invisible emplacements, and quick dashes over streets which were covered by machine guns. During the afternoon, Rubinstein and a few of the men got into one corner of the strongpoint, but they were held there by a concrete wall, over which the Germans threw a stream of hand grenades. A tank which turned up to help them used all its ammunition against the wall without knocking it down, and the troop had to retreat and try again. Rubinstein himself had been sent into battle with a .45 revolver, the conventional and practically useless weapon of an officer, but he had picked up a rifle. There was very little use for that either, but he did once see a German running along a trench, and he raised the rifle and fired. The German jumped like a shot rabbit and disappeared. Rubinstein felt no emotion at all, except surprise that it had been such a good shot. He had discovered by then that in battle the enemy seems impersonal.

By the evening, they had still made very little progress. No doubt they had worn down the strength of the defenders, but their own strength was flagging too. The fact was that the strongpoint was too well planned and too toughly defended for light arms to make any quick impression. Towards dusk, the commanding officer of the commando came up to their corner of the battle. He told Rubinstein that a counter-attack from inland was expected during the night. The commando was therefore to break off the attack, and assemble outside the village to defend itself, and leave the strongpoint till the morning. Rubinstein was glad of the chance of a rest; he was tired, and so was his troop. But one worry was still on his mind: some hours before, he had sent out his friend Sergeant Blyth to make a reconnaissance, and he had never come back. Rubinstein asked his commanding officer if he could stay behind when the troop withdrew, to look for the sergeant.

So the troop went back by the way it had come in the morning, and left him alone on the ground it had fought for so long. Silence fell with the darkness on the wreckage round the crossroads, and shreds of the beauty of a summer night descended. Rubinstein walked all alone down the streets where men had only moved at the risk of their lives in daylight, and as he went along he shouted for Blyth ; but he only heard the echoes of his own voice, and the sound of the sea, and gunfire in the distance. Blyth did not answer. The Germans must have heard him behind their walls, but they gave no sign of it.

When he had sadly given up his search and joined the troop again in their bivouac in an orchard, he found some of the men hysterically angry with the Germans, mainly because of the death of Captain Perry. They swore they would get inside the strongpoint in the morning, and kill any German who tried to surrender. Their unreasoned impulse seemed shocking to him. He had seen too much of death. He had watched his friends die, and rebelled at the waste of their lives ; and he had tried to kill Germans himself, because it seemed it had to be done while they still resisted ; but to kill men in anger, because they had done what he had done himself—that was worse than warfare, it was anarchy.

So he thought as he lay on the ground exhausted, under the apple trees. He had grown up a lot since the morning ; but still, he was only nineteen.

Next day, they captured the strongpoint. Sergeant Blyth was found wounded but alive. They took thirty-one prisoners.

Most of the adverse conditions on Juno Beach in the early stages were also found on Sword Beach, on the eastern flank of the whole invasion area : the rough seas, the abnormally high tide, and the defences which had survived the bombardment. On Sword, there was the added unpleasantness of German artillery fire from beyond the River Orne; for Otway and his parachutists had captured the principal battery at Merville, but other batteries over there, and mobile guns which were hidden in the woods, were still in action, and indeed it was weeks before they were all overrun and the eastern end of Sword Beach was out of artillery range.

Sword was in an area aptly called La Brèche—the Breach— on the outskirts of Ouistreham and the seaside resort of Riva Bella. It was also on the outskirts of particularly heavy fortifications. Ouistreham, on the mouth of the Orne and the Caen Canal, had a port large enough for small naval ships like motor torpedo boats and inshore minesweepers. The Germans had a minor naval base there. Some ships were caught in it and tried to escape by steaming up the canal; but when they came to the bridge which Howard and his glider force had captured, and signalled for the bridge to be opened, the answer was not at all what they seemed to have expected. Round the mouth of this harbour and along the sea-front of Riva Bella, there was a concentration of heavy emplacements, and the bombardment which had done so much damage in the town had left the emplacements still able to fire on the beach. The first to land on this formidable spot were some of the D.D. tanks of the 13th/18th Hussars.

The 13th/18th are a venerable cavalry regiment who had only left their horses behind in India just before the war. Some of them, it was said, still had their hearts in the stables. When tanks broke down or burnt out under them, they still liked to refer to themselves, only half-humorously, as unhorsed. In spite of their inclination, they had taken to tanks with efficiency; but when they had heard they were getting swimming tanks, their first reaction had simply been disbelief: the thing just wouldn't work, they said. Certainly that was not an unreasonable opinion; but it had worked, remarkably well, on rehearsals.

One of their tank commanders was a sergeant called Harry Morris; and probably all the other commanders shared Morris's feelings as they sailed across the Channel. First, he was secretly full of admiration for his own crew, who were all very young ; compared with their jobs down inside the tank, he felt that his own, on top in the open air, was a soft option. Secondly, like the Americans in Rockwell's landing craft much farther west, he was very worried about the weather ; he had never tried to launch a D.D. tank in such a sea. And thirdly, he and everyone else in his troop were suffering an extra refinement of the general misery of seasickness. It was their rations. They opened pack after pack, hoping to find something which seasick men could stomach, but every single one was full of tinned steak and kidney pudding—good nourishing stuff, no doubt, but almost the last thing that anyone would have chosen on a rough night in the English Channel. By morning, these Hussars were hungry and miserable, and when the time had come for launching, what they wanted most in the world was to get off the landing craft and on to dry land, no matter how or where. So they were glad when they heard their commander's decision : the swim was on, but from 4,000 yards off shore instead of the 5,000 which had been planned.

Perhaps the sea off Sword Beach was not quite so rough as off Omaha ; or perhaps the Hussars should be given credit for more success. At any rate, the tanks did not sink at once. But from the moment when they were launched, they began to sink slowly. Whatever course they steered, waves broke over the canvas and washed about on top of the tanks and ran down through the turrets faster than the bilge pumps could empty them out. Sergeant Morris, trying to follow the leader of the troop and to steer his clumsy craft so that it dodged the waves, knew it was only a matter of time, a toss-up whether they would reach the shore before the tank went down. But out in the very front of the assault, there were other hazards too. The bombardment was reaching its climax, and the whole of it was going over the heads of the D.D. tank commanders. Morris found it impossible not to duck. The big shells from the fleet some miles behind were comfortably high, but the tank and infantry landing craft, which were almost on his tail, were firing their cannons at short range on a flat trajectory and their tracers seemed to be only just over his head. Worst of all were the rockets, because he could hear them coming from behind him : and in fact the rockets were partly to blame for a tragic mix-up which sent some of the tank crews to the fate which they must have feared.

In the rough sea, the tanks could not keep up their full speed. The tank landing craft, which should have landed two minutes behind them, began to catch them up, until the leading tank landing craft actually passed the last few of the tanks. At that critical moment, when the ships and tanks were danger-ously close together, a salvo of rockets fell short into the sea just ahead of them all. One or two of the landing craft captains, who saw the rockets falling, altered course abruptly and ran down two of the tanks. They sank at once. Their commanders were picked up, but their crews never came to the surface. Perhaps the tanks turned over as they sank.

But Morris was well in front, and did not know of this tragedy behind him. He was watching the deserted, empty beach, and calculating whether they would reach it. He called his driver on the intercom. to ask how he was getting on. " All right, but—wet," the driver answered. In fact, he was sitting up to his waist in water. In the last few hundred yards, the heavy barrage lifted, but the lighter shot from behind was still going past, and now it was met by small arms and mortar fire from ahead as the Germans began to recover from the shelling. Between the two fires, Morris's tank ploughed on, and a couple of rifle bullets could have sunk it. But he hardly gave a thought to the stuff which was flying around, because now he could see his objective right in front of him—a gun built into the base-ment of a hotel above the beach—and now he felt certain he was going to reach the shore.

The tracks grounded a long way out, and he drove forward till the hull was half out of the water, and gave the order " Down canvas " : and as the canvas dropped, his gunner fired a shot

straight ahead without stopping to aim. With that shot, the
D.D. tank achieved the first of its objects : surprise.

Morris had made it ; but not all the commanders had been
so lucky or quite so skilful. Five had not been able to launch
at sea, two had been rammed. The survivors, on the final
approach to the beach, had not attracted special attention from
the German artillery because they were insignificant targets
among the approaching landing craft ; but as soon as they
beached and dropped their canvas and the German gunners saw
them for what they were, fire was concentrated on them and
several were destroyed before they were out of the water. Some
other commanders, having never landed before in such a surf,
made the fatal mistake, even after they reached the land, of
dropping their canvas too soon, so that waves broke over
their turrets and swamped them. Sergeant Morris dealt with
his strongpoint, but immediately after that he was called back
into the edge of the sea again to try to haul out another tank
of his troop which was half full of water. Through all these
causes, the force of D.D's was halved.

Within two minutes of the landing of the D.D's, the hitherto
deserted beach was covered with tanks and hundreds of milling
men. In fact, the mass of men came too close behind the tanks,
because the tanks were late ; and the first of the infantry found
themselves on the beach before the armour had been able to
cope with the strongpoints or start the job of breaching the
dunes and minefields. To most of these men, the scene appeared
chaotic, but in part at least that appearance was deceptive,
because every man knew what he was supposed to do himself, but nobody knew what all the men he could see were
supposed to be doing. The confusion looked much worse than it
really was.

Part of the job of the D.D's was taken over, without any
orders or hesitation, by flail tanks of the 22nd Hussars which
had landed in the teams of specialised armour. Some of these
teams were equipped to make exits from the beach, and others

to clear the obstacles on it—the work which Gibbons's men had had to do by hand with such sacrifice on Omaha. But the obstacle clearance teams could only do half of their job, because half of the obstacles were already under water when they got there. As the senior engineer of the sector, Colonel R. W. Urquhart, came in to the beach in his landing craft, he saw that the outer stakes and ramps were only just showing their tops above the waves, and that all of them had either a landmine or a shell fixed on to them. Urquhart and his men dropped most of their equipment and went overboard, and swam from stake to stake cutting the mines away and letting them fall to the bottom where for the moment they could not do any harm. In the rough sea, under fire, and with landing craft blundering in among them, the swimmers felt, and were, extremely vulnerable, and there was a limit to what the most gallant of them could do; but this resourceful effort saved many landing craft, for the stakes and ramps, once the mines and shells were off them, were much less dangerous than they looked, and when landing craft hit them, it was often the stake which suffered most. An engineer lieutenant had the idea of mounting a tank and persuading its commander to close his turret and drive into the sea, so that he could stand on it to take the mines off the stakes. This also worked well for a time. Some authority with an extraordinarily economical mind had issued an order that the mines were to be stored for future use; so the lieutenant, as he collected them, stowed them dutifully on top of the tank till a sniper hit him in the shoulder and the tank commander had to open up and haul him out of the sea by his hair.

Above water, the armour got to work and cleared gaps at the top of the beach according to plan. The wooden obstacles were crushed where they stood, and the steel hedgehogs were shackled to hawsers and towed out of the way: a simpler and safer process than attaching charges to them and blowing them up. But in spite of all efforts, it was impossible to get at all the obstacles before the tide covered them, and the beach became lined with the wreckage of landing craft. The engineers on this job had lost one in five of their men by the time the day was over.

The armoured breaching teams, which had the job of forcing exits from the beach, were also having a very hard time. At the back of Sword Beach, there were dunes and then a row of seaside villas and hotels; and behind them a road ran parallel to the beach. In the gaps between the buildings there were sandy tracks which led to the road, but they did not extend through the dunes, and they were mined. Some of the houses were fortified, and most of them seemed to shelter mortar teams or snipers. The work of clearing exits through to the road was therefore done at close quarters with the Germans in the houses, often within the range of a hand grenade.

To this task, the engineers had brought 16 flail tanks, 8 armoured bull-dozers, and 24 other tanks with assorted implements—tanks which laid bridges against the dunes, tanks which laid trackways, and tanks which were fitted with pipes full of explosives which they thrust into the dunes to blow the sand away. Without these machines, the forcing of exits would certainly have been long and have cost many lives : with them, it was quick, and the cost was in machinery rather than lives. Within an hour, five exits were clear and were connected together by the road behind the houses. On the left hand end of the beach, where the artillery fire was heaviest, two more exits had been made but then had been blocked by damaged tanks. In the second hour, at least three more were opened. Traffic was flowing ; but half of the tanks which had done the job were out of action.

The control of traffic on beaches was a novel problem, and novel units had been formed to solve it. By long tradition, the navy's responsibility ends and the army's begins at the line called H.W.O.S. : high water of ordinary spring tides. Both the navy and the army were therefore involved in beach control, and had groups of men on the beaches : the navy to organise the approach of the landing craft and to tell them where to come in, and the army to organise the exits from the beaches and keep

the traffic moving. Most people, before the invasion, had regarded the beaches as death-traps to be crossed and left behind
as soon as possible, so nobody very much envied Beach Control
or anyone else who was expected to have to stay on the beaches
all day.

On the army side of high water mark, each beach had its
beach commander, and under him a beach control group had
been assigned to each exit. Each group had a radio, and beach
control had its own net, so that if one exit was blocked or came
under heavy fire, the beach commander could be told and could
divert the traffic to the others. The job was only expected to last
until $D + 1$, and so most of the officers and men who were
to do it were chosen from regiments which were not scheduled
to land in the first week or so. When the beaches were well
organised and no longer under fire, the beach control units
were to hitch-hike back to England to rejoin their regiments
and prepare to go over again. On Sword Beach, the 3rd Reconnaissance Regiment provided the men for this unpromising
assignment; and among them were Neville Gill and Ivor
Stevens.

Gill and Stevens, rather like Roy Manley and George Dunn,
might be taken as an example of the way in which war can
throw together two men of different background and tempera-
ment, and by giving them experience in common can unite
them in a friendship which they might never have achieved in
peace. Gill was 31, a solicitor from Newcastle, with the learned
interests of his profession : Stevens was 25, the son of the landlord of a pub in Bradford-on-Avon, and he had joined the
Grenadier Guards as a guardsman before the war. Gill had no
interest in sport, and preferred a quiet sedentary life : Stevens,
on the other hand, was an enormous athletic man, as strong as
an ox, who rowed and played football and cricket. Both, it was
true, were alike in being bachelors, but whereas Gill was destined
to remain one, Stevens, on D-Day, was in the middle of a whirl-
wind courtship of a Scottish girl called Connie Bowes. He had
only met her five times ; but the fourth time they met, she had

promised to marry him, so that to him the Normandy campaign was merely a job he had to get done before he could attend to much more interesting prospects.

Those were the obvious differences between the two men. What they shared was the experience of the past four years. Both of them had been at Dunkirk, Gill as a subaltern and Stevens as an unpaid lance-corporal, and they had both come out of it unhurt but feeling shattered by their first experience of war and determined that no power on earth would get them across the Channel again in wartime. But that feeling had worn off. Both of them had been in Britain ever since, endlessly training. By D-Day, Gill was a major, and Stevens was a captain and his second-in-command, and both of them, if not exactly eager for death or glory, would have been disappointed if they had not had the chance to go.

Oddly enough, though neither of them was afraid of the landing, they had both been afraid of what would happen when they tried to take ship to come back to rejoin their regiment. They would be all on their own, and so far as they knew, beach control groups were the only people in the whole invasion force who had anything but a one-way ticket. If two army officers and a dozen men went to the captain of a ship on D+1, and told them they wanted to go home, it was going to look funny, and the more they explained it the worse it was going to be. They had worried so seriously about being taken for deserters that Gill had procured a letter of authority, with a roll of his men, signed by the Corps Commander himself : and he carried it most carefully in the breast pocket of his battle dress. Both of them regarded this letter as the most important possession they took with them, their passport to safety again.

Gill and his group were due to land 19 minutes after the first wave of infantry. If anyone could have observed the small landing craft which carried them from their ship towards the beach, he might have discovered another difference between the two officers ; for Gill was right in the bows, and Stevens was right in the stern. Gill took his command very seriously.

It was a very small command for a major, it was true, only about a dozen men all told; but it was an unusually independent command, because his only link to any senior officer was by radio. And of course responsibility for the lives of a dozen men may weigh as heavily as responsibility for a thousand, because the commander of a dozen men can know them all as individuals and know, rather than merely imagine, the importance to them and to their families of their individual lives. So Gill had rather relished his duty to take the most vulnerable place in the landing craft and be the first to land.

But Stevens, the old soldier of 25, took a down-to-earth view of gratuitous courage. He was one of those people who are brave as any but like to pretend to be cowards. A good soldier, he always said, did what he was told but otherwise took care of his own skin. Nobody in their senses did brave deeds unless they had to; people only won medals, he believed, because some circumstance compelled them to do what afterwards seemed to be brave. It is an arguable point of view, and Stevens liked arguing about it. The stern of the landing craft, as it happened, was the proper place for the second in command, but Stevens took it as if it had been his own choice. "You're welcome to the front, sir," he had said to Gill. "As far back as I can get, that's the place for me." He was rewarded, in the ninety minutes of the run-in to the beach, by the sight of the heaving backs of the men in front of him crouched miserably over the paper bags which the army had wisely provided; and soon he was using his own.

But Gill, peering out over the raised ramp, between the bursts of spray which broke over it, was too worried to be sick; worried not by danger but by the belief that they were heading for the wrong beach. The craft was commanded by a subaltern of the Royal Marines. He had a photograph of the beach, and so had Gill. As they drove on, they could see the row of seaside villas which were shown on their photographs, but by then they had been badly knocked about, and through the fog of the bombardment it was difficult to tell which villa was which. The marine was sure he was right. Gill was sure he was wrong, and was annoyed with him for being so cocksure. But while they were afloat, the marine was in charge, so Gill had to let him have his way. As the craft lurched in towards the end of the line of boats already lying in the breakers, Gill was miserably unsure of himself. The crisis was coming, the very moment when his dozen men would depend on his leadership: and desperately searching the beach and his photograph, he could not discover for certain where he was. He felt he was going to fail them.

The dropping of the ramp gave each man in the boat, before he plunged into the sea, a momentary photographic glimpse of the scene he had imagined for so long: the few yards of breaking waves, lapping the shore in a thin line of foam, the almost level sand, two tanks burning, the stakes with mines on top of them, the swirling smoke, and far away, the line of the dunes and the ruins of the villas.

Gill found he was chest-deep, and he waded forward with only one thought in his head: to find out where they were, which side of the place where they ought to have come ashore. There seemed to be nobody moving on the beach ahead. He supposed the first wave of the infantry were across it and in the dunes: they should have been by then. Stevens and the others came splashing through the waves behind him. "Steve," he shouted above the din, "we're in the wrong place. Get the men under cover. I'm going to find out where we are." And he walked up the beach alone.

Stevens was amazed to see him go, because his first impression of what was going on was quite different. All along the water's edge to his left, as far as he could see, men were crouching or lying in the shallows. To his right, there was nobody at all. Tanks were coming ashore on the left, but the only ones he could see up the beach were burning. It looked to him as if the infantry were stuck and nobody so far had got across the beach. Wondering what on earth to do, he crouched in a couple of feet of water. He was still feeling giddy and weak from seasickness. In his left hand he was holding one end of the group's radio : the other end was carried by a corporal.

Gill went along the beach, puzzling over the photograph and the map and cursing the marine subaltern. Men were milling around the edge of the tide. Shells were falling and machine-gun fire was coming from heaven knew where and the noise was tremendous. In the fog and confusion, he met a man he knew but had not seen for years ; he asked him where they were, but he seemed to have no idea. But one thing at least was perfectly clear to Gill, and that was his duty. Steve could look after the men : his own job, first and foremost, was to find out where to go. Of course, it was dangerous, but he never thought about that because everyone had expected the beach to be dangerous. So he went farther up the beach, to try to get a clear view of the dunes and villas. As he went up it, he met a crowd of Germans coming down it with their hands up. They all made for him, but prisoners were no business of his, so he told them to stay where they were and walked on.

Stevens had soon lost sight of Gill. Staying in the water gave a feeling of being under cover, but he knew quite well it was no protection against the stray shots which were flying around and that he ought to get the men somewhere safer till Gill came back. He made up his mind to make for the nearest derelict tank ahead. And then, before they could move, the corporal on the other end of the radio was shot. He fell in the water. One of the others picked up the radio and Stevens shouted to them all to follow him. Dragging the dying man, the group ran forward to the tank. As they dropped down in this momentary shelter, one of the men called to Stevens : " There's the major." And Stevens looked and saw Gill all alone on the open beach : and in the same second, he saw him fall down and lie still.

Gill felt something like an electric shock and felt himself

falling. He fell flat on his back with his pack under him. He tried to get up again, but he could not move at all : his arms and legs lay where they were, and he could not pick them up. He felt very surprised. He thought : " I'm wounded," but it did not hurt, after the first shock, and he did not know where the wound was.

His brain was quite clear. Just before, he had seen some medical orderlies hiding behind a tank, and he shouted to them to come and give a hand, but they did not come. He turned his head to look for them, and saw, crawling up the sand, head-on, a Sherman tank with an explosive charge on the front of it, the sort which he knew was used for blowing holes in sand dunes. It came straight at him. Had the driver seen him ? he wondered. Did he know he was not dead ? Would he drive over a dead man lying in the way ? He tried with all his will to move, to get out of the way, to wave his arm to make the driver look : but nothing would move except his head. He had time to imagine most clearly what would happen if the track went over him, and time to wonder if there was clearance under the belly of a Sherman, if the tracks passed him one on each side. The roar of the tank increased, and he shut his eyes. And then above all the noise he heard Steve's breathless voice with its friendly familiar west-country intonation. " What happened, sir ? " Steve said.

Stevens had left the lee of the burnt-out tank and run alone across the open beach to where Gill had been shot. It had cost him an effort of self-control. He expected to be shot himself. Whether the infantry were in the dunes or not, there were obviously Germans still within rifle range. But he reached Gill unharmed and as he dropped down beside him the Sherman tank stopped dead and turned in its tracks and went round them. " Steve, I can't move," Gill said. " Where did it get me ? "

Stevens could not see a wound, so he turned him over. There was blood on the back of his battledress. He rolled up the tunic and found a jagged wound below the shoulder blades.

He got out a field dressing and started to put it on, and saw from the corner of his eye that the Sherman tank was butting its way into the dunes.

"Keep your head down," he said. "The tank's going to fire its charge." He lay down beside Gill and waited.

Once on an exercise, Gill had been with a man who was badly injured, and a medical orderly had asked him to hold the man's hand. He had felt a fool, but he had held it while the man's injuries were dressed. Now, as he lay with his face in the sand and the numbness began to recede and the pain to flame up inside him, a feeling of terror and loneliness overcame him like a shadow of death; and then he felt Steve's enormous hand take his and understood the strange comfort of this kind of human contact. The tank's charge exploded and sand showered down on them. "I'd better take the Corps Commander's letter," Stevens said; and Gill knew then that his battle was finished before it was even begun. "It's in my breast pocket," he said, and Stevens rolled him over again and took it out.

Then Stevens went and roused the medical orderlies behind their tank, and made them come out with a stretcher. And there the two men parted: Stevens to find the beach exit which Gill had been looking for; and Gill to lie all day under morphia on the beach, to learn that a bullet had gone right through his chest from front to back and broken his spine, to spend a year in a plaster cast and a lifetime of pain. Fourteen years later, he died as a consequence of his wound.

Stevens never changed his low opinion of martial courage. Of course he never told anybody how he had gone out to help Gill; he would have been very upset if anyone had accused him of being brave. But Gill knew quite well what he had done, and understood his embarrassment. "Of course, you didn't care about me, Steve," he said when they met again. "All you wanted was the Corps Commander's letter."

The contradictory impressions which Gill and Stevens

received when they landed were an example of a widespread dilemma. Men who landed in large units could usually follow the crowd, but for men in small specialised groups, suddenly pitched ashore in the midst of the battle, it was extremely hard, if not impossible, to judge at a glance what was happening, and there was never time to pause to think it out. If they had not been able to get their bearings before they landed, there was nobody, in the early stages, to tell them where they were. The most nightmarish experiences on all the beaches except Utah were not merely of being under fire, but of being lost : lost in a battle, perhaps in a minefield, among crowds of other men who knew what they were doing but were much too busy to bother about one's fate.

Stevens was not in that situation for long. He found his beach exit, and set to work on the job of controlling the traffic through it, and repairing it when it was torn up, and removing by brute force any tanks or trucks which stuck and threatened to hold up the stream. Sword Beach never became a comfortable place to work. German long-range artillery kept it under accurate fire : so accurate that the opinion spread that the gunners were ranging on the barrage balloons which were flying from the beach. As there were no German aircraft to be seen, the R.A.F. men who were flying the balloons began to find themselves unpopular, and in the middle of the morning, the balloons were all cut adrift. By noon, the exceptional tide had risen to within ten yards of the dunes, and the narrow strip of sand above it was dry and soft. Trucks, jeeps, tanks and artillery began to get snarled up together so that none of them could even reach the exits, and landings had to be halted for half an hour while people like Stevens sorted out the jam. But by that time, great forces were already ashore and had passed inland, and the first assault on Sword could already be said to have succeeded. Ouistreham had fallen. The defences of Riva Bella had been overcome in a fierce battle by a commando force which included the two troops of Free French who walked into the first aid post in the town ; and Royal Engineers and other commandos were converging on the

Caen Canal bridge, four miles inland, to join with Howard's glider force, and the parachutists.

There are still, and always will be, rival claims for the honour of having been the first to reach the bridge. A unit of engineers drove there in jeeps by a roundabout route, finding no opposition on the way except from snipers. Their mission was to build a new bridge, whether the original one had been captured intact or not. Their first reconnaissance officers got there at one o'clock and found the place still under shell and sniper fire; and like true technicians they set about their plans without ado. At somewhere about the same moment, the first commandos arrived on bicycles, and crossed the bridge to join the airborne forces. An hour later, the main body of commandos under Brigadier Lord Lovat arrived at the bridge, and with a better eye for the picturesque and perhaps for history, they marched across it with Lovat's personal piper playing a cheerful tune.

With this meeting of seaborne and airborne forces, whoever got there first, the assault on the beaches of Normandy was complete.

VII

THE ANNOUNCEMENT

THE ANNOUNCEMENT was the cause of intense excitement, and of intense anxiety.

The first news came from Germany. At 6.33 a.m., within five minutes, by chance, of the landings on Omaha and Utah, Berlin radio said Le Havre was being bombed, and then gave a reasonably accurate report of Hoffmann's flotilla's action against the British fleet. Every few minutes after that, it added more details, especially of parachute landings, some of which were right and some wrong. News agencies which monitored these broadcasts relayed them round the world, and radio news bulletins repeated them. In Washington, where it was just after midnight, people not in the know were sceptical, and thought they might be some kind of propaganda. For two and a half hours, rumours spread, and could not be confirmed: Eisenhower had refused to authorise any announcement at all until he was certain his troops were ashore. At 9.01, the first guarded official statement was issued. It did not mention any names of places ; but seven minutes later, Berlin said the landings stretched over the whole of the area from Le Havre to Cherbourg. From that time onward, news commentators all over the world were on the air, but still most of their material came from Germany. On the eastern seaboard of America, the official news broke at 3.30 a.m. and the first comment came from Mayor La Guardia of New York who rightly foresaw the mood of his city and indeed of the whole of the Allied world : " We can only wait for bulletins and pray for success. It is the most exciting moment in our lives."

In America, people working on night shift heard it : in England, the day had begun. In both countries, and even in Germany too, there was relief that for better or worse the waiting was over and the blow had been struck at last. But there were no outward signs of rejoicing : everyone everywhere knew the battle had only begun, and while people hoped for success, they feared that success would only come through dreadful slaughter. From New York, it was reported that men and women off night shift were drifting into churches on their way home ; a daily paper threw out its leading articles and printed the Lord's Prayer ; a prayer meeting was held in Madison Square. In London, services were held in St. Paul's and West-minster Abbey ; but some people had a sense of anti-climax because it seemed wrong that life should go on as usual, that buses and trains should run and meals be served in restaurants and business be done while such desperate events, on which all this normal life depended, were happening so few miles away.

Personal anxiety was deeper and more widespread than it need have been. Rumour had said that enormous casualties were expected. The secret official belief was that ten thousand men might be lost in the first assault ; but in fact, the cost in lives was less than a quarter of that. Censorship of letters from troops had been very strict for months, and for some time even men who had no dangerous part to play had not been able to write home at all ; and so mothers and wives who had been waiting for letters and now heard the news of invasion imagined their sons and husbands to be fighting their way ashore at that very moment. Probably for each man in the first assault, ten families suffered the anxiety of believing their man was there.

Joy Howard, the wife of John Howard who had led the glider attack on the Caen Canal bridge, was feeding her baby at home in Oxford, too busy to switch on the radio, when a kindly neighbour came in and asked her to spend the day with her, and said somebody had given her a brace of pheasants which they could have for dinner. Joy was surprised by this sudden invitation, and her mind flew to the problems of taking the pram for the baby and the high chair for the two-year-old. " We thought you'd like company on a day like this," the neighbour said ; and then, seeing her bewilderment she added : " Oh, haven't you heard the news ? "

John had told her weeks before that by the time she heard of an airborne attack, his own part in it would be over ; and so it was, for the moment. Just about then, in fact, he was finding time to laugh. Two Italians had reported for duty at the bridge. They had been working for the Germans, digging the holes and putting up the anti-glider posts in the meadow by the bridge where his gliders had landed. They had finished the holes, but not the posts. Now they did not know what to do, but after they had argued it out between them, they decided they had better carry on. So they went into the field and started putting up the anti-glider posts, all round the gliders which were already there.

Connie Bowes, who had just got engaged to Ivor Stevens of the Beach Control group, heard the news on the radio in the factory where she worked at Hawick in Scotland. It was a stocking factory, turned over to making jettison fuel tanks for aircraft, and all the workers were women ; and almost all of them had a son or a husband or a lover who had not told her for months what he was doing and had not written at all for weeks. Work stopped for a bit, and then went on with extra energy. Almost everyone in the factory was in tears. Connie Bowes kept her feelings to herself, but she wondered what Steve was doing.

Perhaps it was just as well she did not know, because just about then he was lying in a slit trench on top of another man and thought his last moment had come. All morning, since Neville Gill had been wounded, Steve had been looking after his exit from Sword Beach, not caring about anything except to see that traffic kept moving through it. Suddenly he saw men scattering for cover on the beach and looked behind him and saw a row of German bombers tearing along the beach at the height of the villa roof-tops. He dived for his trench and as he fell in on top of the man who had got there first, he saw the first plane hit and swerve towards him. It went over the trench so low that he felt the heat of it, and it hit the dune a few feet beyond him and burst into flames. Expecting to be burnt alive, he jumped up to get out, but the first of the bombs in the aircraft exploded with the heat, and he quickly lay down again. Bombs went on exploding one by one. It was a long time before Steve and the man underneath him agreed that the last had gone off.

Sylvia Ogden Smith, whose husband was the man who swam ashore to sample sand, was also at work in her factory in Wales when she heard the news and understood why Bruce was not coming to Buckingham Palace that afternoon to get his medal. As welfare supervisor, she had been given notices to be posted when the invasion had started, urging the staff to work even harder to support the men at the front. She went round and stuck them on the notice-boards, but they were not at all necessary. She saw a stout elderly mother sobbing over her capstan lathe, but the lathe was still running and her hands were moving as fast as ever. She went to talk to her, and found most of the other women weeping at their work. She tried to cheer them up, and then she went away to have a cry herself.

Her husband, just about then, was trying to help to rescue the crew of a landing craft which was burning furiously aground on Omaha Beach; and somewhere quite close to him, Henry Meyers, the schoolmaster from Brooklyn, who had landed in conditions worse than any of the women had imagined, was waiting to advance with his telephone wire; and his wife Molly, who operated an accounting machine in a New York store, was given time off and went to church to pray for him, with her friends from the office who had husbands and lovers overseas in England.

For a few, the immemorial rôles of men and women in war

were reversed. In concentration camps in Germany, prisoners were not supposed to hear any news at all, but in some of them prisoners who were technicians were kept at work repairing radio sets which belonged to the guards, and they contrived to keep one in working order in the workshops. So Dr. Sustendal of Luc-sur-Mer, in prison in Germany for suspected spying on the Atlantic Wall, heard that his own village was on the invasion shore, at almost the moment when his wife and his two boys were sheltering from the bombardment underneath his car in his garage ; and the news brought both hope and concern to him, hope which was justified ; for he lived through his ordeal and went home to his village in the end.

Some Germans, with special anxiety for men in France, listened secretly, against the Nazi laws, to Swiss radio stations, for fear that their own would not tell them the truth ; but the German radio, in fact, had a new sober air and did not make many extravagant claims that day. It was left to a Japanese spokesman to say " The Germans will now have an opportunity to begin new offensive operations."

In the morning, the House of Commons was packed by members waiting eagerly for a statement by Mr. Churchill ; but nothing whatever disturbs the routine of Parliament. Question time was first. A communist member made a plea for the abolition of banks, and an independent asked the Secretary to the Treasury if he would arrange that members of the Government Minor and Manipulative Grades Association of Office Cleaners should be referred to in future as such, and not as charwomen or charladies. When many matters like these had been disposed of and Churchill rose to speak, he added to the atmosphere of impatient expectancy by talking for ten minutes about the fall of Rome which had been announced the day before. Of course that was only fair to the men who were fighting in Italy ; but he seemed to members to be taking a mischievous delight in keeping them on tenterhooks, and his own account confirms that he enjoyed it. When at last he announced the invasion he added : " So far, the commanders who are engaged report that everything is proceeding according to plan. And what a plan ! This vast operation is undoubtedly the most complicated and difficult that has ever taken place." That afternoon, in a second statement, he reminded the House : " It is a most serious time that we enter upon. Thank God we enter upon it with our great Allies all in good heart and all in good friendship."

The annual meeting of the Channel Tunnel Company was held that day in London, and the chairman reported that the future of the tunnel was impossible to foresee.

By midday, the first eye-witness accounts were coming in from war correspondents who had flown over the beaches : " I feel it is a great privilege to be here. I'll be glad to get home all the same . . . I can see the invasion craft out on the water . . . I feel detached, and that awful feeling that the great history of the world is unfolding before us at this very moment." All day, news from the shore itself was very meagre. But while the public knew little of the progress of the battle, it might be said that the men who were ashore knew even less. There is a military phrase for their experience : battlefield isolation. All that they knew was what they could see, and what their own command radio network told them, and once they were across the beach and in among the lanes and villages and hedgerows, they could see very little. Few of them had the time or a suitable radio to hear what was broadcast from London ; but one American airborne commander, out alone with his unit and wondering whether to attack or not, happened to hear a B.B.C. bulletin which said the airborne operation was going according to plan ; and on that slender evidence, he ordered his attack. All that most men knew was that they were ashore and still alive, and that surprised them.

By nightfall, the issue was decided. The foothold at Omaha Beach was still narrow, General Gavin's airborne troops were still isolated, and the landing of materials had lagged behind the plan ; but the Atlantic Wall was decisively broken and the armies securely ashore. Eisenhower was satisfied, but unwilling to be over-optimistic. One question was answered ; everything now depended on the answer to a second : could the Allies build up their forces more quickly than the Germans ? The answer to this question depended on the weather, and the weather had already brought the project near disaster.

The Allied troops could not afford to be over-confident either. Over there, with the Channel behind them and unknown forces ahead, they felt their dependence on support and material which all had to come by the same long perilous route across the sea and the beaches.

The clearest assessment of the outcome of the day was made by the German front-line troops. They knew their own capabilities, and had also seen the fleet and the weight of allied material thrown against them, and the more clear-headed of them knew they could not win.

The German commanders had not seen the fleet, and no mere military report could have conveyed to them the impression of irresistible power which it gave ; but still, it is likely that before the day was over, they also knew in their inmost thoughts that the invasion could not be defeated. It was only eleven days later that von Rundstedt and Rommel tried to suggest to Hitler that Germany should sue for peace with Britain and America— though not with Russia.

Night fell, and the men who had been the first to land were tiring. War may be mechanised, but battles are limited by the stamina of the human body. Some of the men were still in action, and some could try to sleep ; but in the dark, a hundred German bombers ventured over, and the night on the beachhead was noisy with thousands of anti-aircraft guns. Where the first troops rested, the follow-up troops were passing through. In the Channel, ships with more men and more material were passing ships returning to re-load. In English ports, more ships were being loaded, and all over the south of England still more men and still more material were on the move, southward towards the Channel. The assault was over, the battle of the build-up had begun.

On St. Alban's Head the night before, Mr. Wallace the coastguard had seen the fleet and heard the aircraft and knelt down with his wife to pray ; and now the prayers of the great and humble were united. President Roosevelt broadcast, and then went alone to his room and wrote a prayer for " a peace that will let all men live in freedom, reaping the just rewards of their honest toil." In Britain, King George VI broadcast, and these were his final words : " If from every place of worship, from home and factory, from men and women of all ages and many races and occupations, our supplications rise, then, please God, both now and in a future not remote, the predictions of an ancient psalm may be fulfilled : ' The Lord will give strength unto his people : the Lord will give his people the blessing of peace.' "